Costs and Fees Encyclopaedia 2011–2012

The comprehensive compendium of costs and fees, for civil and criminal lawyers

Editorial Board

Michael Bacon, MA (Cantab), FALCD, MAE, QDR

Peter Rogers LL B, *Deputy Costs Judge of the Senior Courts Costs Office*

Keith Biggs

Wendy Popplewell

Jas Sra

CLASS LEGAL

Class Legal
Owl House, Carr Farm, Cadney, BRIGG,
Lincolnshire, DN20 9HP, UK
Tel: 01652 652222 Fax: 01652 651050
DX 24360 Brigg
Email: Info@ClassLegal.com
Website: www.ClassLegal.com

Class Legal is an imprint of Class Publishing Ltd, a company registered in England No. 2993127. VAT No: GB 503 5208 87

Registered Office: 7 Melrose Terrace, London W6 7RL, UK

PRINTING HISTORY

First published 2011

ISBN 978 1 85959 339 4

A CIP Catalogue for this book is available from the British Library

Typeset by: Stephen Theaker

Printed and bound by: Good News Digital Books

Contents

PART 1 CIVIL PROCEEDINGS

1. Extracts from CPR 1998 relating to costs

PART 43 SCOPE OF COST RULES AND DEFINITIONS

43.1 Scope of this Part

This Part contains definitions and interpretation of certain matters set out in the rules about costs contained in Parts 44 to 48.

(Part 44 contains general rules about costs; Part 45 deals with fixed costs; Part 46 deals with fast track trial costs; Part 47 deals with the detailed assessment of costs and related appeals and Part 48 deals with costs payable in special cases)

43.2 Definitions and application

(1) In Parts 44 to 48, unless the context otherwise requires—

(a) 'costs' includes fees, charges, disbursements, expenses, remuneration, reimbursement allowed to a litigant in person under rule 48.6, any additional liability incurred under a funding arrangement and any fee or reward charged by a lay representative for acting on behalf of a party in proceedings allocated to the small claims track;

(b) 'costs judge' means a taxing master of the Senior Courts;

(ba) 'Costs Office' means the Senior Courts Costs Office;

(c) 'costs officer' means—

(i) a costs judge;

(ii) a district judge; and

(iii) an authorised court officer;

(d) 'authorised court officer' means any officer of—

(i) a county court;

(ii) a district registry;

(iii) the Principal Registry of the Family Division; or

(iv) the Costs Office,

whom the Lord Chancellor has authorised to assess costs.

(e) 'fund' includes any estate or property held for the benefit of any person or class of person and any fund to which a trustee or personal representative is entitled in that capacity ;

(f) 'receiving party' means a party entitled to be paid costs;

(g) 'paying party' means a party liable to pay costs;

(h) 'assisted person' means an assisted person within the statutory provisions relating to legal aid;

(i) 'LSC funded client' means an individual who receives services funded by the Legal Services Commission as part of the Community Legal Service within the meaning of Part I of the Access to Justice Act 1999;

(j) 'fixed costs' means the amounts which are to be allowed in respect of solicitors' charges in the circumstances set out in Section I of Part 45.

(k) 'funding arrangement' means an arrangement where a person has—

(i) entered into a conditional fee agreement or a collective conditional fee agreement which provides for a success fee within the meaning of section 58(2) of the Courts and Legal Services Act 1990[1];

(ii) taken out an insurance policy to which section 29 of the Access to Justice Act 1999 (recovery of insurance premiums by way of costs) applies; or

(iii) made an agreement with a membership organisation to meet that person's legal costs;

(l) 'percentage increase' means the percentage by which the amount of a legal representative's fee can be increased in accordance with a conditional fee agreement which provides for a success fee;

(m) 'insurance premium' means a sum of money paid or payable for insurance against the risk of incurring a costs liability in the proceedings, taken out after the event that is the subject matter of the claim;

(n) 'membership organisation' means a body prescribed for the purposes of section 30 of the Access to Justice Act 1999 (recovery where body undertakes to meet costs liabilities);

(o) 'additional liability' means the percentage increase, the insurance premium, or the additional amount in respect of provision made by a membership organisation, as the case may be;

(p) 'free of charge' has the same meaning as in section 194(10) of the Legal Services Act 2007;

(q) 'pro bono representation' means legal representation provided free of charge; and

(r) 'the prescribed charity' has the same meaning as in section 194(8) of the Legal Services Act 2007.

(2) The costs to which Parts 44 to 48 apply include—

(a) the following costs where those costs may be assessed by the court—

(i) costs of proceedings before an arbitrator or umpire;

(ii) costs of proceedings before a tribunal or other statutory body; and

(iii) costs payable by a client to his solicitor; and

(b) costs which are payable by one party to another party under the terms of a contract, where the court makes an order for an assessment of those costs.

(3) Where advocacy or litigation services are provided to a client under a conditional fee agreement, costs are recoverable under Parts 44 to 48 notwithstanding that the client is liable to pay his legal representative's fees and expenses only to the extent that sums are recovered in respect of the proceedings, whether by way of costs or otherwise.

(4) In paragraph (3), the reference to a conditional fee agreement is to an agreement which satisfies all the conditions applicable to it by virtue of section 58 of the Courts and Legal Services Act 1990.

43.3 Meaning of summary assessment

'Summary assessment' means the procedure by which the court, when making an order about costs, orders payment of a sum of money instead of fixed costs or 'detailed assessment'.

43.4 Meaning of detailed assessment

'Detailed assessment' means the procedure by which the amount of costs is decided by a costs officer in accordance with Part 47.

Part 44 GENERAL RULES ABOUT COSTS

44.1 Scope of this Part

This Part contains general rules about costs, entitlement to costs and orders in respect of pro bono representation.

44.2 Solicitor's duty to notify client

Where—

(a) the court makes a costs order against a legally represented party; and

(b) the party is not present when the order is made,

the party's solicitor must notify his client in writing of the costs order no later than 7 days after the solicitor receives notice of the order.

44.3 Court's discretion and circumstances to be taken into account when exercising its discretion as to costs

(1) The court has discretion as to—

Where the court orders a party to pay costs to another party (other than fixed costs) it may either—

(a) make a summary assessment of the costs; or

(b) order detailed assessment of the costs by a costs officer, unless any rule, practice direction or other enactment provides otherwise.

44.3A Costs orders relating to funding arrangements

(1) The court will not assess any additional liability until the conclusion of the proceedings, or the part of the proceedings, to which the funding arrangement relates.

("Funding arrangement" and "additional liability" are defined in rule 43.2)

(2) At the conclusion of the proceedings, or the part of the proceedings, to which the funding arrangement relates the court may—

(a) make a summary assessment of all the costs, including any additional liability;

(b) make an order for detailed assessment of the additional liability but make a summary assessment of the other costs; or

(c) make an order for detailed assessment of all the costs.

44.3B Limits on recovery under funding arrangements

(1) Unless the court orders otherwise, a party may not recover as an additional liability—

(a) any proportion of the percentage increase relating to the cost to the legal representative of the postponement of the payment of his fees and expenses;

(b) any provision made by a membership organisation which exceeds the likely cost to that party of the premium of an insurance policy against the risk of incurring a liability to pay the costs of other parties to the proceedings;

(c) any additional liability for any period ... during which that party failed to provide information about a funding arrangement in accordance with a rule, practice direction or court order;

(d) any percentage increase where that party has failed to comply with—

(i) a requirement in the Costs Practice Direction; or

(ii) a court order,

to disclose in any assessment proceedings the reasons for setting the percentage increase at the level stated in the conditional fee agreement;

(e) any insurance premium where that party has failed to provide information about the insurance policy in question by the time required by a rule, practice direction or court order.

(2) This rule does not apply in an assessment under rule 48.9 (assessment of a solicitor's bill to his client).

44.3C Orders in respect of pro bono representation]

(1) In this rule, "the 2007 Act" means the Legal Services Act 2007.

(2) Where the court makes an order under section 194(3) of the 2007 Act—

(a) the court may order the payment to the prescribed charity of a sum no greater than the costs specified in Part 45 to which the party with pro bono representation would have been entitled in accordance with that Part and in respect of that representation had it not been provided free of charge; or

(b) where Part 45 does not apply, the court may determine the amount of the payment (other than a sum equivalent to fixed costs) to be made by the paying party to the prescribed charity by—

(i) making a summary assessment; or

(ii) making an order for detailed assessment,

of a sum equivalent to all or part of the costs the paying party would have been ordered to pay to the party with pro bono representation in respect of that representation had it not been provided free of charge.

(3) Where the court makes an order under section 194(3) of the 2007 Act, the order must specify that the payment by the paying party must be made to the prescribed charity.

(4) The receiving party must send a copy of the order to the prescribed charity within 7 days of receipt of the order.

(5) Where the court considers making or makes an order under section 194(3) of the 2007 Act, Parts 43 to 48 apply, where appropriate, with the following modifications—

(a) references to "costs orders", "orders about costs" or "orders for the payment of costs" are to be read, unless otherwise stated, as if they refer to an order under section 194(3);

(b) references to "costs" are to be read, as if they referred to a sum equivalent to the costs that would have been claimed by, incurred by or awarded to the party with pro bono representation in respect of that representation had it not been provided free of charge; and

(c) references to "receiving party" are to be read, as meaning a party who has pro bono representation and who would have been entitled to be paid costs in respect of that representation had it not been provided free of charge.

44.4 Basis of assessment

1) Where the court is to assess the amount of costs (whether by summary or detailed assessment) it will assess those costs—

(a) on the standard basis; or

(b) on the indemnity basis,

but the court will not in either case allow costs which have been unreasonably incurred or are unreasonable in amount.

(2) Where the amount of costs is to be assessed on the standard basis, the court will—

(a) only allow costs which are proportionate to the matters in issue; and

(b) resolve any doubt which it may have as to whether costs were reasonably incurred or reasonable and proportionate in amount in favour of the paying party.

(3) Where the amount of costs is to be assessed on the indemnity basis, the court will resolve any doubt which it may have as to whether costs were reasonably incurred or were reasonable in amount in favour of the receiving party.

(4) Where—

(a) the court makes an order about costs without indicating the basis on which the costs are to be assessed; or

(b) the court makes an order for costs to be assessed on a basis other than the standard basis or the indemnity basis,

the costs will be assessed on the standard basis.

(5) *Revoked*

(6) Where the amount of a solicitor's remuneration in respect of non-contentious business is regulated by any general orders made under the Solicitors Act 1974, the amount of the costs to be allowed in respect of any such business which falls to be assessed by the court will be decided in accordance with those general orders rather than this rule and rule 44.5.

44.5 Factors to be taken into account in deciding the amount of costs

(1) The court is to have regard to all the circumstances in deciding whether costs were—

(a) if it is assessing costs on the standard basis—

(i) proportionately and reasonably incurred; or

(ii) were proportionate and reasonable in amount, or

(b) if it is assessing costs on the indemnity basis—

(i) unreasonably incurred; or

(ii) unreasonable in amount.

(2) In particular the court must give effect to any orders which have already been made.

(3) The court must also have regard to—

(a) the conduct of all the parties, including in particular—

(i) conduct before, as well as during, the proceedings; and

(ii) the efforts made, if any, before and during the proceedings in order to try to resolve the dispute;

(b) the amount or value of any money or property involved;

(c) the importance of the matter to all the parties;

(d) the particular complexity of the matter or the difficulty or novelty of the questions raised;

(e) the skill, effort, specialised knowledge and responsibility involved;

(f) the time spent on the case; and

(g) the place where and the circumstances in which work or any part of it was done.

44.6 Fixed costs

A party may recover the fixed costs specified in Part 45 in accordance with that Part.

44.7 Procedure for assessing costs

Where the court orders a party to pay costs to another party (other than fixed costs) it may either—

(a) make a summary assessment of the costs; or

(b) order detailed assessment of the costs by a costs officer,

unless any rule, practice direction or other enactment provides otherwise.

44.8 Time for complying with an order for costs

A party must comply with an order for the payment of costs within 14 days of—

(a) the date of the judgment or order if it states the amount of those costs;

(b) if the amount of those costs (or part of them) is decided later in accordance with Part 47, the date of the certificate which states the amount; or

(c) in either case, such later date as the court may specify.

44.9 Costs on the small claims track and fast track

(1) Part 27 (small claims) and Part 46 (fast track trial costs) contain special rules about—

(a) liability for costs;

(b) the amount of costs which the court may award; and

(c) the procedure for assessing costs.

(2) Once a claim is allocated to a particular track, those special rules shall apply to the period before, as well as after, allocation except where the court or a practice direction provides otherwise.

44.10 Limitation on amount court may allow where a claim allocated to the fast track settles before trial

(1) Where the court—

(a) assesses costs in relation to a claim which—

(i) has been allocated to the fast track; and

(ii) settles before the start of the trial; and

(b) is considering the amount of costs to be allowed in respect of a party's advocate for preparing for the trial,

it may not allow, in respect of those advocate's costs, an amount that exceeds the amount of fast track trial costs which would have been payable in relation to the claim had the trial taken place.

(2) When deciding the amount to be allowed in respect of the advocate's costs, the court shall have regard to—

(a) when the claim was settled; and

(b) when the court was notified that the claim had settled.

(3) In this rule, 'advocate' and 'fast track trial costs' have the meanings given to them by Part 46.

44.11 Costs following allocation and re-allocation

(1) Any costs orders made before a claim is allocated will not be affected by allocation.

(2) Where—

(a) a claim is allocated to a track; and

(b) the court subsequently re-allocates that claim to a different track,

then unless the court orders otherwise, any special rules about costs applying—

(i) to the first track, will apply to the claim up to the date of re-allocation; and

(ii) to the second track, will apply from the date of re-allocation.

44.12 Cases where costs orders deemed to have been made

(1) Where a right to costs arises under—

(a) rule 3.7 (defendant's right to costs where claim struck out for non-payment of fees);

(b) rule 36.10(1) or (2) (claimant's entitlement to costs where a Part 36 offer is accepted);

(c) Omitted

(d) rule 38.6 (defendant's right to costs where claimant discontinues), a costs order will be deemed to have been made on the standard basis.

(1A) Where such an order is deemed to be made in favour of a party with pro bono representation, that party may apply for an order under section 194(3) of the Legal Services Act 2007.

(2) Interest payable pursuant to section 17 of the Judgments Act 1838[2] or section 74 of the County Courts Act 1984[3] on the costs deemed to have been ordered under paragraph (1) shall begin to run from the date on which the event which gave rise to the entitlement to costs occurred.

44.12A Costs-only proceedings

(1) This rule sets out a procedure which may be followed where—

(a) the parties to a dispute have reached an agreement on all issues (including which party is to pay the costs) which is made or confirmed in writing; but

(b) they have failed to agree the amount of those costs; and

(c) no proceedings have been started.

(2) Either party to the agreement may start proceedings under this rule by issuing a claim form in accordance with Part 8.

(3) The claim form must contain or be accompanied by the agreement or confirmation.

(4) Except as provided in paragraph (4A) (and subject to rule 44.12B), in proceedings to which this rule applies the court—

(a) may (i) make an order for costs to be determined by detailed assessment; or (ii) dismiss the claim; and

(b) must dismiss the claim if it is opposed.

(4A) In proceedings to which Section II or Section VI of Part 45 applies, the court shall assess the costs in the manner set out in that Section.

(5) Rule 48.3 (amount of costs where costs are payable pursuant to a contract) does not apply to claims started under the procedure in this rule. (Rule 7.2 provides that proceedings are started when the court issues a claim form at the request of the claimant)

44.12B Costs-only proceedings – costs in respect of insurance premium in publication cases

(1) If in proceedings to which rule 44.12A applies it appears to the court that—

(a) if proceedings had been started, they would have been publication proceedings;

(b) one party admitted liability and made an offer of settlement on the basis of that admission;

(c) agreement was reached after that admission of liability and offer of settlement; and

(d) either—

(i) the party making the admission of liability and offer of settlement was not provided by the other party with the information about an insurance policy as required by the Practice Direction (Pre-Action Conduct); or

(ii) that party made the admission of liability and offer of settlement before, or within 42 days of, being provided by the other party with that information,

no costs may be recovered by the other party in respect of the insurance premium.

(2) In this rule, 'publication proceedings' means proceedings for—

(a) defamation;

(b) malicious falsehood; or

(c) breach of confidence involving publication to the public at large.

44.12C Costs-only application after a claim is started under Part 8 in accordance with Practice Direction 8B

(1) This rule sets out the procedure where—

(a) the parties to a dispute have reached an agreement on all issues (including which party is to pay the costs) which is made or confirmed in writing; but

(b) they have failed to agree the amount of those costs; and

(c) proceedings have been started under Part 8 in accordance with Practice Direction 8B.

(2) Either party may make an application for the court to determine the costs.

(3) Where an application is made under this rule the court will assess the costs in accordance with rule 45.34 or rule 45.37.

(4) Rule 48.3 (amount of costs where costs are payable pursuant to a contract) does not apply to an application under this rule.

44.13 Special situations

(1) Where the court makes an order which does not mention costs—

(a) subject to paragraphs (1A) and (1B), the general rule is that no party is entitled—

(i) to costs; or

(ii) to seek an order under section 194(3) of the Legal Services Act 2007,

in relation to that order; but

(b) this does not affect any entitlement of a party to recover costs out of a fund held by that party as trustee or personal representative, or pursuant to any lease, mortgage or other security.

(1A) Where the court makes—

(a) an order granting permission to appeal;

(b) an order granting permission to apply for judicial review; or

(c) any other order or direction sought by a party on an application without notice,

and its order does not mention costs, it will be deemed to include an order for applicant's costs in the case.

(1B) Any party affected by a deemed order for costs under paragraph (1A) may apply at any time to vary the order.

(2) The court hearing an appeal may, unless it dismisses the appeal, make orders about the costs of the proceedings giving rise to the appeal as well as the costs of the appeal.

(3) Where proceedings are transferred from one court to another, the court to which they are transferred may deal with all the costs, including the costs before the transfer.

(4) Paragraph (3) is subject to any order of the court which ordered the transfer.

44.14 Court's powers in relation to misconduct

(1) The court may make an order under this rule where—

(a) a party or his legal representative, in connection with a summary or detailed assessment, fails to comply with a rule, practice direction or court order; or

(b) it appears to the court that the conduct of a party or his legal representative, before or during the proceedings which gave rise to the assessment proceedings, was unreasonable or improper.

(2) Where paragraph (1) applies, the court may—

(a) disallow all or part of the costs which are being assessed; or

(b) order the party at fault or his legal representative to pay costs which he has caused any other party to incur.

(3) Where—

(a) the court makes an order under paragraph (2) against a legally represented party; and

(b) the party is not present when the order is made,

the party's solicitor must notify his client in writing of the order no later than 7 days after the solicitor receives notice of the order.

44.15 Providing information about funding arrangements

(1) A party who seeks to recover an additional liability must provide information about the funding arrangement to the court and to other parties as required by a rule, practice direction or court order.

(2) Where the funding arrangement has changed, and the information a party has previously provided in accordance with paragraph (1) is no longer accurate, that party must file notice of the change and serve it on all other parties within 7 days.

(3) Where paragraph (2) applies, and a party has already filed—

(a) an allocation questionnaire; or

(b) a pre-trial check list (listing questionnaire)

he must file and serve a new estimate of costs with the notice.

44.16 Adjournment where legal representative seeks to challenge disallowance of any amount of percentage increase

(1) This rule applies where the Conditional Fee Agreements Regulations 2000 or the Collective Conditional Fee Agreements Regulations 2000 continues to apply to an agreement which provides for a success fee.

(2) Where—

(a) the court disallows any amount of a legal representative's percentage increase in summary or detailed assessment proceedings; and

(b) the legal representative applies for an order that the disallowed amount should continue to be payable by his client,

the court may adjourn the hearing to allow the client to be—

(i) notified of the order sought; and

(ii) separately represented.

44.17 Application of costs rules

This Part and Part 45 (fixed costs), Part 46 (fast track trial costs), Part 47 (procedure for detailed assessment of costs and default provisions) and Part 48 (special cases), do not apply to the assessment of costs in proceedings to the extent that—

(a) section 11 of the Access to Justice Act 1999, and provisions made under that Act, or

(b) regulations made under the Legal Aid Act 1988,

make different provision.

44.18 Costs capping orders – General

(1) A costs capping order is an order limiting the amount of future costs (including disbursements) which a party may recover pursuant to an order for costs subsequently made.

(2) In this rule, 'future costs' means costs incurred in respect of work done after the date of the costs capping order but excluding the amount of any additional liability.

(3) This rule does not apply to protective costs orders.

(4) A costs capping order may be in respect of—

(a) the whole litigation; or

(b) any issues which are ordered to be tried separately.

(5) The court may at any stage of proceedings make a costs capping order against all or any of the parties, if—

(a) it is in the interests of justice to do so;

(b) there is a substantial risk that without such an order costs will be disproportionately incurred; and

(c) it is not satisfied that the risk in sub-paragraph (b) can be adequately controlled by—

(i) case management directions or orders made under Part 3; and

(ii) detailed assessment of costs.

(6) In considering whether to exercise its discretion under this rule, the court will consider all the circumstances of the case, including—

(a) whether there is a substantial imbalance between the financial position of the parties;

(b) whether the costs of determining the amount of the cap are likely to be proportionate to the overall costs of the litigation;

(c) the stage which the proceedings have reached; and

(d) the costs which have been incurred to date and the future costs.

(7) A costs capping order, once made, will limit the costs recoverable by the party subject to the order unless a party successfully applies to vary the order. No such variation will be made unless—

(a) there has been a material and substantial change of circumstances since the date when the order was made; or

(b) there is some other compelling reason why a variation should be made.

44.19 Application for a costs capping order

(1) An application for a costs capping order must be made on notice in accordance with Part 23.

(2) The application notice must—

(a) set out—

(i) whether the costs capping order is in respect of the whole of the litigation or a particular issue which is ordered to be tried separately; and

(ii) why a costs capping order should be made; and

(b) be accompanied by an estimate of costs setting out—

(i) the costs (and disbursements) incurred by the applicant to date; and

(ii) the costs (and disbursements) which the applicant is likely to incur in the future conduct of the proceedings.

(3) The court may give directions for the determination of the application and such directions may—

(a) direct any party to the proceedings—

(i) to file a schedule of costs in the form set out in the Costs Practice Direction;

(ii) to file written submissions on all or any part of the issues arising;

(b) fix the date and time estimate of the hearing of the application;

(c) indicate whether the judge hearing the application will sit with an assessor at the hearing of the application; and

(d) include any further directions as the court sees fit.

44.20 Application to vary a costs capping order

An application to vary a costs capping order must be made by application notice pursuant to Part 23.

Part 45 FIXED COSTS

45.1 Scope of this Section

(1) This Section sets out the amounts which, unless the court orders otherwise, are to be allowed in respect of solicitors' charges in the cases to which this Section applies.

(2) This Section applies where—

(a) the only claim is a claim for a specified sum of money where the value of the claim exceeds £25 and—

(i) judgment in default is obtained under rule 12.4(1);

(ii) judgment on admission is obtained under rule 14.4(3);

(iii) judgment on admission on part of the claim is obtained under rule 14.5(6);

(iv) summary judgment is given under Part 24;

(v) the court has made an order to strike out a defence under rule 3.4(2)(a) as disclosing no reasonable grounds for defending the claim; or

(vi) rule 45.3 applies;

(b) the only claim is a claim where the court gave a fixed date for the hearing when it issued the claim and judgment is given for the delivery of goods, and the value of the claim exceeds £25;

(c) the claim is for the recovery of land, including a possession claim under Part 55, whether or not the claim includes a claim for a sum of money and the defendant gives up possession, pays the amount claimed, if any, and the fixed commencement costs stated in the claim form;

(d) the claim is for the recovery of land, including a possession claim under Part 55, where one of the grounds for possession is arrears of rent, for which the court gave a fixed date for the hearing when it issued the claim and judgment is given for the possession of land (whether or not the order for possession is suspended on terms) and the defendant—

(i) has neither delivered a defence, or counterclaim, nor otherwise denied liability; or

(ii) has delivered a defence which is limited to specifying his proposals for the payment of arrears of rent;

(e) the claim is a possession claim under Section II of Part 55 (accelerated possession claims of land let on an assured shorthold tenancy) and a possession order is made where the defendant has neither delivered a defence, or counterclaim, nor otherwise denied liability;

(f) the claim is a demotion claim under Section III of Part 65 or a demotion claim is made in the same claim form in which a claim for possession is made under Part 55 and that demotion claim is successful; or

(g) a judgment creditor has taken steps under Parts 70 to 73 to enforce a judgment or order.

(3) Any appropriate court fee will be allowed in addition to the costs set out in this Section.

(4) The claim form may include a claim for fixed commencement costs.

45.2 Amount of fixed commencement costs in a claim for the recovery of money or goods

(1) The amount of fixed commencement costs in a claim to which rule 45.1(2)(a) or (b) applies

(a) shall be calculated by reference to Table 1; and

(b) the amount claimed, or the value of the goods claimed if specified, in the claim form is to be used for determining the band in Table 1 that applies to the claim.

(2) The amounts shown in Table 4 are to be allowed in addition, if applicable.

45.2A Amount of fixed commencement costs in a claim for the recovery of land or a demotion claim

(1) The amount of fixed commencement costs in a claim to which rule 45.1(2)(c), (d) or (f) applies shall be calculated by reference to Table 2.

(2) The amounts shown in Table 4 are to be allowed in addition, if applicable.

TABLE 1: Fixed costs on commencement of a claim for the recovery of money or goods			
Relevant band	Where the claim form is served by the court or by any method other than personal service by the claimant	Where the claim form is served personally by the claimant; and there is only one defendant	Where there is more than one defendant, for each additional defendant personally served at separate addresses by the claimant
Where the value of the claim exceeds £25 but does not exceed £500	£50	£60	£15
Where the value of the claim exceeds £500 but does not exceed £1,000	£70	£80	£15
Where • the value of the claim exceeds £1,000 but does not exceed £5,000; or • the only claim is for delivery of goods and no value is specified or stated on the claim form	£80	£90	£15
Where the value of the claim exceeds £5,000	£100	£110	£15

TABLE 2: Fixed costs on commencement of a claim for the recovery of land or a demotion claim		
Where the claim form is served by the court or by any method other than personal service by the claimant	Where - • the claim form is served personally by the claimant; and • there is only one defendant	Where there is more than one defendant, for each additional defendant personally served at separate addresses by the claimant
£69.50	£77.00	£15.00

45.3 When defendant only liable for fixed commencement costs

(1) Where—

(a) the only claim is for a specified sum of money; and

(b) the defendant pays the money claimed within 14 days after service of particulars of claim on him, together with the fixed commencement costs stated in the claim form, the defendant is not liable for any further costs unless the court orders otherwise.

45.4 Costs on entry of judgment in a claim for the recovery of money or goods

Where—

(a) the claimant has claimed fixed commencement costs under rule 45.2; and

(b) judgment is entered in a claim to which rule 45.1(2)(a) or (b) applies in the circumstances specified in Table 3, the amount to be included in the judgment for the claimant's solicitor's charges is the total of-

(i) the fixed commencement costs; and

(ii) the relevant amount shown in Table 3.

45.4A Costs on entry of judgment in a claim for the recovery of land or a demotion claim

(1) Where—

(a) the claimant has claimed fixed commencement costs under rule 45.2A; and

(b) judgment is entered in a claim to which rule 45.1(2)(d) or (f) applies, the amount to be included in the judgment for the claimant's solicitor's charges is the total of—

(i) the fixed commencement costs; and (ii) the sum of £57.25.

(2) Where an order for possession is made in a claim to which rule 45.1(2)(e) applies, the amount allowed for the claimant's solicitor's charges for preparing and filing—

(a) the claim form;

(b) the documents that accompany the claim form; and

(c) the request for possession, is £79.50.

TABLE 3: Fixed Costs on Entry of Judgment in a claim for the recovery of money or goods		
	Where the amount of the judgment exceeds £25 but does not exceed £5,000	**Where the amount of the judgment exceeds £5,000**
Where judgment in default of an acknowledgment of service is entered under rule 12.4(1) (entry of judgment by request on claim for money only)	£22	£30
Where judgment in default of a defence is entered under rule 12.4(1) (entry of judgment by request on claim for money only)	£25	£35
Where judgment is entered under rule 14.4 (judgment on admission), or rule 14.5 (judgment on admission of part of claim) and claimant accepts the defendant's proposal as to the manner of payment	£40	£55
Where judgment is entered under rule 14.4 (judgment on admission), or rule 14.5 (judgment on admission of part of claim) and court decides the date or time of payment	£55	£70
Where summary judgment is given under Part 24 or the court strikes out a defence under rule 3.4(2)(a), in either case, on application by a party	£175	£210
Where judgment is given on a claim for delivery of goods under a regulated agreement within the meaning of the Consumer Credit Act 1974 and no other entry in this table applies	£60	£85

45.5 Miscellaneous fixed costs

Table 4 shows the amount to be allowed in respect of solicitor's charges in the circumstances mentioned.

TABLE 4: Miscellaneous Fixed Costs	
For service by a party of any document required to be served personally including preparing and copying a certificate of service for each individual served	£15.00
Where service by an alternative method or at an alternative place is permitted by an order under rule 6.15 for each individual served	£53.25
Where a document is served out of the jurisdiction –	
(a) in Scotland, Northern Ireland, the Isle of Man or the Channel Islands;	£68.25
(b) in any other place	£77.00

45.6 Fixed enforcement costs

Table 5 shows the amount to be allowed in respect of solicitors' costs in the circumstances mentioned. The amounts shown in Table 4 are to be allowed in addition, if applicable.

TABLE 5: Fixed Enforcement Costs	
For an application under rule 70.5(4) that an award may be enforced as if payable under a court order, where the amount outstanding under the award:	
exceeds £25 but does not exceed £250	£30.75
exceeds £250 but does not exceed £600	£41.00
exceeds £600 but does not exceed £2,000	£69.50
exceeds £2,000	£75.50
On attendance to question a judgment debtor (or officer of a company or other corporation) who has been ordered to attend court under rule 71.2 where the questioning takes place before a court officer, including attendance by a responsible representative of the solicitor	for each half hour or part, £15.00 (When the questioning takes place before a judge, he may summarily assess any costs allowed.)
On the making of a final third party debt order under rule 72.8(6)(a) or an order for the payment to the judgment creditor of money in court under rule 72.10(1)(b):	
if the amount recovered is less than £150	one-half of the amount recovered
otherwise	£98.50
On the making of a final charging order under rule 73.8(2)(a):	£110.00
	The court may also allow reasonable disbursements in respect of search fees and the registration of the order.
Where a certificate is issued and registered under Schedule 6 to the Civil Jurisdiction and Judgments Act 1982, the costs of registration	£39.00
Where permission is given under RSC Order 45, rule 3 to enforce a judgment or order giving possession of land and costs are allowed on the judgment or order, the amount to be added to the judgment or order for costs –	
(a) basic costs	£42.50
(b) where notice of the proceedings is to be to more than one person, for each additional person	£2.75
Where a writ of execution as defined in the RSC Order 46, rule 1, is issued against any party	£51.75
Where a request is filed for the issue of a warrant of execution under CCR Order 26, rule 1, for a sum exceeding £25	£2.25

Where an application for an attachment of earnings order is made and costs are allowed under CCR Order 27, rule 9 or CCR Order 28, rule 10, for each attendance on the hearing of the application	£8.50

II ROAD TRAFFIC ACCIDENTS – FIXED RECOVERABLE COSTS

45.7 Scope and interpretation

(1) This Section sets out the costs which are to be allowed in—

(a) costs-only proceedings under the procedure set out in rule 44.12A; or

(b) proceedings for approval of a settlement or compromise under rule 21.10(2),

in cases to which this Section applies.

(2) This Section applies where—

(a) the dispute arises from a road traffic accident;

(b) the agreed damages include damages in respect of personal injury, damage to property, or both;

(c) the total value of the agreed damages does not exceed £10,000; and

(d) if a claim had been issued for the amount of the agreed damages, the small claims track would not have been the normal track for that claim.

(3) This Section does not apply where—

(a) the claimant is a litigant in person; or

(b) Section VI of this Part applies.

(4) In this Section—

(a) 'road traffic accident' means an accident resulting in bodily injury to any person or damage to property caused by, or arising out of, the use of a motor vehicle on a road or other public place in England and Wales;

(b) 'motor vehicle' means a mechanically propelled vehicle intended for use on roads; and

(c) 'road' means any highway and any other road to which the public has access and includes bridges over which a road passes.

45.8 Application of fixed recoverable costs

Subject to rule 45.12, the only costs which are to be allowed are—

(a) fixed recoverable costs calculated in accordance with rule 45.9;

(b) disbursements allowed in accordance with rule 45.10; and

(c) a success fee allowed in accordance with rule 45.11.

45.9 Amount of fixed recoverable costs

(1) Subject to paragraphs (2) and (3), the amount of fixed recoverable costs is the total of—

(a) £800;

(b) 20% of the damages agreed up to £5,000; and

(c) 15% of the damages agreed between £5,000 and £10,000.

(2) Where the claimant—

(a) lives or works in an area set out in the Costs Practice Direction; and

(b) instructs a solicitor or firm of solicitors who practise in that area,

the fixed recoverable costs shall include, in addition to the costs specified in paragraph (1), an amount equal to 12.5% of the costs allowable under that paragraph.

(3) Where appropriate, value added tax (VAT) may be recovered in addition to the amount of fixed recoverable costs and any reference in this Section to fixed recoverable costs is a reference to those costs net of any such VAT.

45.10 Disbursements

(1) The court—

(a) may allow a claim for a disbursement of a type mentioned in paragraph (2); but

(b) must not allow a claim for any other type of disbursement.

(2) The disbursements referred to in paragraph (1) are—

(a) the cost of obtaining—

(i) medical records;

(ii) a medical report;

(iii) a police report;

(iv) an engineer's report; or

(v) a search of the records of the Driver Vehicle Licensing Authority;

(b) the amount of an insurance premium; or, where a membership organisation undertakes to meet liabilities incurred to pay the costs of other parties to proceedings, a sum not exceeding such additional amount of costs as would be allowed under section 30 in respect of provision made against the risk of having to meet such liabilities;

(c) where they are necessarily incurred by reason of one or more of the claimants being a child or protected party as defined in Part 21—

(i) fees payable for instructing counsel; or

(ii) court fees payable on an application to the court;

(d) any other disbursement that has arisen due to a particular feature of the dispute.

45.11 Success fee

(1) A claimant may recover a success fee if he has entered into a funding arrangement of a type specified in rule 43.2(k)(i).

(2) The amount of the success fee shall be 12.5% of the fixed recoverable costs calculated in accordance with rule 45.9(1), disregarding any additional amount which may be included in the fixed recoverable costs by virtue of rule 45.9(2).

45.12 Claims for an amount of costs exceeding fixed recoverable costs

(1) The court will entertain a claim for an amount of costs (excluding any success fee or disbursements) greater than the fixed recoverable costs but only if it considers that there are exceptional circumstances making it appropriate to do so.

(2) If the court considers such a claim appropriate, it may—

(a) assess the costs; or

(b) make an order for the costs to be assessed.

(3) If the court does not consider the claim appropriate, it must make an order for fixed recoverable costs only.

45.13 Failure to achieve costs greater than fixed recoverable costs

(1) This rule applies where—

(a) costs are assessed in accordance with rule 45.12(2); and

(b) the court assesses the costs (excluding any VAT) as being an amount which is less than 20% greater than the amount of the fixed recoverable costs.

(2) The court must order the defendant to pay to the claimant the lesser of—

(a) the fixed recoverable costs; and

(b) the assessed costs.

45.14 Costs of the costs-only proceedings or the detailed assessment

Where—

(a) the court makes an order for fixed recoverable costs in accordance with rule 45.12(3); or

(b) rule 45.13 applies,

the court must—

(i) make no award for the payment of the claimant's costs in bringing the proceedings under rule 44.12A; and

(ii) order that the claimant pay the defendant's costs of defending those proceedings.

III FIXED PERCENTAGE INCREASE IN ROAD TRAFFIC ACCIDENT CLAIMS

45.15 Scope and interpretation

(1) This Section sets out the percentage increase which is to be allowed in the cases to which this Section applies.

(2) This Section applies where—

(a) the dispute arises from a road traffic accident; and

(b) the claimant has entered into a funding arrangement of a type specified in rule 43.2(k)(i).

(3) This Section does not apply if the proceedings are costs only proceedings to which Section II of this Part applies.

(4) This Section does not apply—

(a) to a claim which has been allocated to the small claims track;

(b) to a claim not allocated to a track, but for which the small claims track is the normal track;

(c) where the road traffic accident which gave rise to the dispute occurred before 6th October 2003; or

(d) to a claim to which Section VI of this Part applies.

(5) The definitions in rule 45.7(4) apply to this Section as they apply to Section II.

(6) In this Section—

(a) a reference to 'fees' is a reference to fees for work done under a conditional fee agreement or collective conditional fee agreement;

(b) a reference to 'trial' is a reference to the final contested hearing or to the contested hearing of any issue ordered to be tried separately;

(c) a reference to a claim concluding at trial is a reference to a claim concluding by settlement after the trial has commenced or by judgment; and

(d) 'trial period' means a period of time fixed by the court within which the trial is to take place and where the court fixes more than one such period in relation to a claim, means the most recent period to be fixed.

45.16 Percentage increase of solicitors' fees

Subject to rule 45.18, the percentage increase which is to be allowed in relation to solicitors' fees is—

(a) 100% where the claim concludes at trial; or

(b) 12.5% where –(i) the claim concludes before a trial has commenced; or

(ii) the dispute is settled before a claim is issued.

45.17 Percentage Increase of counsel's fees

(1) Subject to rule 45.18, the percentage increase which is to be allowed in relation to counsel's fees is—

(a) 100% where the claim concludes at trial;

(b) if the claim has been allocated to the fast track—

(i) 50% if the claim concludes 14 days or less before the date fixed for the commencement of the trial; or

(ii) 12.5% if the claim concludes more than 14 days before the date fixed for the commencement of the trial or before any such date has been fixed;

(c) if the claim has been allocated to the multi-track—

(i) 75% if the claim concludes 21 days or less before the date fixed for the commencement of the trial; or

(ii) 12.5% if the claim concludes more than 21 days before the date fixed for the commencement of the trial or before any such date has been fixed;

(d) 12.5% where—

(i) the claim has been issued but concludes before it has been allocated to a track; or

(ii) in relation to costs-only proceedings, the dispute is settled before a claim is issued.

(2) Where a trial period has been fixed, if—

(a) the claim concludes before the first day of that period; and

(b) no trial date has been fixed within that period before the claim concludes, the first day of that period is treated as the date fixed for the commencement of the trial for the purposes of paragraph (1).

(3) Where a trial period has been fixed, if

(a) the claim concludes before the first day of that period; but

(b) before the claim concludes, a trial date had been fixed within that period, the trial date is the date fixed for the commencement of the trial for the purposes of paragraph (1).

(4) Where a trial period has been fixed and the claim concludes—

(a) on or after the first day of that period; but

(b) before commencement of the trial,

the percentage increase in paragraph (1)(b)(i) or (1)(c)(i) shall apply as appropriate, whether or not a trial date has been fixed within that period.

(5) For the purposes of this rule, in calculating the periods of time, the day fixed for the commencement of the trial (or the first day of the trial period, where appropriate) is not included.

45.18 Application for an alternative percentage increase where the fixed increase is 12.5%

(1) This rule applies where the percentage increase to be allowed—

(a) in relation to solicitors' fees under the provisions of rule 45.16; or

(b) in relation to counsel's fees under rule 45.17, is 12.5%.

(2) A party may apply for a percentage increase greater or less than that amount if—

(a) the parties agree damages of an amount greater than £500,000 or the court awards damages of an amount greater than £500,000; or

(b) the court awards damages of £500,000 or less but would have awarded damages greater than £500,000 if it had not made a finding of contributory negligence; or

(c) the parties agree damages of £500,000 or less and it is reasonable to expect that if the court had made an award of damages, it would have awarded damages greater than £500,000, disregarding any reduction the court may have made in respect of contributory negligence.

(3) In paragraph (2), a reference to a lump sum of damages includes a reference to periodical payments of equivalent value.

(4) If the court is satisfied that the circumstances set out in paragraph (2) apply it must—

(a) assess the percentage increase; or

(b) make an order for the percentage increase to be assessed.

45.19 Assessment of alternative percentage increase

(1) This rule applies where the percentage increase of fees is assessed under rule 45.18(4).

(2) If the percentage increase is assessed as greater than 20% or less than 7.5%, the percentage increase to be allowed shall be that assessed by the court.

(3) If the percentage increase is assessed as no greater than 20% and no less than 7.5%—

(a) the percentage increase to be allowed shall be 12.5%; and

(b) the costs of the application and assessment shall be paid by the applicant.

IV FIXED PERCENTAGE INCREASE IN EMPLOYERS LIABILITY CLAIMS

45.20 Scope and interpretation

(1) Subject to paragraph (2), this Section applies where—

(a) the dispute is between an employee and his employer arising from a bodily injury sustained by the employee in the course of his employment; and

(b) the claimant has entered into a funding arrangement of a type specified in rule 43.2(1)(k)(i).

(2) This Section does not apply—

(a) where the dispute –(i) relates to a disease;

(ii) relates to an injury sustained before 1st October 2004; or

(iii) arises from a road traffic accident (as defined in rule 45.7(4)(a)); or

(iv) relates to an injury to which Section V of this Part applies; or

(b) to a claim –(i) which has been allocated to the small claims track; or

(ii) not allocated to a track, but for which the small claims track is the normal track.

(3) For the purposes of this Section—

(a) 'employee' has the meaning given to it by section 2(1) of the Employers' Liability (Compulsory Insurance) Act 1969[1]; and

(b) a reference to 'fees' is a reference to fees for work done under a conditional fee agreement or collective conditional fee agreement.

45.21 Percentage increase of solicitors' and counsel's fees

In the cases to which this Section applies, subject to rule 45.22 the percentage increase which is to be allowed in relation to solicitors' and counsel's fees is to be determined in accordance with rules 45.16 and 45.17, subject to the modifications that—

(a) the percentage increase which is to be allowed in relation to solicitors' fees under rule 45.16(b) is—

(i) 27.5% if a membership organisation has undertaken to meet the claimant's liabilities for legal costs in accordance with section 30 of the Access to Justice Act 1999; and

(ii) 25% in any other case; and

(b) the percentage increase which is to be allowed in relation to counsel's fees under rule 45.17(1)(b)(ii), (1)(c)(ii) or (1)(d) is 25%.

45.22 Alternative percentage increase

(1) In the cases to which this Section applies, rule 45.18(2)–(4) applies where—

(a) the percentage increase of solicitors' fees to be allowed in accordance with rule 45.21 is 25% or 27.5%; or

(b) the percentage increase of counsel's fees to be allowed is 25%.

(2) Where the percentage increase of fees is assessed by the court under rule 45.18(4) as applied by paragraph (1) above—

(a) if the percentage increase is assessed as greater than 40% or less than 15%, the percentage increase to be allowed shall be that assessed by the court; and

(b) if the percentage increase is assessed as no greater than 40% and no less than 15%—

(i) the percentage increase to be allowed shall be 25% or 27.5% (as the case may be); and

(ii) the costs of the application and assessment shall be paid by the applicant.

V FIXED RECOVERABLE SUCCESS FEES IN EMPLOYER'S LIABILITY DISEASE CLAIMS

45.23 Scope and Interpretation

(1) Subject to paragraph (2), this Section applies where—

(a) the dispute is between an employee (or, if the employee is deceased, the employee's estate or dependants) and his employer (or a person alleged to be liable for the employer's alleged breach of statutory or common law duties of care); and

(b) the dispute relates to a disease with which the employee is diagnosed that is alleged to have been contracted as a consequence of the employer's alleged breach of statutory or common law duties of care in the course of the employee's employment; and

(c) the claimant has entered into a funding arrangement of a type specified in rule 43.2(1)(k)(i).

(2) This Section does not apply where—

(a) the claimant sent a letter of claim to the defendant containing a summary of the facts on which the claim is based and main allegations of fault before 1st October 2005; or

(b) rule 45.20(2)(b) applies.

(3) For the purposes of this Section—

(a) rule 45.15(6) applies;

(b) 'employee' has the meaning given to it by section 2(1) of the Employers' Liability (Compulsory Insurance) Act 1969;

(c) 'Type A claim' means a claim relating to a disease or physical injury alleged to have been caused by exposure to asbestos;

(d) 'Type B claim' means a claim relating to—

(i) a psychiatric injury alleged to have been caused by work-related psychological stress;

(ii) a work-related upper limb disorder which is alleged to have been caused by physical stress or strain, excluding hand/arm vibration injuries; and

(e) 'Type C claim' means a claim relating to a disease not falling within either type A or type B.

45.24 Percentage increase of solicitors' fees

(1) In the cases to which this Section applies, subject to rule 45.26, the percentage increase which is to be allowed in relation to solicitors' fees is—

(a) 100% if the claim concludes at trial; or

(b) where – (i) the claim concludes before a trial has commenced; or

(ii) the dispute is settled before a claim is issued,to be determined by rule 45.24(2).

(2) Where rule 45.24(1)(b) applies, the percentage increase which is to be allowed in relation to solicitors' fees is—

(a) in type A claims—

(i) 30% if a membership organisation has undertaken to meet the claimant's liabilities for legal costs in accordance with section 30 of the Access to Justice Act 1999; and

(ii) 27.5% in any other case;

(b) in type B claims, 100%; and

(c) in type C claims—

(i) 70% if a membership organisation has undertaken to meet the claimant's liabilities for legal costs in accordance with section 30 of the Access to Justice Act 1999; and

(ii) 62.5% in any other case.

45.25 Percentage increase of counsel's fees

(1) In the cases to which this Section applies, subject to rule 45.26, the percentage increase which is to be allowed in relation to counsel's fees is—

(a) 100% if the claim concludes at trial; or

(b) where – (i) the claim concludes before a trial has commenced; or

(ii) the dispute is settled before a claim is issued, to be determined by rule 45.25(2).

(2) Where rule 45.25(1)(b) applies, the percentage increase which is to be allowed in relation to counsel's fees is—

(a) if the claim has been allocated to the fast track, the amount shown in Table 6; and

(b) if the claim has been allocated to the multi-track, the amount shown in Table 7.

(3) Where a trial period has been fixed, rules 45.17(2) to 45.17(5) apply for the purposes of determining the date fixed for the commencement of the trial.

TABLE 6: Claims allocated to the fast track		
	If the claim concludes 14 days or less before the date fixed for commencement of the trial	If the claim concludes more than 14 days before the date fixed for commencement of the trial or before any such date has been fixed
Type A claim	50%	27.5%
Type B claim	100%	100%
Type C claim	62.5%	62.5%

TABLE 7: Claims allocated to the multi-track		
	If the claim concludes 21 days or less before the date fixed for commencement of the trial	If the claim concludes more than 21 days before the date fixed for commencement of the trial or before any such date has been fixed
Type A claim	75%	27.5%
Type B claim	100%	100%
Type C claim	75%	62.5%

45.26 Alternative percentage increase

(1) In cases to which this Section applies and subject to paragraph (2) below, rules 45.18(2) to (4) apply where the percentage increase is the amount allowed under rules 45.24 and 45.25.

(2) For the purposes of this section, the sum of £250,000 shall be substituted for the sum of £500,000 in rules 45.18(2)(a) to (c).

(3) Where the percentage increase of fees is assessed by the court under rule 45.18(4), as applied by paragraph 1 above, the percentage increase to be allowed shall be the amount shown in Table 8.

(4) The percentage increase cannot be varied where the case concludes at trial.

TABLE 8

Type of claim	Amount Allowed	
A	If the percentage increase is assessed as greater than 40% or less than 15%, the percentage increase that is assessed by the court.	If the percentage increase is assessed as no greater than 40% and no less than 15% – (i) 27.5%; and (ii) the costs of the application and assessment shall be paid by the applicant.
B	If the percentage increase is assessed as less than 75%, the percentage increase that is assessed by the court.	If the percentage increase is assessed as no less than 75% – (i) 100%; and (ii) the costs of the application and assessment shall be paid by the applicant.
C	If the percentage increase is assessed as greater than 75% or less than 50%, the percentage increase that is assessed by the court.	If the percentage increase is assessed as no greater than 75% and no less than 50% – (i) 62.5%; and (ii) the costs of the application and assessment shall be paid by the applicant.

VI PRE-ACTION PROTOCOL FOR LOW VALUE PERSONAL INJURY CLAIMS IN ROAD TRAFFIC ACCIDENTS

45.27 Scope and interpretation

(1) This Section applies to claims that have been or should have been started under Part 8 in accordance with Practice Direction 8B ('the Stage 3 Procedure').

(2) Where a party has not complied with the RTA Protocol rule 45.36 will apply.

(3) 'RTA Protocol' means the Pre-Action Protocol for Personal Injury Claims in Road Traffic Accidents.

(4) A reference to 'Claim Notification Form' is a reference to the form used in the RTA Protocol.

45.28 Application of fixed costs, disbursements and success fee

The only costs allowed are—

(a) fixed costs in rule 45.29;

(b) disbursements in accordance with rule 45.30; and

(c) a success fee in accordance with rule 45.31.

45.29 Amount of fixed costs

(1) Subject to paragraph (4), the amount of fixed costs is set out in Table 1.

(2) In Table 1—

(a) 'Type A fixed costs' means the legal representative's costs;

(b) 'Type B fixed costs' means the advocate's costs; and

(c) 'Type C fixed costs' means the costs for the advice on the amount of damages where the claimant is a child.

(3) Advocate has the same meaning as in rule 46.1(2)(a).

(4) Subject to rule 45.36(2) the court will not award more or less than the amounts shown in Table 1.

(5) Where the claimant—

(a) lives or works in an area set out in the Costs Practice Direction; and

(b) instructs a legal representative who practices in that area,

the fixed costs will include, in addition to the costs set out in Table 1, an amount equal to 12.5% of the Stage 1 and 2 and Stage 3 Type A fixed costs.

(6) Where appropriate, value added tax (VAT) may be recovered in addition to the amount of fixed costs and any reference in this Section to fixed costs is a reference to those costs net of any such VAT.

TABLE 1: Fixed costs in relation to the RTA Protocol	
Stage 1 fixed costs	£400
Stage 2 fixed costs	£800
Stage 3 –	
Type A fixed costs	£250
Type B fixed costs	£250
Type C fixed costs	£150

45.30 Disbursements

(1) The court—

(a) may allow a claim for a disbursement of a type mentioned in paragraph (2); but

(b) must not allow a claim for any other type of disbursement.

(2) The disbursements referred to in paragraph (1) are—

(a) the cost of obtaining – (i) medical records;

(ii) a medical report or reports as provided for in the RTA Protocol;

(iii) an engineer's report;

(iv) a search of the records of the—

(aa) Driver Vehicle Licensing Authority;

(bb) Motor Insurance Database;

(b) the amount of the insurance premium or, where a membership organisation undertakes to meet liabilities incurred to pay the costs of other parties to proceedings, a sum not exceeding such additional amount of costs as would be allowed under section 30 of the Access to Justice Act 1999[2] in respect of provision made against the risk of having to meet such liabilities;

(c) court fees as a result of Part 21 being applicable;

(d) court fees payable where proceedings are started as a result of a limitation period that is about to expire;

(e) court fees in respect of the Stage 3 Procedure;

(f) any other disbursement that has arisen due to a particular feature of the dispute.

45.31 Success fee

(1) A party who has entered into a funding arrangement of a type specified in rule 43.2(1)(k)(i) in respect of any element of the fixed costs in rule 45.29 may recover a success fee on that element of the fixed costs.

(2) A reference to a success fee in this Section is a reference to a success fee in accordance with paragraph (1).

(3) Where the court—

(a) determines the claim at a Stage 3 hearing or on the papers; and

(b) awards an amount of damages that is more than the defendant's RTA Protocol offer,

the amount of the claimant's success fee is—

(i) 12.5% of the Stage 1 and 2 fixed costs; and

(ii) 100% of the relevant Stage 3 fixed costs.

(4) Where the court—

(a) determines the claim at a Stage 3 hearing or on the papers; and

(b) awards an amount of damages that is equal to or less than the defendant's RTA Protocol offer,

the amount of the defendant's success fee is 100% of the relevant Stage 3 fixed costs.

(5) Where the claimant is a child and the court—

(a) does not approve a settlement at a settlement hearing;

(b) determines the claim at a Stage 3 hearing; and

(c) awards an amount of damages that is more than the amount of the settlement considered by the court at the first settlement hearing;

the amount of the claimant's success fee is – (i) 12.5% of the Stage 1 and 2 fixed costs;

(ii) 100% of the relevant Stage 3 fixed costs.

(6) Where paragraphs (3) to (5) do not apply the success fee is—

(a) 12.5% of Stage 1 and 2 fixed costs; and

(b) 12.5% of the relevant Stage 3 fixed costs.

(7) The amount of the success fee set out in paragraphs (3) to (6) will be calculated without regard to any additional amount which may be included in the fixed costs by virtue of rule 45.29(5).

45.32 Where the claimant obtains judgment for an amount more than the defendant's RTA Protocol offer

(1) Where rule 36.21(1)(b) or (c) applies, the court will order the defendant to pay—

(a) where not already paid by the defendant, the Stage 1 and 2 fixed costs;

(b) where the claim is determined—

(i) on the papers, Stage 3 Type A fixed costs;

(ii) at a Stage 3 hearing, Stage 3 Type A and B fixed costs; or

(iii) at a Stage 3 hearing and the claimant is a child, Type A, B and C fixed costs;

(c) disbursements allowed in accordance with rule 45.30; and

(d) a success fee in accordance with rule 45.31(3).

45.33 Settlement at Stage 2 where the claimant is a child

(1) This rule applies where—

(a) the claimant is a child;

(b) there is a settlement at Stage 2 of the RTA Protocol; and

(c) an application is made to the court to approve the settlement.

(2) Where the court approves the settlement at a settlement hearing it will order the defendant to pay—

(a) the Stage 1 and 2 fixed costs;

(b) the Stage 3 Type A, B and C fixed costs;

(c) disbursements allowed in accordance with rule 45.30; and

(d) a success fee in accordance with rule 45.31(6).

(3) Where the court does not approve the settlement at a settlement hearing it will order the defendant to pay the Stage 1 and 2 fixed costs.

(4) Paragraphs (5) and (6) apply where the court does not approve the settlement at the first settlement hearing but does approve the settlement at a second settlement hearing.

(5) At the second settlement hearing the court will order the defendant to pay—

(a) the Stage 3 Type A and C fixed costs for the first settlement hearing;

(b) disbursements allowed in accordance with rule 45.30;

(c) the Stage 3 Type B fixed costs for one of the hearings; and

(d) a success fee in accordance with rule 45.31(6) on the Stage 1 and 2 fixed costs and the Stage 3 Type A, B and C fixed costs.

(6) The court in its discretion may also order—

(a) the defendant to pay—

(i) an additional amount of either or both the Stage 3—

(aa) Type A fixed costs;

(bb) Type B fixed costs; and

(ii) a success fee in accordance with rule 45.31(6) on the additional Stage 3 fixed costs in sub-paragraph (a)(i); or

(b) the claimant to pay an amount equivalent to either or both the Stage 3—

(i) Type A fixed costs;

(ii) Type B fixed costs.

45.34 Settlement at Stage 3 where the claimant is a child

(1) This rule applies where—

(a) the claimant is a child;

(b) there is a settlement after proceedings are started under the Stage 3 Procedure;

(c) the settlement is more than the defendant's RTA Protocol offer; and

(d) an application is made to the court to approve the settlement.

(2) Where the court approves the settlement at the settlement hearing it will order the defendant to pay—

(a) the Stage 1 and 2 fixed costs;

(b) the Stage 3 Type A, B and C fixed costs;

(c) disbursements allowed in accordance with rule 45.30; and

(d) a success fee in accordance with rule 45.31(6).

(3) Where the court does not approve the settlement at the settlement hearing it will order the defendant to pay the Stage 1 and 2 fixed costs.

(4) Paragraphs (5) and (6) apply where the court does not approve the settlement at the first settlement hearing but does approve the settlement at the Stage 3 hearing.

(5) At the Stage 3 hearing the court will order the defendant to pay—

(a) the Stage 3 Type A and C fixed costs for the settlement hearing;

(b) disbursements allowed in accordance with rule 45.30;

(c) the Stage 3 Type B fixed costs for one of the hearings; and

(d) a success fee in accordance with rule 45.31(6) on the Stage 1 and 2 fixed costs and the Stage 3 Type A, B and C fixed costs.

(6) The court in its discretion may also order—

(a) the defendant to pay—

(i) an additional amount of either or both the Stage 3—

(aa) Type A fixed costs;

(bb) Type B fixed costs; and

(ii) a success fee in accordance with rule 45.31(6) on the additional Stage 3 fixed costs in sub-paragraph (a)(i); or

(b) the claimant to pay an amount equivalent to either or both of the Stage 3—

(i) Type A fixed costs;

(ii) Type B fixed costs.

(7) Where the settlement is not approved at the Stage 3 hearing the court will order the defendant to pay the Stage 3 Type A fixed costs.

45.35 Where the court orders the claim is not suitable to be determined under the Stage 3 Procedure and the claimant is a child

Where—

(a) the claimant is a child; and

(b) at a settlement hearing or the Stage 3 hearing the court orders that the claim is not suitable to be determined under the Stage 3 Procedure,

the court will order the defendant to pay—

(i) the Stage 1 and 2 fixed costs; and

(ii) the Stage 3 Type A, B and C fixed costs.

45.36 Failure to comply or electing not to continue with the RTA Protocol – costs consequences

(1) This rule applies where the claimant—

(a) does not comply with the process set out in the RTA Protocol; or

(b) elects not to continue with that process,

and starts proceedings under Part 7.

(2) Where a judgment is given in favour of the claimant but—

(a) the court determines that the defendant did not proceed with the process set out in the RTA Protocol because the claimant provided insufficient information on the Claim Notification Form;

(b) the court considers that the claimant acted unreasonably—

(i) by discontinuing the process set out in the RTA Protocol and starting proceedings under Part 7;

(ii) by valuing the claim at more than £10,000, so that the claimant did not need to comply with the RTA Protocol; or

(iii) except for paragraph (2)(a), in any other way that caused the process in the RTA Protocol to be discontinued; or

(c) the claimant did not comply with the RTA Protocol at all despite the claim falling within the scope of the RTA Protocol;

the court may order the defendant to pay no more than the fixed costs in rule 45.29 together with the disbursements allowed in accordance with rule 45.30 and success fee in accordance with rule 45.31(3).

(3) Where the claimant starts proceedings under paragraph 7.22 of the RTA Protocol and the court orders the defendant to make an interim payment of no more than the interim payment made under paragraph 7.14(2) or (3) of that Protocol the court will, on the final determination of the proceedings, order the defendant to pay no more than—

(a) the Stage 1 and 2 fixed costs;

(b) the disbursements allowed in accordance with rule 45.30; and

(c) a success fee in accordance with rule 45.31(3).

45.37 Where the parties have settled after proceedings have started

(1) This rule applies where an application is made under rule 44.12C (costs-only application after a claim is started under Part 8 in accordance with Practice Direction 8B).

(2) Where the settlement is more than the defendant's RTA Protocol offer the court will order the defendant to pay—

(a) the Stage 1 and 2 fixed costs where not already paid by the defendant;

(b) the Stage 3 Type A fixed costs;

(c) disbursements allowed in accordance with rule 45.30; and

(d) a success fee in accordance with rule 45.31(6).

(3) Where the settlement is less than or equal to the defendant's RTA Protocol offer the court will order the defendant to pay—

(a) the Stage 1 and 2 fixed costs where not already paid by the defendant;

(b) disbursements allowed in accordance with rule 45.30; and

(c) success fee in accordance with rule 45.31(6).

(4) The court may, in its discretion, order either party to pay the costs of the application.

45.38 Where the claimant obtains judgment for an amount equal to or less than the defendant's RTA Protocol offer

Where rule 36.21(1)(a) applies, the court will order the claimant to pay—

(a) where the claim is determined – (i) on the papers, Stage 3 Type A fixed costs; or

(ii) at a hearing, Stage 3 Type A and B fixed costs;

(b) disbursements allowed in accordance with rule 45.30; and

(c) a success fee in accordance with rule 45.31(4).

45.39 Adjournment

Where the court adjourns a settlement hearing or a Stage 3 hearing it may, in its discretion, order a party to pay—

(a) an additional amount of the Stage 3 Type B fixed costs; and

(b) any court fee for that adjournment.

45.40 Account of payment of Stage 1 fixed costs

Where a claim no longer continues under the RTA Protocol the court will, when making any order as to costs including an order for fixed recoverable costs under Section II of this Part, take into account the Stage 1 fixed costs together with any success fee on those costs that have been paid by the defendant.

VII SCALE COSTS FOR CLAIMS IN A PATENTS COUNTY COURT

45.41 Scope and interpretation

(1) Subject to paragraph (2) this Section applies to proceedings in a patents county court.

(2) This Section does not apply where—

(a) the court considers that a party has behaved in a manner which amounts to an abuse of the court's process; or

(b) the claim concerns the infringement or revocation of a patent or registered design the validity of which has been certified by a court in earlier proceedings.

(3) The court will make a summary assessment of the costs of the party in whose favour any order for costs is made. Rules 44.3(8), 44.3A(2)(b) and (c), 44.7(b) and Part 47 do not apply to this Section.

(4) 'Scale costs' means costs as defined in rule 43.2(1)(a).

45.42 Amount of scale costs

(1) Subject to rule 45.43 the court will not order a party to pay total costs of more than—

(a) £50,000 on the final determination of a claim in relation to liability; and

(b) £25,000 on an inquiry as to damages or account of profits.

(2) The amounts in paragraph (1) apply after the court has applied the provision on set off in accordance with rule 44.3(9)(a).

(3) The maximum amount of scale costs that the court will award for each stage of the claim is set out in the Costs Practice Direction.

(4) The amount of the scale costs awarded by the court in accordance with paragraph (3) will depend on the nature and complexity of the claim.

(5) Where appropriate, value added tax (VAT) may be recovered in addition to the amount of the scale costs and any reference in this Section to scale costs is a reference to those costs net of any such VAT.

45.43 Summary assessment of the costs of an application where a party has behaved unreasonably

Costs awarded to a party under rule 63.26(2) are in addition to the total costs that may be awarded to that party under rule 45.42.

45.44.—Scope Interpretation and application

(1) This Section sets out the amounts which, unless the court orders otherwise, are to be allowed in respect of HM Revenue & Customs charges ("HMRC charges") in the cases to which this Section applies.

(2) For the purpose of this Section—

"HMRC Officer" means a person appointed by the Commissioners under section 2 of the Commissioners for Revenue and Customs Act 2005 and authorised to conduct county court proceedings for recovery of debt under section 25(1A) of that Act;

"debt" means any sum payable to the Commissioners under or by virtue of an enactment or under a contract settlement; and

"HMRC charges" means the fixed costs set out in Tables 9 and 10 in this Section.

(3) HMRC charges shall, for the purpose of this Section, be claimed as "solicitor costs" on relevant court forms.

(4) This Section applies where the only claim is a claim conducted by an HMRC Officer in the county court for recovery of a debt and the Commissioners obtain judgment on the claim.

(5) Any appropriate court fee will be allowed in addition to the costs set out in this Section.

(6) The claim form may include a claim for fixed commencement costs.

45.45. Amount of fixed commencement costs in a county court claim for the recovery of money.

The amount of fixed commencement costs in a claim to which rule 45.44 applies—

(a) shall be calculated by reference to Table 9; and

(b) the amount claimed in the claim form is to be used for determining which claim band in Table 9 applies.

TABLE 9: Fixed costs on commencement of a county court claim conducted by an HMRC officer	
Where the value of the claim exceeds £25 but does not exceed £500	£33
Where the value of the claim exceeds £500 but does not exceed £1,000	£47
Where the value of the claim exceeds £1,000 but does not exceed £5,000	£53
Where the value of the claim exceeds £5,000 but does not exceed £15,000	£67
Where the value of the claim exceeds £15,000 but does not exceed £50,000	£90
Where the value of the claim exceeds £50,000 but does not exceed £100,000	£113
Where the value of the claim exceeds £100,000 but does not exceed £150,000	£127
Where the value of the claim exceeds £150,000 but does not exceed £200,000	£140
Where the value of the claim exceeds £200,000 but does not exceed £250,000	£153
Where the value of the claim exceeds £250,000 but does not exceed £300,000	£167
Where the value of the claim exceeds £300,000	£180

45.46. Costs on entry of judgment in a county court claim for recovery of money

Where—

(a) an HMRC Officer has claimed fixed commencement costs under Rule 45.45; and

(b) judgment is entered in a claim to which rule 45.44 applies the amount to be included in the judgment for HMRC charges is the total of—

(i) the fixed commencement costs; and

(ii) the amount in Table 10 relevant to the value of the claim.

TABLE 10: Fixed costs on entry of judgment in a county court claim conducted by an HMRC officer	
Where the value of the claim does not exceed £5,000	£15
Where the value of the claim exceeds £5,000	£20

45.47 When the defendant is only liable for fixed commencement costs

Where—

(a) the only claim is for a specified sum of money; and

(b) the defendant pays the money claimed within 14 days after service of the particulars of claim, together with the fixed commencement costs stated in the claim form,

the defendant is not liable for any further costs unless the court orders otherwise.

Part 46 FAST TRACK TRIAL COSTS

46.1 Scope of this Part

(1) This Part deals with the amount of costs which the court may award as the costs of an advocate for preparing for and appearing at the trial of a claim in the fast track (referred to in this rule as 'fast track trial costs').

(2) For the purposes of this Part—

(a) 'advocate' means a person exercising a right of audience as a representative of, or on behalf of, a party;

(b) 'fast track trial costs' means the costs of a party's advocate for preparing for and appearing at the trial, but does not include – (i) any other disbursements; or

(ii) any value added tax payable on the fees of a party's advocate; and

(c) 'trial' includes a hearing where the court decides an amount of money or the value of goods following a judgment under Part 12 (default judgment) or Part 14 (admissions) but does not include – (i) the hearing of an application for summary judgment under Part 24; or

(ii) the court's approval of a settlement or other compromise under rule 21.10.

46.2 Amount of fast track trial costs

(1) The following table shows the amount of fast track trial costs which the court may award (whether by summary or detailed assessment).

Value of the claim	Amount of fast track trial costs which the court may award
No more than £3,000	£485
More than £3,000 but not more than £10,000	£690
More than £10,000 but not more than £15,000	£1,035
For proceedings issued on or after 6th April 2009, more than £15,000	£1,650

(2) The court may not award more or less than the amount shown in the table except where—

(a) it decides not to award any fast track trial costs; or

(b) rule 46.3 applies,

but the court may apportion the amount awarded between the parties to reflect their respective degrees of success on the issues at trial.

(3) Where the only claim is for the payment of money—

(a) for the purpose of quantifying fast track trial costs awarded to a claimant, the value of the claim is the total amount of the judgment excluding—

(i) interest and costs; and

(ii) any reduction made for contributory negligence.

(b) for the purpose of quantifying fast track trial costs awarded to a defendant, the value of the claim is—

(i) the amount specified in the claim form (excluding interest and costs);

(ii) if no amount is specified, the maximum amount which the claimant reasonably expected to recover according to the statement of value included in the claim form under rule 16.3; or

(iii) more than £15,000, if the claim form states that the claimant cannot reasonably say how much is likely to be recovered.

(4) Where the claim is only for a remedy other than the payment of money the value of the claim is deemed to be more than £3,000 but not more than £10,000, unless the court orders otherwise.

(5) Where the claim includes both a claim for the payment of money and for a remedy other than the payment of money, the value of the claim is deemed to be the higher of—

(a) the value of the money claim decided in accordance with paragraph (3); or

(b) the deemed value of the other remedy decided in accordance with paragraph (4),

unless the court orders otherwise.

(6) Where—

(a) a defendant has made a counterclaim against the claimant;

(b) the counterclaim has a higher value than the claim; and

(c) the claimant succeeds at trial both on the claim and the counterclaim,

for the purpose of quantifying fast track trial costs awarded to the claimant, the value of the claim is the value of the defendant's counterclaim calculated in accordance with this rule.

46.3 Power to award more or less than the amount of fast track trial costs

(1) This rule sets out when a court may award—

(a) an additional amount to the amount of fast track trial costs shown in the table in rule 46.2(1); and

(b) less than those amounts.

(2) If – (a) in addition to the advocate, a party's legal representative attends the trial;

(b) the court considers that it was necessary for a legal representative to attend to assist the advocate; and

(c) the court awards fast track trial costs to that party,

the court may award an additional £345 in respect of the legal representative's attendance at the trial.

(2A) The court may in addition award a sum representing an additional liability.

(3) If the court considers that it is necessary to direct a separate trial of an issue then the court may award an additional amount in respect of the separate trial but that amount is limited in accordance with paragraph (4) of this rule.

(4) The additional amount the court may award under paragraph 3 must not exceed two-thirds of the amount payable for that claim, subject to a minimum award of £485.

(5) Where the party to whom fast track trial costs are to be awarded is a litigant in person, the court will award—

(a) if the litigant in person can prove financial loss, two-thirds of the amount that would otherwise be awarded; or

(b) if the litigant in person fails to prove financial loss, an amount in respect of the time spent reasonably doing the work at the rate specified in the Costs Practice Direction.

(6) Where a defendant has made a counterclaim against the claimant, and—

(a) the claimant has succeeded on his claim; and

(b) the defendant has succeeded on his counterclaim,

the court will quantify the amount of the award of fast track trial costs to which—

(i) but for the counterclaim, the claimant would be entitled for succeeding on his claim; and

(ii) but for the claim, the defendant would be entitled for succeeding on his counterclaim,

and make one award of the difference, if any, to the party entitled to the higher award of costs.

(7) Where the court considers that the party to whom fast track trial costs are to be awarded has behaved unreasonably or improperly during the trial, it may award that party an amount less than would otherwise be payable for that claim, as it considers appropriate.

(8) Where the court considers that the party who is to pay the fast track trial costs has behaved improperly during the trial the court may award such additional amount to the other party as it considers appropriate.

46.4 Fast track trial costs where there is more than one claimant or defendant

(1) Where the same advocate is acting for more than one party—

(a) the court may make only one award in respect of fast track trial costs payable to that advocate; and

(b) the parties for whom the advocate is acting are jointly entitled to any fast track trial costs awarded by the court.

(2) Where – (a) the same advocate is acting for more than one claimant; and

(b) each claimant has a separate claim against the defendant,

the value of the claim, for the purpose of quantifying the award in respect of fast track trial costs is to be ascertained in accordance with paragraph (3).

(3) The value of the claim in the circumstances mentioned in paragraph (2) is—

(a) where the only claim of each claimant is for the payment of money—

(i) if the award of fast track trial costs is in favour of the claimants, the total amount of the judgment made in favour of all the claimants jointly represented; or

(ii) if the award is in favour of the defendant, the total amount claimed by the claimants,

and in either case, quantified in accordance with rule 46.2(3);

(b) where the only claim of each claimant is for a remedy other than the payment of money, deemed to be more than £3,000 but not more than £10,000; and

(c) where claims of the claimants include both a claim for the payment of money and for a remedy other than the payment of money, deemed to be—

(i) more than £3,000 but not more than £10,000; or

(ii) if greater, the value of the money claims calculated in accordance with sub paragraph (a) above.

(4) Where – (a) there is more than one defendant; and

(b) any or all of the defendants are separately represented,

the court may award fast track trial costs to each party who is separately represented.

(5) Where – (a) there is more than one claimant; and

(b) a single defendant,

the court may make only one award to the defendant of fast track trial costs, for which the claimants are jointly and severally liable.

(6) For the purpose of quantifying the fast track trial costs awarded to the single defendant under paragraph (5), the value of the claim is to be calculated in accordance with paragraph (3) of this rule.

Part 47 PROCEDURE FOR DETAILED ASSESSMENT OF COSTS AND DEFAULT PROVISIONS

I GENERAL RULES ABOUT DETAILED ASSESSMENT

47.1 Time when detailed assessment may be carried out

The general rule is that the costs of any proceedings or any part of the proceedings are not to be assessed by the detailed procedure until the conclusion of the proceedings but the court may order them to be assessed immediately.

47.2 No stay of detailed assessment where there is an appeal

Detailed assessment is not stayed pending an appeal unless the court so orders.

47.3 Powers of an authorised court officer

(1) An authorised court officer has all the powers of the court when making a detailed assessment, except—

(a) power to make a wasted costs order as defined in rule 48.7;

(b) power to make an order under—

(i) rule 44.14 (powers in relation to misconduct);

(ii) rule 47.8 (sanction for delay in commencing detailed assessment proceedings);

(iii) paragraph (2) (objection to detailed assessment by authorised court officer); and

(c) power to make a detailed assessment of costs payable to a solicitor by his client, unless the costs are being assessed under rule 48.5 (costs where money is payable to a child or protected party).

(2) Where a party objects to the detailed assessment of costs being made by an authorised court officer, the court may order it to be made by a costs judge or a district judge.

47.4 Venue for detailed assessment proceedings

(1) All applications and requests in detailed assessment proceedings must be made to or filed at the appropriate office.

(2) The court may direct that the appropriate office is to be the Costs Office.

(3) A county court may direct that another county court is to be the appropriate office.

(4) A direction under paragraph (3) may be made without proceedings being transferred to that court.

II COSTS PAYABLE BY ONE PARTY TO ANOTHER – COMMENCEMENT OF DETAILED ASSESSMENT PROCEEDINGS

47.5 Application of this Section

This Section of Part 47 applies where a cost officer is to make a detailed assessment of—

(a) costs which are payable by one party to another; or

(b) the sum which is payable by one party to the prescribed charity pursuant to an order under section 194(3) of the Legal Services Act 2007.

47.6 Commencement of detailed assessment proceedings

(1) Detailed assessment proceedings are commenced by the receiving party serving on the paying party—

(a) notice of commencement in the relevant practice form; and

(b) a copy of the bill of costs.

(2) The receiving party must also serve a copy of the notice of commencement and the bill on any other relevant persons specified in the Costs Practice Direction.

(3) A person on whom a copy of the notice of commencement is served under paragraph (2) is a party to the detailed assessment proceedings (in addition to the paying party and the receiving party).

47.7 Period for commencing detailed assessment proceedings

The following table shows the period for commencing detailed assessment proceedings.

Source of right to detailed assessment	Time by which detailed assessment proceedings must be commenced
Judgment, direction, order, award or other determination	3 months after the date of the judgment etc. Where detailed assessment is stayed pending an appeal, 3 months after the date of the order lifting the stay
Discontinuance under Part 38	3 months after the date of service of notice of discontinuance under rule 38.3; or 3 months after the date of the dismissal of application to set the notice of discontinuance aside under rule 38.4
Acceptance of an offer to settle under Part 36	3 months after the date when the right to costs arose

47.8 Sanction for delay in commencing detailed assessment proceedings

(1) Where the receiving party fails to commence detailed assessment proceedings within the period specified – (a) in rule 47.7; or

(b) by any direction of the court,

the paying party may apply for an order requiring the receiving party to commence detailed assessment proceedings within such time as the court may specify.

(2) On an application under paragraph (1), the court may direct that, unless the receiving party commences detailed

assessment proceedings within the time specified by the court, all or part of the costs to which the receiving party would otherwise be entitled will be disallowed.

(3) If – (a) the paying party has not made an application in accordance with paragraph (1); and

(b) the receiving party commences the proceedings later than the period specified in rule 47.7,

the court may disallow all or part of the interest otherwise payable to the receiving party under—

(i) section 17 of the Judgments Act 1838; or

(ii) section 74 of the County Courts Act 1984,

but must not impose any other sanction except in accordance with rule 44.14 (powers in relation to misconduct).

(4) Where the costs to be assessed in a detailed assessment are payable out of the Community Legal Service Fund, this rule applies as if the receiving party were the solicitor to whom the costs are payable and the paying party were the Legal Services Commission.

47.9 Points of dispute and consequence of not serving

(1) The paying party and any other party to the detailed assessment proceedings may dispute any item in the bill of costs by serving points of dispute on—

(a) the receiving party; and

(b) every other party to the detailed assessment proceedings.

(2) The period for serving points of dispute is 21 days after the date of service of the notice of commencement.

(3) If a party serves points of dispute after the period set out in paragraph (2), he may not be heard further in the detailed assessment proceedings unless the court gives permission.

(4) The receiving party may file a request for a default costs certificate if—

(a) the period set out in rule 47.9 (2) for serving points of dispute has expired; and

(b) he has not been served with any points of dispute.

(5) If any party (including the paying party) serves points of dispute before the issue of a default costs certificate the court may not issue the default costs certificate.

47.10 Procedure where costs are agreed

(1) If the paying party and the receiving party agree the amount of costs, either party may apply for a costs certificate (either interim or final) in the amount agreed.

(Rule 47.15 and rule 47.16 contain further provisions about interim and final costs certificates respectively)

(2) An application for a certificate under paragraph (1) must be made to the court which would be the venue for detailed assessment proceedings under rule 47.4.

III COSTS PAYABLE BY ONE PARTY TO ANOTHER – DEFAULT PROVISIONS

47.11 Default costs certificate

(1) Where the receiving party is permitted by rule 47.9 to obtain a default costs certificate, that party does so by filing a request in the relevant practice form.

(2) A default costs certificate will include an order to pay the costs to which it relates.

(3) Where a receiving party obtains a default costs certificate, the costs payable to that party for the commencement of detailed assessment proceedings will be the sum set out in the Costs Practice Direction.

(4) A receiving party who obtains a default costs certificate in detailed assessment proceedings pursuant to an order under section 194(3) of the Legal Services Act 2007 must send a copy of the default costs certificate to the prescribed charity.

47.12 Setting aside default costs certificate

(1) The court must set aside a default costs certificate if the receiving party was not entitled to it.

(2) In any other case, the court may set aside or vary a default costs certificate if it appears to the court that there is some good reason why the detailed assessment proceedings should continue.

(3) Where—

(a) the receiving party has purported to serve the notice of commencement on the paying party;

(b) a default costs certificate has been issued; and

(c) the receiving party subsequently discovers that the notice of commencement did not reach the paying party at least 21 days before the default costs certificate was issued,

the receiving party must—

(i) file a request for the default costs certificate to be set aside; or

(ii) apply to the court for directions.

(4) Where paragraph (3) applies, the receiving party may take no further step in—

(a) the detailed assessment proceedings; or

(b) the enforcement of the default costs certificate,

until the certificate has been set aside or the court has given directions.

(5) Where the court sets aside or varies a default costs certificate in detailed assessment proceedings pursuant to an order under section 194(3) of the Legal Services Act 2007, the receiving party must send a copy of the order setting aside or varying the default costs certificate to the prescribed charity.

IV COSTS PAYABLE BY ONE PARTY TO ANOTHER – PROCEDURE WHERE POINTS OF DISPUTE ARE SERVED

47.13 Optional reply

(1) Where any party to the detailed assessment proceedings serves points of dispute, the receiving party may serve a reply on the other parties to the assessment proceedings.

(2) He may do so within 21 days after service on him of the points of dispute to which his reply relates.

47.14 Detailed assessment hearing

(1) Where points of dispute are served in accordance with this Part, the receiving party must file a request for a detailed assessment hearing.

(2) He must file the request within 3 months of the expiry of the period for commencing detailed assessment proceedings as specified – (a) in rule 47.7; or

(b) by any direction of the court.

(3) Where the receiving party fails to file a request in accordance with paragraph (2), the paying party may apply for an order requiring the receiving party to file the request within such time as the court may specify.

(4) On an application under paragraph (3), the court may direct that, unless the receiving party requests a detailed assessment hearing within the time specified by the court, all or part of the costs to which the receiving party would otherwise be entitled will be disallowed.

(5) If – (a) the paying party has not made an application in accordance with paragraph (3); and

(b) the receiving party files a request for a detailed assessment hearing later than the period specified in paragraph (2),

the court may disallow all or part of the interest otherwise payable to the receiving party under

(i) section 17 of the Judgments Act 1838[3]; or

(ii) section 74 of the County Courts Act 1984,

but must not impose any other sanction except in accordance with rule 44.14 (powers in relation to misconduct).

(6) No party other than – (a) the receiving party;

(b) the paying party; and

(c) any party who has served points of dispute under rule 47.9,

may be heard at the detailed assessment hearing unless the court gives permission.

(7) Only items specified in the points of dispute may be raised at the hearing, unless the court gives permission.

V INTERIM COSTS CERTIFICATE AND FINAL COSTS CERTIFICATE

47.15 Power to issue an interim certificate

(1) The court may at any time after the receiving party has filed a request for a detailed assessment hearing – (a) issue an interim costs certificate for such sum as it considers appropriate;

(b) amend or cancel an interim certificate.

(2) An interim certificate will include an order to pay the costs to which it relates, unless the court orders otherwise.

(3) The court may order the costs certified in an interim certificate to be paid into court.

(4) Where the court – (a) issues an interim costs certificate; or

(b) amends or cancels an interim certificate,

in detailed assessment proceedings pursuant to an order under section 194(3) of the Legal Services Act 2007, the receiving party must send a copy of the interim costs certificate or the order amending or cancelling the interim costs certificate to the prescribed charity.

47.16 Final costs certificate

(1) In this rule a completed bill means a bill calculated to show the amount due following the detailed assessment of the costs.

(2) The period for filing the completed bill is 14 days after the end of the detailed assessment hearing.

(3) When a completed bill is filed the court will issue a final costs certificate and serve it on the parties to the detailed assessment proceedings.

(4) Paragraph (3) is subject to any order made by the court that a certificate is not to be issued until other costs have been paid.

(5) A final costs certificate will include an order to pay the costs to which it relates, unless the court orders otherwise.

(6) Where the court issues a final costs certificate in detailed assessment proceedings pursuant to an order under section 194(3) of the Legal Services Act 2007, the receiving party must send a copy of the final costs certificate to the prescribed charity.

VI DETAILED ASSESSMENT PROCEDURE FOR COSTS OF A LSC FUNDED CLIENT OR AN ASSISTED PERSON WHERE COSTS ARE PAYABLE OUT OF THE COMMUNITY LEGAL SERVICE FUND

47.17 Detailed assessment procedure for costs of a lsc funded client or an assisted person where costs are payable out of the community legal service fund

(1) Where the court is to assess costs of a LSC funded client or an assisted person which are payable out of the Community Legal Services Fund, that person's solicitor may commence detailed assessment proceedings by filing a request in the relevant practice form.

(2) A request under paragraph (1) must be filed within 3 months after the date when the right to detailed assessment arose.

(3) The solicitor must also serve a copy of the request for detailed assessment on the LSC funded client or the assisted person, if notice of that person's interest has been given to the court in accordance with community legal service or legal aid regulations.

(4) Where the solicitor has certified that the LSC funded client or that person wishes to attend an assessment hearing, the court will, on receipt of the request for assessment, fix a date for the assessment hearing.

(5) Where paragraph (3) does not apply, the court will, on receipt of the request for assessment provisionally assess the costs without the attendance of the solicitor, unless it considers that a hearing is necessary.

(6) After the court has provisionally assessed the bill, it will return the bill to the solicitor.

(7) The court will fix a date for an assessment hearing if the solicitor informs the court, within 14 days after he receives the provisionally assessed bill, that he wants the court to hold such a hearing.

47.17A Detailed assessment procedure where costs are payable out of a fund other than the community legal service fund

(1) Where the court is to assess costs which are payable out of a fund other than the Community Legal Service Fund, the receiving party may commence detailed assessment proceedings by filing a request in the relevant practice form.

(2) A request under paragraph (1) must be filed within 3 months after the date when the right to detailed assessment arose.

(3) The court may direct that the party seeking assessment serve a copy of the request on any person who has a financial interest in the outcome of the assessment.

(4) The court will, on receipt of the request for assessment, provisionally assess the costs without the attendance of the receiving party, unless it considers that a hearing is necessary.

(5) After the court has provisionally assessed the bill, it will return the bill to the receiving party.

(6) The court will fix a date for an assessment hearing if the party informs the court, within 14 days after he receives the provisionally assessed bill, that he wants the court to hold such a hearing.

VII COSTS OF DETAILED ASSESSMENT PROCEEDINGS

47.18 Liability for costs of detailed assessment proceedings

(1) The receiving party is entitled to the costs of the detailed assessment proceedings except where—

(a) the provisions of any Act, any of these Rules or any relevant practice direction provide otherwise; or

(b) the court makes some other order in relation to all or part of the costs of the detailed assessment proceedings.

(1A) Paragraph (1) does not apply where the receiving party has pro bono representation in the detailed assessment proceedings but that party may apply for an order in respect of that representation under section 194(3) of the Legal Services Act 2007.

(2) In deciding whether to make some other order, the court must have regard to all the circumstances, including—

(a) the conduct of all the parties;

(b) the amount, if any, by which the bill of costs has been reduced; and

(c) whether it was reasonable for a party to claim the costs of a particular item or to dispute that item.

47.19 Offers to settle without prejudice save as to costs of the detailed assessment proceedings

(1) Where—

(a) a party (whether the paying party or the receiving party) makes a written offer to settle the costs of the proceedings which gave rise to the assessment proceedings; and

(b) the offer is expressed to be without prejudice[(GL)] save as to the costs of the detailed assessment proceedings, the court will take the offer into account in deciding who should pay the costs of those proceedings.

(2) The fact of the offer must not be communicated to the costs officer until the question of costs of the detailed assessment proceedings falls to be decided.

VIII APPEALS FROM AUTHORISED COURT OFFICERS IN DETAILED ASSESSMENT PROCEEDINGS

47.20 Right to appeal

(1) Any party to detailed assessment proceedings may appeal against a decision of an authorised court officer in those proceedings.

(2) For the purposes of this Section, a LSC funded client or an assisted person is not a party to detailed assessment proceedings.

47.21 Court to hear appeal

An appeal against a decision of an authorised court officer is to a costs judge or a district judge of the High Court.

47.22 Appeal procedure

(1) The appellant must file an appeal notice within 21 days after the date of the decision he wishes to appeal against.

(2) On receipt of the appeal notice, the court will—

(a) serve a copy of the notice on the parties to the detailed assessment proceedings; and

(b) give notice of the appeal hearing to those parties.

47.23 Powers of the court on appeal

On an appeal from an authorised court officer the court will—

(a) re-hear the proceedings which gave rise to the decision appealed against; and

(b) make any order and give any directions as it considers appropriate.

Part 48 COSTS – SPECIAL CASES

I COSTS PAYABLE BY OR TO PARTICULAR PERSONS

48.1 Pre-commencement disclosure and orders for disclosure against a person who is not a party

(1) This paragraph applies where a person applies—

(a) for an order under – (i) section 33 of the Senior Courts Act 1981; or

(ii) section 52 of the County Courts Act 1984,

(which give the court powers exercisable before commencement of proceedings); or

(b) for an order under – (i) section 34 of the Supreme Court Act 1981; or

(ii) section 53 of the County Courts Act 1984,

(which give the court power to make an order against a non-party for disclosure of documents, inspection of property etc.).

(2) The general rule is that the court will award the person against whom the order is sought his costs—

(a) of the application; and

(b) of complying with any order made on the application.

(3) The court may however make a different order, having regard to all the circumstances, including—

(a) the extent to which it was reasonable for the person against whom the order was sought to oppose the application; and

(b) whether the parties to the application have complied with any relevant pre-action protocol.

48.2 Costs orders in favour of or against non-parties

(1) Where the court is considering whether to exercise its power under section 51 of the Supreme Court Act 1981 (costs are in the discretion of the court) to make a costs order in favour of or against a person who is not a party to proceedings—

(a) that person must be added as a party to the proceedings for the purposes of costs only; and

(b) he must be given a reasonable opportunity to attend a hearing at which the court will consider the matter further.

(2) This rule does not apply—

(a) where the court is considering whether to—

(i) make an order against the Legal Services Commission;

(ii) make a wasted costs order (as defined in 48.7); and

(b) in proceedings to which rule 48.1 applies (pre-commencement disclosure and orders for disclosure against a person who is not a party).

48.3 Amount of costs where costs are payable pursuant to a contract

(1) Where the court assesses (whether by the summary or detailed procedure) costs which are payable by the paying party to the receiving party under the terms of a contract, the costs payable under those terms are, unless the contract expressly provides otherwise, to be presumed to be costs which—

(a) have been reasonably incurred; and

(b) are reasonable in amount, and the court will assess them accordingly.

(The Costs Practice Direction sets out circumstances where the court may order otherwise)

(2) This rule does not apply where the contract is between a solicitor and his client.

48.4 Limitations on court's power to award costs in favour of trustee or personal representative

(1) This rule applies where—

(a) a person is or has been a party to any proceedings in the capacity of trustee or personal representative; and

(b) rule 48.3 does not apply.

(2) The general rule is that he is entitled to be paid the costs of those proceedings, insofar as they are not recovered from or paid by any other person, out of the relevant trust fund or estate.

(3) Where he is entitled to be paid any of those costs out of the fund or estate, those costs will be assessed on the indemnity basis.

48.5 Costs where money is payable by or to a child or protected party

(1) This rule applies to any proceedings where a party is a child or protected party and—

(a) money is ordered or agreed to be paid to, or for the benefit of, that party; or

(b) money is ordered to be paid by him or on his behalf.

('Child' and 'protected party' have the same meaning as in rule 21.1(2)

(2) The general rule is that—

(a) the court must order a detailed assessment of the costs payable by, or out of money belonging to, any party who is a child or protected party; and

(b) on an assessment under paragraph (a), the court must also assess any costs payable to that party in the proceedings, unless—

(i) the court has issued a default costs certificate in relation to those costs under rule 47.11; or

(ii) the costs are payable in proceedings to which Section II or Section VI of Part 45 applies.

(3) The court need not order detailed assessment of costs in the circumstances set out in the Costs Practice Direction.

(4) Where—

(a) a claimant is a child or protected party; and

(b) a detailed assessment has taken place under paragraph (2)(a), the only amount payable by the child or protected party is the amount which the court certifies as payable.

48.6 Litigants in person

(1) This rule applies where the court orders (whether by summary assessment or detailed assessment) that the costs of a litigant in person are to be paid by any other person.

(2) The costs allowed under this rule must not exceed, except in the case of a disbursement, two-thirds of the amount which would have been allowed if the litigant in person had been represented by a legal representative.

(3) The litigant in person shall be allowed—

(a) costs for the same categories of—

(i) work; and

(ii) disbursements,

which would have been allowed if the work had been done or the disbursements had been made by a legal representative on the litigant in person's behalf;

(b) the payments reasonably made by him for legal services relating to the conduct of the proceedings; and

(c) the costs of obtaining expert assistance in assessing the costs claim.

(4) The amount of costs to be allowed to the litigant in person for any item of work claimed shall be—

(a) where the litigant can prove financial loss, the amount that he can prove he has lost for time reasonably spent on doing the work; or

(b) where the litigant cannot prove financial loss, an amount for the time reasonably spent on doing the work at the rate set out in the Costs Practice Direction.

(5) A litigant who is allowed costs for attending at court to conduct his case is not entitled to a witness allowance in respect of such attendance in addition to those costs.

(6) For the purposes of this rule, a litigant in person includes—

(a) a company or other corporation which is acting without a legal representative; and

(b) a barrister, solicitor, solicitor's employee, manager of a body recognised under section 9 of the Administration of Justice Act 1985 or a person who, for the purposes of the Legal Services Act 2007, is an authorised person in relation to an activity which constitutes the conduct of litigation (within the meaning of that Act) who is acting for himself.

48.6A Costs where the court has made a group litigation order

(1) This rule applied where the court has made a Group Litigation Order ('GLO').

(2) In this rule—

(a) 'individual costs' means costs incurred in relation to an individual claim on the group register;

(b) 'common costs' means—

(i) costs incurred in relation to the GLO issues;

(ii) individual costs incurred in a claim while it is proceeding as a test claim, and

(iii)costs incurred by the lead solicitor in administering the group litigation; and

(c) 'group litigant' means a claimant or defendant, as the case may be, whose claim is entered on the group register.

(3) Unless the court orders otherwise, any order for common costs against group litigants imposes on each group litigant several liability for an equal proportion of those common costs.

(4) The general rule is that where a group litigant is the paying party, he will, in addition to any costs he is liable to pay to the receiving party, be liable for—

(a) the individual costs of his claim; and

(b) an equal proportion, together with all the other group litigants, of the common costs.

(5) Where the court makes an order about costs in relation to any application or hearing which involved—

(a) one or more GLO issues; and

(b) issues relevant only to individual claims,

the court will direct the proportion of the costs that is to relate to common costs and the proportion that is to relate to individual costs.

(6) Where common costs have been incurred before a claim is entered on the group register, the court may order the group litigant to be liable for a proportion of those costs.

(7) Where a claim is removed from the group register, the court may make an order for costs in that claim which includes a proportion of the common costs incurred up to the date on which the claim is removed from the group register.

II COSTS RELATING TO SOLICITORS AND OTHER LEGAL REPRESENTATIVES

48.7 Personal liability of legal representative for costs – wasted costs orders

(1) This rule applies where the court is considering whether to make an order under section 51(6) of the Senior Courts Act 1981 (court's power to disallow or (as the case may be) order a legal representative to meet, 'wasted costs').

(2) The court must give the legal representative a reasonable opportunity to attend a hearing to give reasons why it should not make such an order.

(3) Revoked

(4) When the court makes a wasted costs order, it must—

(a) specify the amount to be disallowed or paid; or

(b) direct a costs judge or a district judge to decide the amount of costs to be disallowed or paid.

(5) The court may direct that notice must be given to the legal representative's client, in such manner as the court may direct—

(a) of any proceedings under this rule; or

(b) of any order made under it against his legal representative.

(6) Before making a wasted costs order, the court may direct a costs judge or a district judge to inquire into the matter and report to the court.

(7) The court may refer the question of wasted costs to a costs judge or a district judge, instead of making a wasted costs order.

48.8 Basis of detailed assessment of solicitor and client costs

(1) This rule applies to every assessment of a solicitor's bill to his client except a bill which is to be paid out of the Community Legal Service Fund under the Legal Aid Act 1988 or the Access to Justice Act 1999 and

(1A) Section 74(3) of the Solicitors Act 1974 applies unless the solicitor and client have entered into a written agreement which expressly permits payment to the solicitor of an amount of costs greater than that which the client could have recovered from another party to the proceedings.

(2) Subject to paragraph (1A), costs are to be assessed on the indemnity basis but are to be presumed—

(a) to have been reasonably incurred if they were incurred with the express or implied approval of the client;

(b) to be reasonable in amount if their amount was expressly or impliedly approved by the client;

(c) to have been unreasonably incurred if –(i) they are of an unusual nature or amount; and

(ii) the solicitor did not tell his client that as a result he might not recover all of them from the other party.

(3) Where the court is considering a percentage increase, whether on the application of the legal representative under rule 44.16 or on the application of the client, the court will have regard to all the relevant factors as they reasonably appeared to the solicitor or counsel when the conditional fee agreement was entered into or varied.

(4) In paragraph (3), 'conditional fee agreement' means an agreement enforceable under section 58 of the Courts and Legal Services Act 1990 at the date on which that agreement was entered into or varied.

48.9 Revoked

48.10 Assessment procedure

(1) This rule sets out the procedure to be followed where the court has made an order under Part III of the Solicitors Act 1974 for the assessment of costs payable to a solicitor by his client.

(2) The solicitor must serve a breakdown of costs within 28 days of the order for costs to be assessed.

(3) The client must serve points of dispute within 14 days after service on him of the breakdown of costs.

(4) If the solicitor wishes to serve a reply, he must do so within 14 days of service on him of the points of dispute.

(5) Either party may file a request for a hearing date—

(a) after points of dispute have been served; but

(b) no later than 3 months after the date of the order for the costs to be assessed.

(6) This procedure applies subject to any contrary order made by the court.

PRACTICE DIRECTION 43–48

SECTION 1 INTRODUCTION

1.1 This Practice Direction supplements Parts 43 to 48 of the Civil Procedure Rules. It applies to all proceedings to which those Parts apply.

1.2 Paragraphs 57.1 to 57.9 of this Practice Direction deal with various transitional provisions affecting proceedings about costs.

1.3 Attention is drawn to the powers to make orders about costs conferred on the Senior Courts and any county court by Section 51 of the Senior Courts Act 1981.

1.4 In these Directions

'counsel' means a barrister or other person with a right of audience in relation to proceedings in the High Court or in the County Courts in which he is instructed to act.

'LSC' means Legal Services Commission.

'solicitor' means a solicitor of the Senior Courts or other person with a right of audience in relation to proceedings, who is conducting the claim or defence (as the case may be) on behalf of a party to the proceedings and, where the context admits, includes a patent agent.

1.5 In respect of any document which is required by these Directions to be signed by a party or his legal representative Practice Direction 22 will apply as if the document in question was a statement of truth. (Practice Direction 22 makes provision for cases in which a party is a child, a protected party or a company or other corporation and cases in which a document is signed on behalf of a partnership).

SECTION 2 SCOPE OF COSTS RULES AND DEFINITIONS

Rule 43.2 Definitions and Application

2.1 Where the court makes an order for costs and the receiving party has entered into a funding arrangement as defined in rule 43.2, the costs payable by the paying party include any additional liability (also defined in rule 43.2) unless the court orders otherwise.

2.2 In the following paragraphs—

'funding arrangement', 'percentage increase', 'insurance premium', 'membership organisation' and 'additional liability' have the meanings given to them by rule 43.2 .

* A 'conditional fee agreement' is an agreement with a person providing advocacy or litigation services which provides for his fees and expenses, or part of them, to be payable only in specified circumstances, whether or not it provides for a success fee as mentioned in section 58(2)(b) of the Courts and Legal Services Act 1990.

'base costs' means costs other than the amount of any additional liability.

2.3 Rule 44.3A(1) provides that the court will not assess any additional liability until the conclusion of the proceedings or the part of the proceedings to which the funding arrangement relates. (As to the time when detailed assessment may be carried out see paragraph 27.1 below).

2.4 For the purposes of the following paragraphs of this practice direction and rule 44.3A proceedings are concluded when the court has finally determined the matters in issue in the claim, whether or not there is an appeal. The making of an award of provisional damages under Part 41 will also be treated as a final determination of the matters in issue.

2.5 The court may order or the parties may agree in writing that, although the proceedings are continuing, they will nevertheless be treated as concluded.

SECTION 3 MODEL FORMS FOR CLAIMS FOR COSTS

RULE 43.3 MEANING OF SUMMARY ASSESSMENT

3.1 Rule 43.3 defines summary assessment. When carrying out a summary assessment of costs where there is an additional liability the court may assess the base costs alone, or the base costs and the additional liability.

3.2 Form N260 is a model form of Statement of Costs to be used for summary assessments.

3.3 Further details about Statements of Costs are given in paragraph 13.5 below.

RULE 43.4 MEANING OF DETAILED ASSESSMENT

3.4 Rule 43.4 defines detailed assessment. When carrying out a detailed assessment of costs where there is an additional liability the court will assess both the base costs and the additional liability, or, if the base costs have already been assessed, the additional liability alone.

3.5 Precedents A, B, C and D in the Schedule of Costs Precedents annexed to this Practice Direction are model forms of bills of costs to be used for detailed assessments.

3.6 Further details about bills of costs are given in the next section of these Directions and in paragraphs 28.1 to 49.1, below.

3.7 Precedents A, B, C and D in the Schedule of Costs Precedents and the next section of this Practice Direction all refer to a model form of bill of costs. The use of a model form is not compulsory, but is encouraged. A party wishing to rely upon a bill which departs from the model forms should include in the background information of the bill an explanation for that departure.

3.8 In any order of the court (whether made before or after 26 April 1999) the word 'taxation' will be taken to mean 'detailed assessment' and the words 'to be taxed' will be taken to mean 'to be decided by detailed assessment' unless in either case the context otherwise requires.

SECTION 4 FORM AND CONTENTS OF BILLS OF COSTS

4.1 A bill of costs may consist of such of the following sections as may be appropriate:

(1) title page;

(2) background information;

(3) items of costs claimed under the headings specified in paragraph 4.6;

(4) summary showing the total costs claimed on each page of the bill;

(5) schedules of time spent on non-routine attendances; and

(6) the certificates referred to in paragraph 4.15.

4.2 Where it is necessary or convenient to do so, a bill of costs may be divided into two or more parts, each part containing sections (2), (3) and (4) above. Circumstances in which it will be necessary or convenient to divide a bill into parts include:

(1) Where the receiving party acted in person during the course of the proceedings (whether or not that party also had a legal representative at that time) the bill must be divided into different parts so as to distinguish between;

(a) the costs claimed for work done by the legal representative; and

(b) the costs claimed for work done by the receiving party in person.

(1A) Where the receiving party had pro bono representation for part of the proceedings and an order under section 194(3) of the Legal Services Act 2007 has been made, the bill must be divided into different parts so as to distinguish between:

(a) the sum equivalent to the costs claimed for work done by the legal representative acting free of charge; and

(b) the costs claimed for work done by the legal representative not acting free of charge.

(2) Where the receiving party was represented by different solicitors during the course of the proceedings, the bill must be divided into different parts so as to distinguish between the costs payable in respect of each solicitor.

(3) Where the receiving party obtained legal aid or LSC funding in respect of all or part of the proceedings the bill must be divided into separate parts so as to distinguish between;

(a) costs claimed before legal aid or LSC funding was granted;

(b) costs claimed after legal aid or LSC funding was granted; and

(c) any costs claimed after legal aid or LSC funding ceased.

(4) Where value added tax (VAT) is claimed and there was a change in the rate of VAT during the course of the proceedings, the bill must be divided into separate parts so as to distinguish between;

(a) costs claimed at the old rate of VAT; and

(b) costs claimed at the new rate of VAT.

(5) Where the bill covers costs payable under an order or orders under which there are different paying parties the bill must be divided into parts so as to deal separately with the costs payable by each paying party.

(*6) Where the bill covers costs payable under an order or orders, in respect of which the receiving party wishes to claim interest from different dates, the bill must be divided to enable such interest to be calculated.

4.3 Where a party claims costs against another party and also claims costs against the LSC only for work done in the same period, the costs claimed against the LSC only can be claimed either in a separate part of the bill or in additional columns in the same part of the bill. Precedents C and D in the Schedule of Costs Precedents annexed to this Practice Direction show how bills should be drafted when costs are claimed against the LSC only.

4.4 The title page of the bill of costs must set out:

(1) the full title of the proceedings;

(2) the name of the party whose bill it is and a description of the document showing the right to assessment (as to which see paragraph 40.4, below);

(3) if VAT is included as part of the claim for costs, the VAT number of the legal representative or other person in respect of whom VAT is claimed;

(4) details of all legal aid certificates, LSC certificates and relevant amendment certificates in respect of which claims for costs are included in the bill.

4.5 The background information included in the bill of costs should set out:

(1) a brief description of the proceedings up to the date of the notice of commencement;

(2) a statement of the status of the solicitor or solicitor's employee in respect of whom costs are claimed and (if those costs are calculated on the basis of hourly rates) the hourly rates claimed for each such person.

It should be noted that 'legal executive' means a Fellow of the Institute of Legal Executives.

Other clerks, who are fee earners of equivalent experience, may be entitled to similar rates. It should be borne in mind that Fellows of the Institute of Legal Executives will have spent approximately 6 years in practice, and taken both general and specialist examinations. The Fellows have therefore acquired considerable practical and academic experience. Clerks without the equivalent experience of legal executives will normally be treated as being the equivalent of trainee solicitors and para-legals.

(3) a brief explanation of any agreement or arrangement between the receiving party and his solicitors, which affects the costs claimed in the bill.

4.6 The bill of costs may consist of items under such of the following heads as may be appropriate:

(1) attendances on the court and counsel up to the date of the notice of commencement;

(2) attendances on and communications with the receiving party;

(3) attendances on and communications with witnesses including any expert witness;

(4) attendances to inspect any property or place for the purposes of the proceedings;

(5) attendances on and communications with other persons, including offices of public records;

(6) communications with the court and with counsel;

(7) work done on documents: preparing and considering documentation, including documentation necessary to comply with Practice Direction (Pre-Action Conduct) or any relevant pre-action protocols where appropriate, work done in connection with arithmetical calculations of compensation and/or interest and time spent collating documents;

(8) work done in connection with negotiations with a view to settlement if not already covered in the heads listed above;

(9) attendances on and communications with London and other agents and work done by them;

(10) other work done which was of or incidental to the proceedings and which is not already covered in the heads listed above.

4.7 In respect of each of the heads of costs:

(1) 'communications' means letters out e-mails out and telephone calls;

(2) communications, which are not routine communications, must be set out in chronological order;

(3) routine communications must be set out as a single item at the end of each head;

4.8 Routine communications are letters out, e-mails out and telephone calls which because of their simplicity should not be regarded as letters or e-mails of substance or telephone calls which properly amount to an attendance.

4.9 Each item claimed in the bill of costs must be consecutively numbered.

4.10 In each part of the bill of costs which claims items under head (1) (attendances on court and counsel) a note should be made of:

(1) all relevant events, including events which do not constitute chargeable items;

(2) any orders for costs which the court made (whether or not a claim is made in respect of those costs in this bill of costs).

4.11 The numbered items of costs may be set out on paper divided into columns. Precedents A, B, C and D in the Schedule of Costs Precedents annexed to this Practice Direction illustrate various model forms of bills of costs.

4.12 In respect of heads (2) to (10) in paragraph 4.6 above, if the number of attendances and communications other than routine communications is twenty or more, the claim for the costs of those items in that section of the bill of costs should be for the total only and should refer to a schedule in which the full record of dates and details is set out. If the bill of costs contains more than one schedule each schedule should be numbered consecutively.

4.13 The bill of costs must not contain any claims in respect of costs or court fees which relate solely to the detailed assessment proceedings other than costs claimed for preparing and checking the bill.

4.14 The summary must show the total profit costs and disbursements claimed separately from the total VAT claimed. Where the bill of costs is divided into parts the summary must also give totals for each part. If each page of the bill gives a page total the summary must also set out the page totals for each page.

4.15 The bill of costs must contain such of the certificates, the texts of which are set out in Precedent F of the Schedule of Costs Precedents annexed to this Practice Direction, as are appropriate.

4.16 The following provisions relate to work done by solicitors:

(1) Routine letters out routine e-mails out and routine telephone calls will in general be allowed on a unit basis of 6 minutes each, the charge being calculated by reference to the appropriate hourly rate. The unit charge for letters out and e-mails out will include perusing and considering the relevant letters in or e-mails in and accordingly no separate charge is to be made for in-coming letters or e-mails.

(2) The court may, in its discretion, allow an actual time charge for preparation of electronic communications other than e-mails sent by solicitors, which properly amount to attendances provided that the time taken has been recorded.

(3) Local travelling expenses incurred by solicitors will not be allowed. The definition of 'local' is a matter for the discretion of the court. While no absolute rule can be laid down, as a matter of guidance, 'local' will, in general, be taken to mean within a radius of 10 miles from the court dealing with the case at the relevant time. Where travelling and waiting time is claimed, this should be allowed at the rate agreed with the client unless this is more than the hourly rate on the assessment.

(4) The cost of postage, couriers, out-going telephone calls, fax and telex messages will in general not be allowed but the court may exceptionally in its discretion allow such expenses in unusual circumstances or where the cost is unusually heavy.

(5) The cost of making copies of documents will not in general be allowed but the court may exceptionally in its discretion make an allowance for copying in unusual circumstances or where the documents copied are unusually numerous in relation to the nature of the case. Where this discretion is invoked the number of copies made, their purpose and the costs claimed for them must be set out in the bill.

(6) Agency charges as between principal solicitors and their agents will be dealt with on the principle that such charges, where appropriate, form part of the principal solicitor's charges. Where these charges relate to head (1) in paragraph 4.6 (attendances at court and on counsel) they must be included in their chronological order in that head. In other cases they must be included in head (9) (attendances on London and other agents).

4.17

(1) Where a claim is made for a percentage increase in addition to an hourly rate or base fee, the amount of the increase must be shown separately, either in the appropriate arithmetic column or in the narrative column. (For an example see Precedent A or Precedent B.)

(2) Where a claim is made against the LSC only and includes enhancement and where a claim is made in family proceedings and includes a claim for uplift or general care and conduct, the amount of enhancement uplift and general care and conduct must be shown, in respect of each item upon which it is claimed, as a separate amount either in the appropriate arithmetic column or in the narrative column. (For an example, see Precedent C.)

'Enhancement' means the increase in prescribed rates which may be allowed by a costs officer in accordance with the Legal Aid in Civil Proceedings (Remuneration) Regulations 1994 or the Legal Aid in Family Proceedings Regulations 1991.

4.18 Costs of preparing the bill

A claim may be made for the reasonable costs of preparing and checking the bill of costs.

SECTION 5 SPECIAL PROVISIONS RELATING TO VAT

5.1 This section deals with claims for value added tax (VAT) which are made in respect of costs being dealt with by way of summary assessment or detailed assessment.

5.2 VAT Registration Number

The number allocated by HM Revenue and Customs to every person registered under the Value Added Tax Act 1983 (except a Government Department) must appear in a prominent place at the head of every statement, bill of costs, fee sheet, account or voucher on which VAT is being included as part of a claim for costs.

5.3 Entitlement to VAT on Costs

VAT should not be included in a claim for costs if the receiving party is able to recover the VAT as input tax. Where the receiving party is able to obtain credit from HM Revenue and Customs for a proportion of the VAT as input tax, only that proportion which is not eligible for credit should be included in the claim for costs.

5.4 The receiving party has responsibility for ensuring that VAT is claimed only when the receiving party is unable to recover the VAT or a proportion thereof as input tax.

5.5 Where there is a dispute as to whether VAT is properly claimed the receiving party must provide a certificate signed by the solicitors or the auditors of the receiving party substantially in the form illustrated in Precedent F in the Schedule of

Costs Precedents annexed to this Practice Direction. Where the receiving party is a litigant in person who is claiming VAT, reference should be made by him to HM Revenue and Customs and wherever possible a Statement to similar effect produced at the hearing at which the costs are assessed.

5.6 Where there is a dispute as to whether any service in respect of which a charge is proposed to be made in the bill is zero rated or exempt, reference should be made to HM Revenue and Customs and wherever possible the view of HM Revenue and Customs obtained and made known at the hearing at which the costs are assessed. Such application should be made by the receiving party. In the case of a bill from a solicitor to his own client, such application should be made by the client.

Form of bill of costs where VAT rate changes

5.7 Where there is a change in the rate of VAT, suppliers of goods and services are entitled by ss 88 (1) and 88(2) of the VAT Act 1994 in most circumstances to elect whether the new or the old rate of VAT should apply to a supply where the basic and actual tax points span a period during which there has been a change in VAT rates.

5.8 It will be assumed, unless a contrary indication is given in writing, that an election to take advantage of the provisions mentioned in paragraph 5.7 above and to charge VAT at the lower rate has been made. In any case in which an election to charge at the lower rate is not made, such a decision must be justified to the court assessing the costs.

Apportionment

5.9 All bills of costs, fees and disbursements on which VAT is included must be divided into separate parts so as to show work done before, on and after the date or dates from which any change in the rate of VAT takes effect. Where, however, a lump sum charge is made for work which spans a period during which there has been a change in VAT rates, and paragraphs 5.7 and 5.8 above do not apply, reference should be made to paragraphs 8 and 9 of Appendix F of Customs' Notice 700 (or any revised edition of that notice), a copy of which should be in the possession of every registered trader. If necessary, the lump sum should be apportioned. The totals of profit costs and disbursements in each part must be carried separately to the summary.

5.10 Should there be a change in the rate between the conclusion of a detailed assessment and the issue of the final costs certificate, any interested party may apply for the detailed assessment to be varied so as to take account of any increase or reduction in the amount of tax payable. Once the final costs certificate has been issued, no variation under this paragraph will be permitted.

Disbursements not classified as such for VAT purposes

5.11

(1) Legal representatives often make payments to third parties for the supply of goods or services where no VAT was chargeable on the supply by the third party: for example, the cost of meals taken and travel costs. The question whether legal representatives should include VAT in respect of these payments when invoicing their clients or in claims for costs between litigants should be decided in accordance with this Direction and with the criteria set out in the VAT Guide (Notice 700) published by HM Revenue and Customs.

(2) Payments to third parties which are normally treated as part of the legal representative's overheads (for example, postage costs and telephone costs) will not be treated as disbursements. The third party supply should be included as part of the costs of the legal representatives' legal services and VAT must be added to the total bill charged to the client.

(3) Disputes may arise in respect of payments made to a third party which the legal representative shows as disbursements in the invoice delivered to the receiving party. Some payments, although correctly described as disbursements for some purposes, are not classified as disbursements for VAT purposes. Items not classified as disbursements for VAT purposes must be shown as part of the services provided by the legal representative and, therefore, VAT must be added in respect of them whether or not VAT was chargeable on the supply by the third party.

(4) Guidance as to the circumstances in which disbursements may or may not be classified as disbursements for VAT purposes is given in the VAT Guide (Notice 700, paragraph 25.1). One of the key issues is whether the third party supply (i) was made to the legal representative (and therefore subsumed in the onward supply of legal services), or (ii) was made direct to the receiving party (the third party having no right to demand payment from the legal representative, who makes the payment only as agent for the receiving party).

(5) Examples of payments under (i) are: travelling expenses, such as an airline ticket, and subsistence expenses, such as the cost of meals, where the person travelling and receiving the meals is the legal representative. The supplies by the airline and the restaurant are supplies to the legal representative, not to the client.

(6) Payments under (ii) are classified as disbursements for VAT purposes and, therefore, the legal representative need not add VAT in respect of them. Simple examples are payments by a legal representative of court fees and payment of fees to an expert witness.

5.12. Omitted

Legal Aid/LSC Funding

5.13

(1) VAT will be payable in respect of every supply made pursuant to a legal aid/LSC certificate where—

(a) the person making the supply is a taxable person; and

(b) the assisted person/LSC funded client—

(i) belongs in the United Kingdom or another member state of the European Union; and

(ii) is a private individual or receives the supply for non-business purposes.

(2) Where the assisted person/LSC funded client belongs outside the European Union, VAT is generally not payable unless the supply relates to land in the United Kingdom.

(3) For the purpose of sub-paragraphs (1) and (2), the place where a person belongs is determined by section 9 of the Value Added Tax Act 1994.

(4) Where the assisted person/LSC funded client is registered for VAT and the legal services paid for by the LSC are in connection with that person's business, the VAT on those services will be payable by the LSC only.

5.14 Any summary of costs payable by the LSC must be drawn so as to show the total VAT on Counsel's fees as a separate item from the VAT on other disbursements and the VAT on profit costs.

Tax invoice

5.15 A bill of costs filed for detailed assessment is always retained by the court. Accordingly if a solicitor waives his solicitor and client costs and accepts the costs certified by the court as payable by the unsuccessful party in settlement, it will be necessary for a short statement as to the amount of the certified costs and the VAT thereon to be prepared for use as the tax invoice.

Vouchers

5.16 Where receipted accounts for disbursements made by the solicitor or his client are retained as tax invoices a photostat copy of any such receipted account may be produced and will be accepted as sufficient evidence of payment when disbursements are vouched.

Certificates

5.17 In a costs certificate payable by the LSC, the VAT on solicitor's costs, Counsel's fees and disbursements will be shown separately.

Litigants acting in person

5.18 Where a litigant acts in litigation on his own behalf he is not treated for the purposes of VAT as having supplied services and therefore no VAT is chargeable in respect of work done by that litigant (even where, for example, that litigant is a solicitor or other legal representative).

5.19 Consequently in the circumstances described in the preceding paragraph, a bill of costs presented for agreement or assessment should not claim any VAT which will not be allowed on assessment.

Government Departments

5.20 On an assessment between parties, where costs are being paid to a Government Department in respect of services rendered by its legal staff, VAT should not be added.

Payment pursuant to an order under section 194(3) of the Legal Services Act 2007

5.21 Where an order is made under section 194(3) of the Legal Services Act 2007 any bill presented for agreement or assessment pursuant to that order must not include a claim for VAT.

SECTION 6 ESTIMATES OF COSTS

6.1 This section sets out certain steps which parties and their legal representatives must take in order to keep the parties informed about their potential liability in respect of costs and in order to assist the court to decide what, if any, order to make about costs and about case management.

6.2

(1) In this Section an 'estimate of costs' means—

(a) an estimate of costs of—

(i) base costs (including disbursements) already incurred; and

(ii) base costs (including disbursements) to be incurred,

which a party, if successful in the proceedings, intends to seek to recover from any other party under an order for costs; or

(b) in proceedings where the party has pro bono representation and intends, if successful in the proceedings, to seek an order under section 194(3) of the Legal Services Act 2007, an estimate of the sum equivalent to—

(i) the base costs (including disbursements) that the party would have already incurred had the legal representation provided to that party not been free of charge; and

(ii) the base costs (including disbursements) that the party would incur if the legal representation to be provided to that party were not free of charge.

('Base costs' are defined in paragraph 2.2 of this Practice Direction.)

(2) A party who intends to recover an additional liability (defined in rule 43.2) need not reveal the amount of that liability in the estimate.

6.3 The court may at any stage in a case order any party to file an estimate of costs and to serve copies of the estimate on all other parties. The court may direct that the estimate be prepared in such a way as to demonstrate the likely effects of giving or not giving a particular case management direction which the court is considering, for example a direction for a split trial or for the trial of a preliminary issue. The court may specify a time limit for filing and serving the estimate. However, if no time limit is specified the estimate should be filed and served within 28 days of the date of the order.

6.4

(1) When—

(a) a party to a claim which is outside the financial scope of either the small claims track or the fast track files an allocation questionnaire; or

(b) a party to a claim which is being dealt with on the fast track or the multi track files a pre-trial check list (listing questionnaire),

that party must also file an estimate of costs and serve a copy of it on every other party, unless the court otherwise directs. Where a party is represented, that party's legal representative must in addition serve a copy of the estimate on that party.

(2) Where a party who is required to file and serve a new estimate of costs in accordance with Rule 44.15(3) is represented; and the legal representative must in addition serve the new estimate on that party.

(3) This paragraph does not apply to litigants in person.

6.5 An estimate of costs should be substantially in the form illustrated in Precedent H in the Schedule of Costs Precedents annexed to the Practice Direction.

6.5A

(1) If there is a difference of 20% or more between the base costs claimed by a receiving party on detailed assessment and the costs shown in an estimate of costs filed by that party, the receiving party must provide a statement of the reasons for the difference with his bill of costs.

(2) If a paying party—

(a) claims that he reasonably relied on an estimate of costs filed by a receiving party; or

(b) wishes to rely upon the costs shown in the estimate in order to dispute the reasonableness or proportionality of the costs claimed,

the paying party must serve a statement setting out his case in this regard in his points of dispute.

6.6

(1) On an assessment of the costs of a party, the court may have regard to any estimate previously filed by that party, or by any other party in the same proceedings. Such an estimate may be taken into account as a factor among others, when assessing the reasonableness and proportionality of any costs claimed.

(2) In particular, where—

(a) there is a difference of 20% or more between the base costs claimed by a receiving party and the costs shown in an estimate of costs filed by that party; and

(b) it appears to the court that—

(i) the receiving party has not provided a satisfactory explanation for that difference; or

(ii) the paying party reasonably relied on the estimate of costs;

the court may regard the difference between the costs claimed and the costs shown in the estimate as evidence that the costs claimed are unreasonable or disproportionate.

DIRECTIONS RELATING TO PART 44 GENERAL RULES ABOUT COSTS

SECTION 7 SOLICITOR'S DUTY TO NOTIFY CLIENT: RULE 44.2

7.1 For the purposes of rule 44.2 'client' includes a party for whom a solicitor is acting and any other person (for example, an insurer, a trade union or the LSC) who has instructed the solicitor to act or who is liable to pay his fees.

7.2 Where a solicitor notifies a client of an order under that rule, he must also explain why the order came to be made.

7.3 Although rule 44.2 does not specify any sanction for breach of the rule the court may, either in the order for costs itself or in a subsequent order, require the solicitor to produce to the court evidence showing that he took reasonable steps to comply with the rule.

SECTION 8 COURT'S DISCRETION AND CIRCUMSTANCES TO BE TAKEN INTO ACCOUNT WHEN EXERCISING ITS DISCRETION AS TO COSTS: RULE 44.3

8.1 Attention is drawn to the factors set out in this rule which may lead the court to depart from the general rule stated in rule 44.3(2) and to make a different order about costs.

8.2 In a probate claim where a defendant has in his defence given notice that he requires the will to be proved in solemn form (see paragraph 8.3 of Practice Direction 57), the court will not make an order for costs against the defendant unless it appears that there was no reasonable ground for opposing the will. The term 'probate claim' is defined in rule 57.1(2).

8.3 (1) The court may make an order about costs at any stage in a case.

(2) In particular the court may make an order about costs when it deals with any application, makes any order or holds any hearing and that order about costs may relate to the costs of that application, order or hearing.

(3) * Rule 44.3A(1) provides that the court will not assess any additional liability until the conclusion of the proceedings or the part of the proceedings to which the funding arrangement relates. (Paragraphs 2.4 and 2.5 above explain when proceedings are concluded. As to the time when detailed assessment may be carried out see paragraphs 28.1, below.)

8.4 In deciding what order to make about costs the court is required to have regard to all the circumstances including any payment into court or admissible offer to settle made by a party which is drawn to the court's attention, and which is not an offer to which costs consequences under Part 36 apply.

8.5 There are certain costs orders which the court will commonly make in proceedings before trial. The following table sets out the general effect of these orders. The table is not an exhaustive list of the orders which the court may make.

Term	Effect
• Costs • Costs in any event	The party in whose favour the order is made is entitled to the costs in respect of the part of the proceedings to which the order relates, whatever other costs orders are made in the proceedings.
• Costs in the case • Costs in the application	The party in whose favour the court makes an order for costs at the end of the proceedings is entitled to his costs of the part of the proceedings to which the order relates.
• Costs reserved	The decision about costs is deferred to a later occasion, but if no later order is made the costs will be costs in the case.
• Claimant's/Defendant's costs in case/application	If the party in whose favour the costs order is made is awarded costs at the end the proceedings, that party is entitled to his costs of the part of the proceedings to which the order relates. If any other party is awarded costs at the end of the proceedings, the party in whose favour the final costs order is made is not liable to pay the costs of any other party in respect of the part of the proceedings to which the order relates.

Term	Effect
• Costs thrown away	Where, for example, a judgment or order is set aside, the party in whose favour the costs order is made is entitled to the costs which have been incurred as a consequence. This includes the costs of – • preparing for and attending any hearing at which the judgment or order which has been set aside was made; • preparing for and attending any hearing to set aside the judgment or order in question; • preparing for and attending any hearing at which the court orders the proceedings or the part in question to be adjourned; • any steps taken to enforce a judgment or order which has subsequently been set aside.
• Costs of and caused by	Where, for example, the court makes this order on an application to amend a statement of case, the party in whose favour the costs order is made is entitled to the costs of preparing for and attending the application and the costs of any consequential amendment to his own statement of case.
• Costs here and below	The party in whose favour the costs order is made is entitled not only to his costs in respect of the proceedings in which the court makes the order but also to his costs of the proceedings in any lower court. In the case of an appeal from a Divisional Court the party is not entitled to any costs incurred in any court below the Divisional Court.
• No order as to costs • Each party to pay his own costs	Each party is to bear his own costs of the part of the proceedings to which the order relates whatever costs order the court makes at the end of the proceedings.

8.6 Where, under rule 44.3(8), the court orders an amount to be paid before costs are assessed—

(1) the order will state that amount, and

(2) if no other date for payment is specified in the order, rule 44.8 (Time for complying with an order for costs) will apply.

Fees of counsel

8.7

(1) This paragraph applies where the court orders the detailed assessment of the costs of a hearing at which one or more counsel appeared for a party.

(2) Where an order for costs states the opinion of the court as to whether or not the hearing was fit for the attendance of one or more counsel, a costs officer conducting a detailed assessment of costs to which that order relates will have regard to the opinion stated.

(3) The court will generally express an opinion only where:

(a) the paying party asks it to do so;

(b) more than one counsel appeared for a party or,

(c) the court wishes to record its opinion that the case was not fit for the attendance of counsel.

Fees payable to conveyancing counsel appointed by the court to assist it

8.8

(1) Where the court refers any matter to the conveyancing counsel of the court the fees payable to counsel in respect of the work done or to be done will be assessed by the court in accordance with rule 44.3.

(2) An appeal from a decision of the court in respect of the fees of such counsel will be dealt with under the general rules as to appeals set out in Part 52. If the appeal is against the decision of an authorised court officer, it will be dealt with in accordance with rules 47.20 to 47.23.

SECTION 9 COSTS ORDERS RELATING TO FUNDING ARRANGEMENTS: RULE 44.3A

9.1 Under an order for payment of 'costs' the costs payable will include an additional liability incurred under a funding arrangement.

9.2

(1) If before the conclusion of the proceedings the court carries out a summary assessment of the base costs it may identify separately the amount allowed in respect of: solicitors' charges; counsels' fees; other disbursements; and any value added tax (VAT). (Sections 13 and 14 of this Practice Direction deal with summary assessment.)

(2) If an order for the base costs of a previous application or hearing did not identify separately the amounts allowed for solicitor's charges, counsel's fees and other disbursements, a court which later makes an assessment of an additional liability may apportion the base costs previously ordered.

SECTION 10 LIMITS ON RECOVERY UNDER FUNDING ARRANGEMENTS: RULE 44.3B

10.1 In a case to which rule 44.3B(1)(c) or (d) applies the party in default may apply for relief from the sanction. He should do so as quickly as possible after he becomes aware of the default. An application, supported by evidence, should be made under Part 23 to a costs judge or district judge of the court which is dealing with the case. (Attention is drawn to rules 3.8 and 3.9 which deal with sanctions and relief from sanctions).

10.2 Where the amount of any percentage increase recoverable by counsel may be affected by the outcome of the application, the solicitor issuing the application must serve on counsel a copy of the application notice and notice of the hearing as soon as practicable and in any event at least 2 days before the hearing. Counsel may make written submissions or may attend and make oral submissions at the hearing. (Paragraph 1.4 contains definitions of the terms 'counsel' and 'solicitor'.)

SECTION 10A ORDERS IN RESPECT OF PRO BONO REPRESENTATION: RULE 44.3C

10A.1 Rule 44.3C(2) sets out how the court may determine the amount of payment when making an order under section 194(3) of the Legal Services Act 2007. Paragraph 13.2 of this Practice Direction provides that the general rule is that the court will make a summary assessment of costs in the circumstances outlined in that paragraph unless there is good reason not to do so. This will apply to rule 44.3C(2)(b) with the modification that the summary assessment of the costs is to be read as meaning the summary assessment of the sum equivalent to the costs that would have been claimed by the party with pro bono representation in respect of that representation had it not been provided free of charge.

10A.2 Where an order under section 194(3) of the Legal Services Act 2007 is sought, to assist the court in making a summary assessment of the amount payable to the prescribed charity, the party who has pro bono representation must prepare, file and serve in accordance with paragraph 13.5(2) a written statement of the sum equivalent to the costs that party would have claimed for that legal representation had it not been provided free of charge.

SECTION 11 FACTORS TO BE TAKEN INTO ACCOUNT IN DECIDING THE AMOUNT OF COSTS: RULE 44.5

11.1 In applying the test of proportionality the court will have regard to rule 1.1(2)(c). The relationship between the total of the costs incurred and the financial value of the claim may not be a reliable guide. A fixed percentage cannot be applied in all cases to the value of the claim in order to ascertain whether or not the costs are proportionate.

11.2 In any proceedings there will be costs which will inevitably be incurred and which are necessary for the successful conduct of the case. Solicitors are not required to conduct litigation at rates which are uneconomic. Thus in a modest claim the proportion of costs is likely to be higher than in a large claim, and may even equal or possibly exceed the amount in dispute.

11.3 Where a trial takes place, the time taken by the court in dealing with a particular issue may not be an accurate guide to the amount of time properly spent by the legal or other representatives in preparation for the trial of that issue.

11.4 Where a party has entered into a funding arrangement the costs claimed may, subject to rule 44.3B include an additional liability.

11.5 In deciding whether the costs claimed are reasonable and (on a standard basis assessment) proportionate, the court will consider the amount of any additional liability separately from the base costs.

11.6 In deciding whether the base costs are reasonable and (if relevant) proportionate the court will consider the factors set out in rule 44.5.

11.7 When the court is considering the factors to be taken into account in assessing an additional liability, it will have regard to the facts and circumstances as they reasonably appeared to the solicitor or counsel when the funding arrangement was entered into and at the time of any variation of the arrangement.

11.8

(1) In deciding whether a percentage increase is reasonable relevant factors to be taken into account may include:

(a) the risk that the circumstances in which the costs, fees or expenses would be payable might or might not occur;

(b) the legal representative's liability for any disbursements;

(c) what other methods of financing the costs were available to the receiving party.

(2) Omitted.

11.9 A percentage increase will not be reduced simply on the ground that, when added to base costs which are reasonable and (where relevant) proportionate, the total appears disproportionate.

11.10 In deciding whether the cost of insurance cover is reasonable, relevant factors to be taken into account include:

(1) where the insurance cover is not purchased in support of a conditional fee agreement with a success fee, how its cost compares with the likely cost of funding the case with a conditional fee agreement with a success fee and supporting insurance cover;

(2) the level and extent of the cover provided;

(3) the availability of any pre-existing insurance cover;

(4) whether any part of the premium would be rebated in the event of early settlement;

(5) the amount of commission payable to the receiving party or his legal representatives or other agents.

11.11 Where the court is considering a provision made by a membership organisation, rule 44.3B(1) (b) provides that any such provision which exceeds the likely cost to the receiving party of the premium of an insurance policy against the risk of incurring a liability to pay the costs of other parties to the proceedings is not recoverable. In such circumstances the court will, when assessing the additional liability, have regard to the factors set out in paragraph 11.10 above, in addition to the factors set out in rule 44.5.

SECTION 12 PROCEDURE FOR ASSESSING COSTS: RULE 44.7

12.1 Where the court does not order fixed costs (or no fixed costs are provided for) the amount of costs payable will be assessed by the court. This rule allows the court making an order about costs either

(a) to make a summary assessment of the amount of the costs, or

(b) to order the amount to be decided in accordance with Part 47 (a detailed assessment).

12.2 An order for costs will be treated as an order for the amount of costs to be decided by a detailed assessment unless the order otherwise provides.

12.3 Whenever the court awards costs to be assessed by way of detailed assessment it should consider whether to exercise the power in rule 44.3(8) (Courts Discretion as to Costs) to order the paying party to pay such sum of money as it thinks just on account of those costs.

SECTION 13 SUMMARY ASSESSMENT: GENERAL PROVISIONS

13.1 Whenever a court makes an order about costs which does not provide for fixed costs to be paid the court should consider whether to make a summary assessment of costs.

13.2 The general rule is that the court should make a summary assessment of the costs:

(1) at the conclusion of the trial of a case which has been dealt with on the fast track, in which case the order will deal with the costs of the whole claim, and

(2) at the conclusion of any other hearing, which has lasted not more than one day, in which case the order will deal with the costs of the application or matter to which the hearing related. If this hearing disposes of the claim, the order may deal with the costs of the whole claim;

(3) in hearings in the Court of Appeal to which Paragraph 14 of Practice Direction 52 applies;

unless there is good reason not to do so e.g. where the paying party shows substantial grounds for disputing the sum claimed for costs that cannot be dealt with summarily or there is insufficient time to carry out a summary assessment.

13.3 The general rule in paragraph 13.2 does not apply to a mortgagee's costs incurred in mortgage possession proceedings or other proceedings relating to a mortgage unless the mortgagee asks the court to make an order for his costs to be paid by another party. Paragraphs 50.3 and 50.4 deal in more detail with costs relating to mortgages.

13.4 Where an application has been made and the parties to the application agree an order by consent without any party attending, the parties should agree a figure for costs to be inserted in the consent order or agree that there should be no order for costs. If the parties cannot agree the costs position, attendance on the appointment will be necessary but, unless good reason can be shown for the failure to deal with costs as set out above, no costs will be allowed for that attendance.

13.5

(1) It is the duty of the parties and their legal representatives to assist the judge in making a summary assessment of costs in any case to which paragraph 13.2 above applies, in accordance with the following paragraphs.

(2) Each party who intends to claim costs must prepare a written statement of those costs showing separately in the form of a schedule:

(a) the number of hours to be claimed,

(b) the hourly rate to be claimed,

(c) the grade of fee earner;

(d) the amount and nature of any disbursement to be claimed, other than counsel's fee for appearing at the hearing,

(e) the amount of solicitor's costs to be claimed for attending or appearing at the hearing,

(f) the fees of counsel to be claimed in respect of the hearing, and

(g) any value added tax (VAT) to be claimed on these amounts.

(*3) The statement of costs should follow as closely as possible Form N260 and must be signed by the party or the party's legal representative. Where a litigant is an assisted person or is a LSC funded client or is represented by a solicitor in the litigant's employment the statement of costs need not include the certificate appended at the end of Form N260.

(4) The statement of costs must be filed at court and copies of it must be served on any party against whom an order for payment of those costs is intended to be sought. The statement of costs must be filed and the copies of it must be served as soon as possible and in any event—

(a) for a fast track trial, not less than 2 days before the trial; and

(b) for all other hearings, not less than 24 hours before the time fixed for the hearing.

(5) *Where the litigant is or may be entitled to claim an additional liability the statement filed and served need not reveal the amount of that liability.

13.6 The failure by a party, without reasonable excuse, to comply with the foregoing paragraphs will be taken into account by the court in deciding what order to make about the costs of the claim, hearing or application, and about the costs of any further hearing or detailed assessment hearing that may be necessary as a result of that failure.

13.7 If the court makes a summary assessment of costs at the conclusion of proceedings the court will specify separately

(1) the base costs, and if appropriate, the additional liability allowed as solicitor's charges, counsel's fees, other disbursements and any VAT; and

(2) the amount which is awarded under Part 46 (Fast Track Trial Costs).

13.8 The court awarding costs cannot make an order for a summary assessment of costs by a costs officer. If a summary assessment of costs is appropriate but the court awarding costs is unable to do so on the day, the court must give directions as to a further hearing before the same judge.

13.9 * The court will not make a summary assessment of the costs of a receiving party who is an assisted person or LSC funded client.

13.10 * A summary assessment of costs payable by an assisted person or LSC funded client is not by itself a determination of that person's liability to pay those costs (as to which see rule 44.17 and paragraphs 21.1 to 23.17 of this Practice Direction).

13.11

(1) The court will not make a summary assessment of the costs of a receiving party who is a child or protected party within the meaning of Part 21 unless the solicitor acting for the child or protected party has waived the right to further costs (see paragraph 51.1 below).

(2) The court may make a summary assessment of costs payable by a child or protected party.

13.12

(1) Attention is drawn to rule 44.3A which prevents the court from making a summary assessment of an additional liability before the conclusion of the proceedings or the part of the proceedings to which the funding arrangement relates. Where this applies, the court should nonetheless make a summary assessment of the base costs of the hearing or application unless there is a good reason not to do so.

(2) Where the court makes a summary assessment of the base costs all statements of costs and costs estimates put before the judge will be retained on the court file.

13.13 The court will not give its approval to disproportionate and unreasonable costs. Accordingly:

(a) When the amount of the costs to be paid has been agreed between the parties the order for costs must state that the order is by consent.

(b) If the judge is to make an order which is not by consent, the judge will, so far as possible, ensure that the final figure is not disproportionate and/or unreasonable having regard to Part 1 of the CPR. The judge will retain this responsibility notwithstanding the absence of challenge to individual items in the make-up of the figure sought. The fact that the paying party is not disputing the amount of costs can however be taken as some indication that the amount is proportionate and reasonable. The judge will therefore intervene only if satisfied that the costs are so disproportionate that it is right to do so.

SECTION 14 SUMMARY ASSESSMENT WHERE COSTS CLAIMED INCLUDE AN ADDITIONAL LIABILITY

Orders made before the conclusion of the proceedings

14.1 The existence of a conditional fee agreement or other funding arrangement within the meaning of rule 43.2 is not by itself a sufficient reason for not carrying out a summary assessment.

14.2 Where a legal representative acting for the receiving party has entered into a conditional fee agreement the court may summarily assess all the costs (other than any additional liability).

14.3 Where costs have been summarily assessed an order for payment will not be made unless the court has been satisfied that in respect of the costs claimed, the receiving party is at the time liable to pay to his legal representative an amount equal to or greater than the costs claimed. A statement in the form of the certificate appended at the end of Form N260 may be sufficient proof of liability. The giving of information under rule 44.15 (where that rule applies) is not sufficient.

14.4 The court may direct that any costs, for which the receiving party may not in the event be liable, shall be paid into court to await the outcome of the case, or shall not be enforceable until further order, or it may postpone the receiving party's right to receive payment in some other way.

Orders made at the conclusion of the proceedings

14.5 Where there has been a trial of one or more issues separately from other issues, the court will not normally order detailed assessment of the additional liability until all issues have been tried unless the parties agree.

14.6 Rule 44.3A(2) sets out the ways in which the court may deal with the assessment of the costs where there is a funding arrangement. Where the court makes a summary assessment of the base costs:

(1) The order may state separately the base costs allowed as (a) solicitor's charges, (b) counsel's fees, (c) any other disbursements and (d) any VAT;

(2) the statements of costs upon which the judge based his summary assessment will be retained on the court file.

14.7 Where the court makes a summary assessment of an additional liability at the conclusion of proceedings, that assessment must relate to the whole of the proceedings; this will include any additional liability relating to base costs allowed by the court when making a summary assessment on a previous application or hearing.

14.8 Paragraph 13.13 applies where the parties are agreed about the total amount to be paid by way of costs, or are agreed about the amount of the base costs that will be paid. Where they disagree about the additional liability the court may summarily assess that liability or make an order for a detailed assessment.

14.9 In order to facilitate the court in making a summary assessment of any additional liability at the conclusion of the proceedings the party seeking such costs must prepare and have available for the court a bundle of documents which must include—

(1) a copy of every notice of funding arrangement (Form N251) which has been filed by him;

(2) a copy of every estimate and statement of costs filed by him;

(3) a copy of the risk assessment prepared at the time any relevant funding arrangement was entered into and on the basis of which the amount of the additional liability was fixed.

SECTION 15 COSTS ON THE SMALL CLAIMS TRACK AND FAST TRACK: RULE 44.9

15.1

(1) Before a claim is allocated to one of those tracks the court is not restricted by any of the special rules that apply to that track.

(2) Where a claim has been allocated to one of those tracks, the special rules which relate to that track will apply to work done before as well as after allocation save to the extent (if any) that an order for costs in respect of that work was made before allocation.

(3)

(i) This paragraph applies where a claim, issued for a sum in excess of the normal financial scope of the small claims track, is allocated to that track only because an admission of part of the claim by the defendant reduces the amount in dispute to a sum within the normal scope of that track.

(See also paragraph 7.4 of Practice Direction 26)

(ii) On entering judgment for the admitted part before allocation of the balance of the claim the court may allow costs in respect of the proceedings down to that date.

SECTION 16 COSTS FOLLOWING ALLOCATION AND RE-ALLOCATION: RULE 44.11

16.1 This paragraph applies where the court is about to make an order to re-allocate a claim from the small claims track to another track.

16.2 Before making the order to re-allocate the claim, the court must decide whether any party is to pay costs to any other party down to the date of the order to re-allocate in accordance with the rules about costs contained in Part 27 (The Small Claims Track).

16.3 If it decides to make such an order about costs, the court will make a summary assessment of those costs in accordance with that Part.

SECTION 17 COSTS-ONLY PROCEEDINGS: RULE 44.12A

17.1 A claim form under this rule should not be issued in the High Court unless the dispute to which the agreement relates was of such a value or type that had proceedings been begun they would have been commenced in the High Court.

17.2 A claim form which is to be issued in the High Court at the Royal Courts of Justice will be issued in the Costs Office.

17.3 Attention is drawn to rule 8.2 (in particular to paragraph (b)(ii)) and to rule 44.12A(3). The claim form must:

(1) identify the claim or dispute to which the agreement to pay costs relates;

(2) state the date and terms of the agreement on which the claimant relies;

(3) set out or have attached to it a draft of the order which the claimant seeks;

(4) state the amount of the costs claimed; and,

(5) state whether the costs are claimed on the standard or indemnity basis. If no basis is specified the costs will be treated as being claimed on the standard basis.

17.4 The evidence to be filed and served with the claim form under Rule 8.5 must include copies of the documents on which the claimant relies to prove the defendant's agreement to pay costs.

17.5 A costs judge or a district judge has jurisdiction to hear and decide any issue which may arise in a claim issued under this rule irrespective of the amount of the costs claimed or of the value of the claim to which the agreement to pay costs relates. A costs officer may make an order by consent under paragraph 17.7, or an order dismissing a claim under paragraph 17.9 below.

17.6 When the time for filing the defendant's acknowledgement of service has expired, the claimant may by letter request the court to make an order in the terms of his claim, unless the defendant has filed an acknowledgement of service stating that he intends to contest the claim or to seek a different order.

17.7 Rule 40.6 applies where an order is to be made by consent. An order may be made by consent in terms which differ from those set out in the claim form.

17.8 (1) An order for costs made under this rule will be treated as an order for the amount of costs to be decided by a detailed assessment to which Part 47 and the practice directions relating to it apply. Rule 44.4(4) (determination of basis of assessment) also applies to the order.

17.9 (1) For the purposes of rule 44.12A(4)(b)—

(a) a claim will be treated as opposed if the defendant files an acknowledgment of service stating that he intends to contest the making of an order for costs or to seek a different remedy; and

(b) a claim will not be treated as opposed if the defendant files an acknowledgment of service stating that he disputes the amount of the claim for costs.

(2) An order dismissing the claim will be made as soon as an acknowledgment of service opposing the claim is filed. The dismissal of a claim under rule 44.12A(4) does not prevent the claimant from issuing another claim form under Part 7 or Part 8 based on the agreement or alleged agreement to which the proceedings under this rule related.

17.10 (1) Rule 8.9 (which provides that claims issued under Part 8 shall be treated as allocated to the multi-track) shall not apply to claims issued under this rule. A claim issued under this rule may be dealt with without being allocated to a track.

(2) Rule 8.1(3) and Part 24 do not apply to proceedings brought under rule 44.12A.

17.11 Nothing in this rule prevents a person from issuing a claim form under Part 7 or Part 8 to sue on an agreement made in settlement of a dispute where that agreement makes provision for costs, nor from claiming in that case an order for costs or a specified sum in respect of costs.

SECTION 18 COURT'S POWERS IN RELATION TO MISCONDUCT: RULE 44.14

18.1 Before making an order under rule 44.14 the court must give the party or legal representative in question a reasonable opportunity to attend a hearing to give reasons why it should not make such an order.

18.2 Conduct before or during the proceedings which gave rise to the assessment which is unreasonable or improper includes steps which are calculated to prevent or inhibit the court from furthering the overriding objective.

18.3 Although rule 44.14(3) does not specify any sanction for breach of the obligation imposed by the rule the court may, either in the order under paragraph (2) or in a subsequent order, require the solicitor to produce to the court evidence that he took reasonable steps to comply with the obligation.

SECTION 19 PROVIDING INFORMATION ABOUT FUNDING ARRANGEMENTS: RULE 44.15

19.1

(1) A party who wishes to claim an additional liability in respect of a funding arrangement must give any other party information about that claim if he is to recover the additional liability. There is no requirement to specify the amount of the additional liability separately nor to state how it is calculated until it falls to be assessed. That principle is reflected in rules 44.3A and 44.15, in the following paragraphs and in Sections 6, 13, 14 and 31 of this Practice Direction. Section 6 deals with estimates of costs, Sections 13 and 14 deal with summary assessment and Section 31 deals with detailed assessment.

(2) In the following paragraphs a party who has entered into a funding arrangement is treated as a person who intends to recover a sum representing an additional liability by way of costs.

(3) Attention is drawn to paragraph 57.9 of this Practice Direction which sets out time limits for the provision of information where a funding arrangement is entered into between 31 March and 2 July 2000 and proceedings relevant to that arrangement are commenced before 3 July 2000.

Method of giving information

19.2

(1) In this paragraph, 'claim form' includes petition and application notice, and the notice of funding to be filed or served is a notice containing the information set out in Form N251.

(2)

(a) A claimant who has entered into a funding arrangement before starting the proceedings to which it relates must provide information to the court by filing the notice when he issues the claim form.

(b) He must provide information to every other party by serving the notice. If he serves the claim form himself he must serve the notice with the claim form. If the court is to serve the claim form, the court will also serve the notice if the claimant provides it with sufficient copies for service.

(3) A defendant who has entered into a funding arrangement before filing any document

(a) must provide information to the court by filing notice with his first document. A 'first document' may be an acknowledgement of service, a defence, or any other document, such as an application to set aside a default judgment.

(b) must provide information to every party by serving notice. If he serves his first document himself he must serve the notice with that document. If the court is to serve his first document the court will also serve the notice if the defendant provides it with sufficient copies for service.

(4) In all other circumstances a party must file and serve notice within 7 days of entering into the funding arrangement concerned.

(Practice Direction (Pre-Action Conduct) provides that a party must inform any other party as soon as possible about a funding arrangement entered into prior to the start of proceedings.)

Notice of change of information

19.3

(1) Rule 44.15 imposes a duty on a party to give notice of change if the information he has previously provided is no longer accurate. To comply he must file and serve notice containing the information set out in Form N251. Rule 44.15(3) may impose other duties in relation to new estimates of costs.

(2) Further notification need not be provided where a party has already given notice:

(a) that he has entered into a conditional fee agreement with a legal representative and during the currency of that agreement either of them enters into another such agreement with an additional legal representative; or

(b) of some insurance cover, unless that cover is cancelled or unless new cover is taken out with a different insurer.

(3) Part 6 applies to the service of notices.

(4) The notice must be signed by the party or by his legal representative.

Information which must be provided

19.4

(1) Unless the court otherwise orders, a party who is required to supply information about a funding arrangement must state whether he has—

- entered into a conditional fee agreement which provides for a success fee within the meaning of section 58(2) of the Courts and Legal Services Act 1990;
- taken out an insurance policy to which section 29 of the Access to Justice Act 1999 applies;
- made an arrangement with a body which is prescribed for the purpose of section 30 of that Act;
- or more than one of these.

(2) Where the funding arrangement is a conditional fee agreement, the party must state the date of the agreement and identify the claim or claims to which it relates (including Part 20 claims if any).

(3) Where the funding arrangement is an insurance policy, the party must—

(a) state the name and address of the insurer, the policy number and the date of the policy and identify the claim or claims to which it relates (including Part 20 claims if any);

(b) state the level of cover provided by the insurance; and

(c) state whether the insurance premiums are staged and, if so, the points at which an increased premium is payable.

(4) Where the funding arrangement is by way of an arrangement with a relevant body the party must state the name of the body and set out the date and terms of the undertaking it has given and must identify the claim or claims to which it relates (including Part 20 claims if any).

(5) Where a party has entered into more than one funding arrangement in respect of a claim, for example a conditional fee agreement and an insurance policy, a single notice containing the information set out in Form N251 may contain the required information about both or all of them.

19.5 Where the court makes a Group Litigation Order, the court may give directions as to the extent to which individual parties should provide information in accordance with rule 44.15.

Transitional Provision

19.6 The amendments to the parenthesis below paragraph 19.2 and to paragraph 19.4(3) do not apply where the funding arrangement was entered into before 1st October 2009 and the parenthesis below paragraph 19.2 and paragraph 19.4(3) in force immediately before that date will continue to apply to that funding arrangement as if those amendments had not been made.

SECTION 20 PROCEDURE WHERE LEGAL REPRESENTATIVE WISHES TO RECOVER FROM HIS CLIENT AN AGREED PERCENTAGE INCREASE WHICH HAS BEEN DISALLOWED OR REDUCED ON ASSESSMENT: RULE 44.16

20.1

(1) Attention is drawn to Regulation 3(2)(b) of the Conditional Fee Agreements Regulations 2000 and to Regulation 5(2)(b) of the Collective Conditional Fee Agreements Regulations 2000, which provide that some or all of a success fee ceases to be payable in certain circumstances. [Both sets of regulations were revoked by the Conditional Fee Agreements (Revocation) Regulations 2005 but continue to have effect in relation to conditional fee agreements and collective conditional fee agreements entered into before 1" November 2005]

(2) Rule 44.16 allows the court to adjourn a hearing at which the legal representative acting for the receiving party applies for an order that a disallowed amount should continue to be payable under the agreement.

20.2 In the following paragraphs 'counsel' means counsel who has acted in the case under a conditional fee agreement which provides for a success fee. A reference to counsel includes a reference to any person who appeared as an advocate in the case and who is not a partner or employee of the solicitor or firm which is conducting the claim or defence (as the case may be) on behalf of the receiving party.

Procedure following Summary Assessment

20.3

(1) If the court disallows any amount of a legal representative's percentage increase, the court will, unless sub-paragraph (2) applies, give directions to enable an application to be made by the legal representative for the disallowed amount to be payable by his client, including, if appropriate, a direction that the application will be determined by a costs judge or district judge of the court dealing with the case.

(2) The court that has made the summary assessment may then and there decide the issue whether the disallowed amount should continue to be payable, if:

(a) the receiving party and all parties to the relevant agreement consent to the court doing so;

(b) the receiving party (or, if corporate, an officer) is present in court; and

(c) the court is satisfied that the issue can be fairly decided then and there.

Procedure following Detailed Assessment

20.4

(1) Where detailed assessment proceedings have been commenced, and the paying party serves points of dispute (as to which see Section 34 of this Practice Direction), which show that he is seeking a reduction in any percentage increase charged by counsel on his fees, the solicitor acting for the receiving party must within 3 days of service deliver to counsel a copy of the relevant points of dispute and the bill of costs or the relevant parts of the bill.

(2) Counsel must within 10 days thereafter inform the solicitor in writing whether or not he will accept the reduction sought or some other reduction. Counsel may state any points he wishes to have made in a reply to the points of dispute, and the solicitor must serve them on the paying party as or as part of a reply.

(3) Counsel who fails to inform the solicitor within the time limits set out above will be taken to accept the reduction unless the court otherwise orders.

20.5 Where the paying party serves points of dispute seeking a reduction in any percentage increase charged by a legal representative acting for the receiving party, and that legal representative intends, if necessary, to apply for an order that any amount of the percentage disallowed as against the paying party shall continue to be payable by his client, the solicitor acting for the receiving party must, within 14 days of service of the points of dispute, give to his client a clear written explanation of the nature of the relevant point of dispute and the effect it will have if it is upheld in whole or in part by the court, and of the client's right to attend any subsequent hearings at court when the matter is raised.

20.6 Where the solicitor acting for a receiving party files a request for a detailed assessment hearing it must if appropriate, be accompanied by a certificate signed by him stating:

(1) that the amount of the percentage increase in respect of counsel's fees or solicitor's charges is disputed;

(2) whether an application will be made for an order that any amount of that increase which is disallowed should continue to be payable by his client;

(3) that he has given his client an explanation in accordance with paragraph 20.5; and,

(4) whether his client wishes to attend court when the amount of any relevant percentage increase may be decided.

20.7

(1) The solicitor acting for the receiving party must within 7 days of receiving from the court notice of the date of the assessment hearing, notify his client, and if appropriate, counsel in writing of the date, time and place of the hearing.

(2) Counsel may attend or be represented at the detailed assessment hearing and may make oral or written submissions.

20.8

(1) At the detailed assessment hearing, the court will deal with the assessment of the costs payable by one party to another, including the amount of the percentage increase, and give a certificate accordingly.

(2) The court may decide the issue whether the disallowed amount should continue to be payable under the relevant conditional fee agreement without an adjournment if:

(a) the receiving party and all parties to the relevant agreement consent to the court deciding the issue without an adjournment,

(b) the receiving party (or, if corporate, an officer or employee who has authority to consent on behalf of the receiving party) is present in court, and

(c) the court is satisfied that the issue can be fairly decided without an adjournment.

(3) In any other case the court will give directions and fix a date for the hearing of the application.

SECTION 21 APPLICATION OF COSTS RULES: RULE 44.17

21.1 Rule 44.17(b) excludes the costs rules to the extent that regulations under the Legal Aid Act 1988 make different provision. The primary examples of such regulations are the regulations providing prescribed rates (with or without enhancement).

21.2 Rule 44.17(a) provides that the procedure for detailed assessment does not apply to the extent that section 11 of the Access to Justice Act 1999 and provisions made under that Act make different provision.

21.3 Section 11 of the Access to Justice Act 1999 provides special protection against liability for costs for litigants who receive funding by the LSC (Legal Services Commission) as part of the Community Legal Service. Any costs ordered to be paid by a LSC funded client must not exceed the amount which is reasonable for him to pay having regard to all the circumstances including:

(a) the financial resources of all the parties to the proceedings, and

(b) their conduct in connection with the dispute to which the proceedings relate.

21.4 In this Practice Direction

'cost protection' means the limit on costs awarded against a LSC funded client set out in Section 11(1) of the Access to Justice Act 1999.

'partner' has the meaning given by the Community Legal Service (Costs) Regulations 2000.

21.5 Whether or not cost protection applies depends upon the 'level of service' for which funding was provided by the LSC in accordance with the Funding Code approved under section 9 of the Access to Justice Act 1999. The levels of service referred to are:

(1) Legal Help – advice and assistance about a legal problem, not including representation or advocacy in proceedings.

(2) Help at Court – advocacy at a specific hearing, where the advocate is not formally representing the client in the proceedings.

(3) Family Mediation.

(4) Legal Representation – representation in actual or contemplated proceedings. Legal Representation can take the form of Investigative Help (limited to investigating the merits of a potential claim) or Full Representation.

(5) General Family Help and Help with Mediation.

(6) Omitted

21.6 Levels of service (4) and (5) are provided under a certificate (similar to a legal aid certificate). The certificate will state which level of service is covered. Where there are proceedings, a copy of the certificate will be lodged with the court.

21.7 Cost protection does not apply where—

(1) The LSC funded client receives Help at Court;

(2) The LSC funded client receives Legal Help only i.e. where the solicitor is advising, but not representing a litigant in person. However, where the LSC funded client receives Legal Help e.g. to write a letter before action, but later receives Legal Representation or General Family Help or Help with Mediation in respect of the same dispute, other than in family proceedings, cost protection does apply to all costs incurred by the receiving party in the funded proceedings or prospective proceedings;

(3) The LSC funded client receives General Family Help or Help with Mediation in family proceedings;

(4) The LSC funded client receives Legal Representation in family proceedings.

21.8 Where cost protection does not apply, the court may award costs in the normal way.

21.9 Where work is done before the issue of a certificate, cost protection does not apply to those costs, except where:

(1) pre-action Legal Help is given and the LSC funded client subsequently receives Legal Representation or General Family Help or Help with Mediation in respect of the same dispute, other than in family proceedings; or

(2) where urgent work is undertaken immediately before the grant of an emergency certificate, other than in family proceedings, when no emergency application could be made as the LSC's offices were closed, provided that the solicitor seeks an emergency certificate at the first available opportunity and the certificate is granted.

21.10 If a LSC funded client's certificate is revoked, costs protection does not apply to work done before or after revocation.

21.11 If a LSC funded client's certificate is discharged, costs protection only applies to costs incurred before the date on which funded services ceased to be provided under the certificate. This may be a date before the date on which the certificate is formally discharged by the LSC (Burridge v Stafford: Khan v Ali [2000] 1 WLR 927, [1999] 4 All ER 660 CA).

21.11A Where an LSC funded client has cost protection, the procedure described in sections 22 and 23 of this Practice Direction applies. However that procedure does not apply in relation to costs claimed during any periods in the proceedings when the LSC funded client did not have cost protection, and the procedure set out in CPR Parts 45 to 47 will apply (as appropriate) in relation to those periods.

Assessing a LSC Funded Client's Resources

21.12 The first £100,000 of the value of the LSC funded client's interest in the main or only home is disregarded when assessing his or her financial resources for the purposes of S.11 and cannot be the subject of any enforcement process by the receiving party. The receiving party cannot apply for an order to sell the LSC funded client's home, but could secure the debt against any value exceeding £100,000 by way of a charging order.

21.13 The court may only take into account the value of the LSC funded client's clothes, household furniture, tools and implements of trade to the extent that it considers that having regard to the quantity or value of the items, the circumstances are exceptional.

21.14 The LSC funded client's resources include the resources of his partner, unless the partner has a contrary interest in the dispute in respect of which funded services are provided.

Party acting in a Representative, Fiduciary or Official Capacity

21.15

(1) Where a LSC funded client is acting in a representative, fiduciary or official capacity, the court shall not take the personal resources of the party into account for the purposes of either a Section 11 order or costs against the Commission, but shall have regard to the value of any property or estate or the amount of any fund out of which the party is entitled to be indemnified, and may also have regard to the resources of any persons who are beneficially interested in the property, estate or fund.

(2) Similarly, where a party is acting as a litigation friend to a client who is a child or a protected party, the court shall not take the personal resources of the litigation friend into account in assessing the resources of the client.

(3) The purpose of this provision is to ensure that any liability is determined with reference to the value of the property or fund being used to pay for the litigation, and the financial position of those who may benefit from or rely on it.

Costs against the LSC

21.16 Regulation 5 of the Community Legal Service (Cost Protection) Regulations 2000 governs when costs can be awarded against the LSC. This provision only applies where cost protection applies and the costs ordered to be paid by the LSC funded client do not fully meet the costs that would have been ordered to be paid by him if cost protection did not apply.

21.17 In this Section and the following two Sections of this Practice Direction 'non-funded party' means a party to proceedings who has not received LSC funded services in relation to these proceedings under a legal aid certificate or a certificate issued under the LSC Funding Code other than a certificate which has been revoked.

21.18 The following criteria set out in Regulation 5 must be satisfied before the LSC can be ordered to pay the whole or any part of the costs incurred by a non-funded party:

(1) the proceedings are finally decided in favour of a non-funded party;

(2) unless there is good reason for delay the non-funded party provides written notice of intention to seek an order against the LSC within three months of the making of the section 11(1) costs order;

(3) the court is satisfied that it is just and equitable in the circumstances that provision for the costs should be made out of public funds; and

(4) where costs are incurred in a court of first instance, the following additional criteria must also be met:

(i) the proceedings were instituted by the LSC funded client;

(ii) the non-funded party is an individual; and

(iii) the non-funded party will suffer financial hardship unless the order is made.

('Section 11(1) costs order' is defined in paragraph 22.1, below).

21.19 In determining whether conditions (3) and (4) are satisfied, the court shall take into account the resources of the non-funded party and his partner, unless the partner has a contrary interest.

21.19A An order under Regulation 5 may be made in relation to proceedings in the Court of Appeal, High Court or a County Court, by a Costs Judge or a District Judge.

Effect of Appeals

21.20

(1) An order for costs can only be made against the LSC when the proceedings (including any appeal) are finally decided. Therefore, where a court of first instance decides in favour of a non-funded party and an appeal lies, any order made against the LSC shall not take effect unless:

(a) where permission to appeal is required, the time limit for permission to appeal expires, without permission being granted;

(b) where permission to appeal is granted or is not required, the time limit for appeal expires without an appeal being brought.

(2) Accordingly, if the LSC funded client appeals, any earlier order against the LSC can never take effect. If the appeal is unsuccessful, an application can be made to the appeal court for a fresh order.

SECTION 22 ORDERS FOR COSTS TO WHICH SECTION 11 OF THE ACCESS TO JUSTICE ACT 1999 APPLIES

22.1 In this Practice Direction:

'order for costs to be determined' means an order for costs to which Section 11 of the Access to Justice Act 1999 applies under which the amount of costs payable by the LSC funded client is to be determined by a costs judge or district judge under Section 23 of this Practice Direction.

'order specifying the costs payable' means an order for costs to which Section 11 of the Act applies and which specifies the amount which the LSC funded client is to pay.

'full costs' means, where an order to which Section 11 of the Act applies is made against a LSC funded client, the amount of costs which that person would, had cost protection not applied, have been ordered to pay.

'determination proceedings' means proceedings to which paragraphs 22.1 to 22.10 apply.

'Section 11(1) costs order' means an order for costs to be determined or an order specifying the costs payable other than an order specifying the costs payable which was made in determination proceedings.

'statement of resources' means

(1) a statement, verified by a statement of truth, made by a party to proceedings setting out:

(a) his income and capital and financial commitments during the previous year and, if applicable, those of his partner;

(b) his estimated future financial resources and expectations and, if applicable, those of his partner ('partner' is defined in paragraph 21.4, above);

(c) a declaration that he and, if applicable, his partner, has not deliberately foregone or deprived himself of any resources or expectations;

(d) particulars of any application for funding made by him in connection with the proceedings; and,

(e) any other facts relevant to the determination of his resources; or

(2) a statement, verified by a statement of truth, made by a client receiving funded services, setting out the information provided by the client under Regulation 6 of the Community Legal Service (Financial) Regulations 2000, and stating that there has been no significant change in the client's financial circumstances since the date on which the information was provided or, as the case may be, details of any such change.

'Regional Director' means any Regional Director appointed by the LSC and any member of his staff authorised to act on his behalf.

22.2 Regulations 8 to 13 of the Community Legal Service (Costs) Regulations 2000 as amended set out the procedure for seeking costs against a funded client and the LSC. The effect of these Regulations is set out in this section and the next section of this Practice Direction.

22.3 As from 5 June 2000, Regulations 9 to13 of the Community Legal Service (Costs) Regulations 2000 as amended also apply to certificates issued under the Legal Aid Act 1988 where costs against the assisted person fall to be assessed under Regulation 124 of the Civil Legal Aid (General) Regulations 1989. In this section and the next section of this Practice Direction the expression 'LSC funded client' includes an assisted person (defined in rule 43.2).

22.4 Regulation 8 of the Community Legal Service (Costs) Regulations 2000 as amended provides that a party intending to seek an order for costs against a LSC funded client may at any time file and serve on the LSC funded client a statement of resources. If that statement is served 7 or more days before a date fixed for a hearing at which an order for costs may be made, the LSC funded client must also make a statement of resources and produce it at the hearing.

22.5 If the court decides to make an order for costs against a LSC funded client to whom cost protection applies it may either:

(1) make an order for costs to be determined, or

(2) make an order specifying the costs payable.

22.6 If the court makes an order for costs to be determined it may also

(1) state the amount of full costs, or

(2) make findings of facts, e.g., concerning the conduct of all the parties which are to be taken into account by the court in the subsequent determination proceedings.

22.7 The court will not make an order specifying the costs payable unless:

(1) it considers that it has sufficient information before it to decide what amount is a reasonable amount for the LSC funded client to pay in accordance with Section 11 of the Act, and

(2) either

(a) the order also states the amount of full costs, or

(b) the court considers that it has sufficient information before it to decide what amount is a reasonable amount for the LSC funded client to pay in accordance with Section 11 of the Act and is satisfied that, if it were to determine the full costs at that time, they would exceed the amounts specified in the order.

22.8 Where an order specifying the costs payable is made and the LSC funded client does not have cost protection in respect of all of the costs awarded in that order, the order must identify the sum payable (if any) in respect of which the LSC funded client has cost protection and the sum payable (if any) in respect of which he does not have cost protection.

22.9 The court cannot make an order under Regulations 8 to 13 of the Community Legal Service (Costs) Regulations 2000 as amended except in proceedings to which the next section of this Practice Direction applies.

SECTION 23 DETERMINATION PROCEEDINGS AND SIMILAR PROCEEDINGS UNDER THE COMMUNITY LEGAL SERVICE (COSTS) REGULATIONS 2000

23.1 This section of this Practice Direction deals with

(1) proceedings subsequent to the making of an order for costs to be determined,

(2) variations in the amount stated in an order specifying the amount of costs payable and

(3) the late determination of costs under an order for costs to be determined;

(4) appeals in respect of determination.

23.2 In this section of this Practice Direction 'appropriate court office' means:

(1) the district registry or county court in which the case was being dealt with when the Section 11(1) order was made, or to which it has subsequently been transferred; or

(2) in all other cases, the Costs Office.

23.2A

(1) This paragraph applies where the appropriate office is any of the following county courts: Barnet, Bow, Brentford, Bromley, Central London, Clerkenwell and Shoreditch, Croydon, Edmonton, Ilford, Kingston, Lambeth, Mayors and City of London, Romford, Uxbridge, Wandsworth, West London, Willesden and Woolwich.

(2) Where this paragraph applies:–

(i) a receiving party seeking an order specifying costs payable by an LSC funded client and/or by the Legal Services Commission under this section must file his application in the Costs Office and, for all purposes relating to that application, the Costs Office will be treated as the appropriate office in that case; and

(ii) unless an order is made transferring the application to the Costs Office as part of the High Court, an appeal from any decision made by a costs judge shall lie to the Designated Civil Judge for the London Group of County Courts or such judge as he shall nominate. The appeal notice and any other relevant papers should be lodged at the Central London Civil Justice Centre.

23.3

(1) A receiving party seeking an order specifying costs payable by an LSC funded client and/or by the LSC may within 3 months of an order for costs to be determined, file in the appropriate court office an application in Form N244 accompanied by

(a) the receiving party's bill of costs (unless the full costs have already been determined);

(b) the receiving party's statement of resources (unless the court is determining an application against a costs order against the LSC and the costs were not incurred in the court of first instance); and

(c) if the receiving party intends to seek costs against the LSC, written notice to that effect.

(2) If the LSC funded client's liability has already been determined and is less than the full costs, the application will be for costs against the LSC only. If the LSC funded client's liability has not yet been determined, the receiving party must indicate if costs will be sought against the LSC if the funded client's liability is determined as less than the full costs.

23.4 The receiving party must file the above documents in the appropriate court office and (where relevant) serve copies on the LSC funded client and the Regional Director. In respect of applications for funded services made before 3 December

2001 a failure to file a request within the 3 months time limit specified in Regulation 10(2) is an absolute bar to the making of a costs order against the LSC. Where the application for funded services was made on or after 3 December 2001 the court does have power to extend the 3 months time limit, but only if the applicant can show good reason for the delay.

23.5 On being served with the application, the LSC funded client must respond by filing a statement of resources and serving a copy of it on the receiving party (and the Regional Director where relevant) within 21 days. The LSC funded client may also file and serve written points disputing the bill within the same time limit. (Under rule 3.1 the court may extend or shorten this time limit.)

23.6 If the LSC funded client fails to file a statement of resources without good reason, the court will determine his liability (and the amount of full costs if relevant) and need not hold an oral hearing for such determination.

23.7 When the LSC funded client files a statement or the 21 day period for doing so expires, the court will fix a hearing date and give the relevant parties at least 14 days notice. The court may fix a hearing without waiting for the expiry of the 21 day period if the application is made only against the LSC.

23.8 Determination proceedings will be listed for hearing before a costs judge or district judge. The determination of the liability on the LSC funded client will be listed as a private hearing.

23.9 Where the LSC funded client does not have cost protection in respect of all of the costs awarded, the order made by the costs judge or district judge must in addition to specifying the costs payable, identify the full costs in respect of which cost protection applies and the full costs in respect of which cost protection does not apply.

23.10 The Regional Director may appear at any hearing at which a costs order may be made against the LSC. Instead of appearing, he may file a written statement at court and serve a copy on the receiving party. The written statement should be filed and a copy served, not less than 7 days before the hearing.

Variation of an order specifying the costs payable

23.11

(1) This paragraph applies where the amount stated in an order specifying the costs payable plus the amount ordered to be paid by the LSC is less than the full costs to which cost protection applies.

(2) The receiving party may apply to the court for a variation of the amount which the LSC funded client is required to pay on the ground that there has been a significant change in the client's circumstances since the date of the order.

23.12 On an application under paragraph 23.11, where the order specifying the costs payable does not state the full costs

(1) the receiving party must file with his application the receiving party's statement of resources and bill of costs and copies of these documents should be served with the application.

(2) The LSC funded client must respond to the application by making a statement of resources which must be filed at court and served on the receiving party within 21 days thereafter. The LSC funded client may also file and serve written points disputing the bill within the same time limit.

(3) The court will, when determining the application assess the full costs identifying any part of them to which cost protection does apply and any part of them to which cost protection does not apply.

23.13 On an application under paragraph 23.11 the order specifying the costs payable may be varied as the court thinks fit. That variation must not increase:

(1) the amount of any costs ordered to be paid by the LSC, and

(2) the amount payable by the LSC funded client,

to a sum which is greater than the amount of the full costs plus the costs of the application.

23.14

(1) Where an order for costs to be determined has been made but the receiving party has not applied, within the three month time limit under paragraph 23.2, the receiving party may apply on any of the following grounds for a determination of the amount which the funded client is required to pay:

   (a) there has been a significant change in the funded client's circumstances since the date of the order for costs to be determined; or

   (b) material additional information about the funded client's financial resources is available which could not with reasonable diligence have been obtained by the receiving party at the relevant time; or

   (c) there were other good reasons for the failure by the receiving party to make an application within the time limit.

(2) An application for costs payable by the LSC cannot be made under this paragraph.

23.15

(1) Where the receiving party has received funded services in relation to the proceedings, the LSC may make an application under paragraphs 23.11 and 23.14 above.

(2) In respect of an application under paragraph 23.11 made by the LSC, the LSC must file and serve copies of the documents described in paragraph 23.12(1)

23.16 An application under paragraph 23.11, 23.14 and 23.15 must be commenced before the expiration of 6 years from the date on which the court made the order specifying the costs payable, or (as the case may be) the order for costs to be determined.

23.17 Applications under paragraphs 23.11, 23.14 and 23.15 should be made in the appropriate court office and should be made in Form N244 to be listed for a hearing before a costs judge or district judge.

Appeals

23.18

(1) Save as mentioned above any determination made under Regulation 9 or 10 of the Costs Regulations is final (Regulation 11(1)). Any party with a financial interest in the assessment of the full costs, other than a funded party, may appeal against that assessment in accordance with CPR Part 52 (Regulation 11(2) and CPR rule 47.20).

(2) The receiving party or the Commission may appeal on a point of law against the making of a costs order against the Commission, against the amount of costs the Commission is required to pay or against the court's refusal to make such an order (Regulation 11(4)).

SECTION 23A COSTS CAPPING ORDERS

When to make an application

23A.1 The court will make a costs capping order only in exceptional circumstances.

23A.2 An application for a costs capping order must be made as soon as possible, preferably before or at the first case management hearing or shortly afterwards. The stage which the proceedings have reached at the time of the application will be one of the factors the court will consider when deciding whether to make a costs capping order.

Estimate of costs

23A.3 The estimate of costs required by rule 44.19 must be in the form illustrated in Precedent H in the Schedule of Costs Precedents annexed to this Practice Direction.

Schedule of costs

23A.4 The schedule of costs referred to in rule 44.19(3)—

(a) must set out—

- (i) each sub-heading as it appears in the applicant's estimate of costs (column 1);
- (ii) alongside each sub-heading, the amount claimed by the applicant in the applicant's estimate of costs (column 2); and
- (iii) alongside the figures referred to in sub-paragraph (ii) the amount that the respondent proposes should be allowed under each sub-heading (column 3); and

(b) must be supported by a statement of truth.

Assessing the quantum of the costs cap

23A.5 When assessing the quantum of a costs cap, the court will take into account the factors detailed in rule 44.5 and the relevant provisions supporting that rule in this Practice Direction. The court may also take into account when considering a party's estimate of the costs they are likely to incur in the future conduct of the proceedings a reasonable allowance on costs for contingencies.

DIRECTIONS RELATING TO PART 45 FIXED COSTS

SECTION 24 FIXED COSTS IN SMALL CLAIMS

24.1 Under Rule 27.14 the costs which can be awarded to a claimant in a small claims track case include the fixed costs payable under Part 45 attributable to issuing the claim.

24.2 Those fixed costs shall be the sum of

(a) the fixed commencement costs calculated in accordance with Table 1 of Rule 45.2 and;

(b) the appropriate court fee or fees paid by the claimant.

SECTION 24A CLAIMS TO WHICH PART 45 DOES NOT APPLY

24A In a claim to which Part 45 does not apply, no amount shall be entered on the claim form for the charges of the claimant's solicitor, but the words "to be assessed" shall be inserted.

SECTION 25 FIXED COSTS ON THE ISSUE OF A DEFAULT COSTS CERTIFICATE

25.1 Unless paragraph 24.2 applies or unless the court orders otherwise, the fixed costs to be included in a default costs certificate are £80 plus a sum equal to any appropriate court fee payable on the issue of the certificate.

25.2 The fixed costs included in a certificate must not exceed the maximum sum specified for costs and court fee in the notice of commencement.

SECTION 25A ROAD TRAFFIC ACCIDENTS: FIXED RECOVERABLE COSTS IN COSTS-ONLY PROCEEDINGS

Scope

25A.1 Section II of Part 45 ('the Section') provides for certain fixed costs to be recoverable between parties in respect of costs incurred in disputes which are settled prior to proceedings being issued. The Section applies to road traffic accident disputes as defined in rule 45.7(4)(a), where the accident which gave rise to the dispute occurred on or after 6th October 2003.

25A.2 The Section does not apply to diputes where the total agreed value of the damages is within the small claims limit or exceeds £10,000. Rule 26.8(2) sets out how the financial value of a claim is assessed for the purposes of allocation to track.

25A.3 Fixed recoverable costs are to be calculated by reference to the amount of agreed damages which are payable to the receiving party. In calculating the amount of these damages—

(a) account must be taken of both general and special damages and interest;

(b) any interim payments made must be included;

(c) where the parties have agreed an element of contributory negligence, the amount of damages attributed to that negligence must be deducted;

(d) any amount required by statute to be paid by the compensating party directly to a third party (such as sums paid by way of compensation recovery payments and National Health Service expenses) must not be included.

25A.4 The Section applies to cases which fall within the scope of the Uninsured Drivers Agreement dated 13 August 1999. The section does not apply to cases which fall within the scope of the Untraced Drivers Agreement dated 14 February 2003.

Fixed recoverable costs formula

25A.5 The amount of fixed costs recoverable is calculated by totalling the following—

(a) the sum of £800;

(b) 20% of the agreed damages up to £5,000; and

(c) 15% of the agreed damages between £5,000 and £10,000.

For example, agreed damages of £7,523 would result in recoverable costs of £2,178.45 i.e.

£800 + (20% of £5,000) + (15% of £2,523).

Additional costs for work in specified areas

25A.6 The area referred to in rules 45.9(2) and 45.29(5) consists of (within London) the county court districts of Barnet, Bow, Brentford, Central London, Clerkenwell and Shoreditch, Edmonton, Ilford, Lambeth, Mayors and City of London, Romford, Wandsworth, West London, Willesden and Woolwich and (outside London) the county court districts of Bromley, Croydon, Dartford, Gravesend and Uxbridge.

Multiple claimants

25A.7 Where there is more than one potential claimant in relation to a dispute and two or more claimants instruct the same solicitor or firm of solicitors, the provisions of the section apply in respect of each claimant.

Information to be included in the claim form

25A.8 Costs only proceedings are commenced using the procedure set out in rule 44.12A. A claim form should be issued in accordance with Part 8. Where the claimant is claiming an amount of costs which exceed the amount of the fixed recoverable costs he must include on the claim form details of the exceptional circumstances which he considers justifies the additional costs.

25A.9 The claimant must also include on the claim form details of any disbursements or success fee he wishes to claim. The disbursements that may be claimed are set out in rule 45.10(1). If the disbursement falls within 45.10(2)(d) (disbursements that have arisen due to a particular feature of the dispute) the claimant must give details of the particular feature of the dispute and why he considers the disbursement to be necessary.

Disbursements and success fee

25A.10 If the parties agree the amount of the fixed recoverable costs and the only dispute is as to the payment of, or amount of, a disbursement or as to the amount of a success fee, then proceedings should be issued under rule 44.12A in the normal way and not by reference to Section II of Part 45.

SECTION 25B FIXED RECOVERABLE SUCCESS FEES IN EMPLOYER'S LIABILITY DISEASE CLAIMS

25B.1 The following table is a non-exclusive list of the conditions that will fall within Type A and Type B claims for the purposes of Rule 45.23.

Claim type	Description
A	Asbestosis
	Mesothelioma
	Bilateral Pleural Thickening
	Pleural Plaques
B	Repetitive Strain Injury/WRULD
	Carpal Tunnel Syndrome caused by Repetitive Strain Injury
	Occupational Stress

SECTION 25C SCALE COSTS FOR PROCEEDINGS IN A PATENTS COUNTY COURT

25C.1 Tables A and B set out the maximum amount of scale costs which the court will award for each stage of a claim in a patents county court.

25C.2 Table A sets out the scale costs for each stage of a claim up to determination of liability.

25C.3 Table B sets out the scale costs for each stage of an inquiry as to damages or account of profits.

Table A

Stage of a claim	Maximum amount of costs
Particulars of claim	£6,125
Defence and counterclaim	£6,125
Reply and defence to counterclaim	£6,125
Reply to defence to counterclaim	£3,000
Attendance at a case management conference	£2,500
Making or responding to an application	£2,500
Providing or inspecting disclosure or product/process description	£5,000
Performing or inspecting experiments	£2,500
Preparing witness statements	£5,000
Preparing experts' report	£7,500
Preparing for and attending trial and judgment	£15,000
Preparing for determination on the papers	£5,000

Table B

Stage of a claim	Maximum amount of costs
Points of claim	£2,500
Points of defence	£2,500
Attendance at a case management conference	£2,500

Making or responding to an application	£2,500
Providing or inspecting disclosure	£2,500
Preparing witness statements	£5,000
Preparing experts' report	£5,000
Preparing for and attending trial and judgment	£7,500
Preparing for determination on the papers	£2,500

DIRECTIONS RELATING TO PART 46 FAST TRACK TRIAL COSTS

SECTION 26 SCOPE OF PART 46: RULE 46.1

26.1 Part 46 applies to the costs of an advocate for preparing for and appearing at the trial of a claim in the fast track.

26.2 It applies only where, at the date of the trial, the claim is allocated to the fast track. It does not apply in any other case, irrespective of the final value of the claim.

26.3 In particular it does not apply to:

(a) the hearing of a claim which is allocated to the small claims track with the consent of the parties given under rule 26.7(3); or

(b) a disposal hearing at which the amount to be paid under a judgment or order is decided by the court (see paragraph 12.4 of Practice Direction 26)).

Cases which settle before trial

26.4 Attention is drawn to rule 44.10 (limitation on amount court may award where a claim allocated to the fast track settles before trial).

SECTION 27 POWER TO AWARD MORE OR LESS THAN THE AMOUNT OF FAST TRACK TRIAL COSTS: RULE 46.3

27.1 Rule 44.15 (providing information about funding arrangements) sets out the requirement to provide information about funding arrangements to the court and other parties. Section 19 of this Practice Direction sets out the information to be provided and when this is to be done.

27.2 Section 11, of this Practice Direction explains how the court will approach the question of what sum to allow in respect of additional liability.

27.3 The court has the power, when considering whether a percentage increase is reasonable, to allow different percentages for different items of costs or for different periods during which costs were incurred.

DIRECTIONS RELATING TO PART 47 PROCEDURE FOR DETAILED ASSESSMENT OF COSTS AND DEFAULT PROVISIONS

SECTION 28 TIME WHEN ASSESSMENT MAY BE CARRIED OUT: RULE 47.1

28.1

(1) For the purposes of rule 47.1, proceedings are concluded when the court has finally determined the matters in issue in the claim, whether or not there is an appeal.

(2) For the purposes of this rule, the making of an award of provisional damages under Part 41 will be treated as a final determination of the matters in issue.

(3) The court may order or the parties may agree in writing that, although the proceedings are continuing, they will nevertheless be treated as concluded.

(4)

(a) A party who is served with a notice of commencement (see paragraph 32.3 below) may apply to a costs judge or a district judge to determine whether the party who served it is entitled to commence detailed assessment proceedings.

(b) On hearing such an application the orders which the court may make include: an order allowing the detailed assessment proceedings to continue, or an order setting aside the notice of commencement.

(5) A costs judge or a district judge may make an order allowing detailed assessment proceedings to be commenced where there is no realistic prospect of the claim continuing.

SECTION 29 NO STAY OF DETAILED ASSESSMENT WHERE THERE IS AN APPEAL: RULE 47.2

29.1

(1) Rule 47.2 provides that detailed assessment is not stayed pending an appeal unless the court so orders.

(2) An application to stay the detailed assessment of costs pending an appeal may be made to the court whose order is being appealed or to the court who will hear the appeal.

SECTION 30 POWERS OF AN AUTHORISED COURT OFFICER: RULE 47.3

30.1

(1) The court officers authorised by the Lord Chancellor to assess costs in the Costs Office and the Principal Registry of the Family Division are authorised to deal with claims for costs not exceeding £30,000 (excluding VAT) in the case of senior executive officers, or their equivalent, and £75,000 (excluding VAT) in the case of principal officers.

(2) In calculating whether or not a bill of costs is within the authorised amounts, the figure to be taken into account is the total claim for costs including any additional liability.

(3) Where the receiving party, paying party and any other party to the detailed assessment proceedings who has served points of dispute are agreed that the assessment should not be made by an authorised court officer, the receiving party should so inform the court when requesting a hearing date. The court will then list the hearing before a costs judge or a district judge.

(4) In any other case a party who objects to the assessment being made by an authorised court officer must make an application to the costs judge or district judge under Part 23 (General Rules about Applications for Court Orders) setting out the reasons for the objection and if sufficient reason is shown the court will direct that the bill be assessed by a costs judge or district judge.

SECTION 31 VENUE FOR DETAILED ASSESSMENT PROCEEDINGS: RULE 47.4

31.1 For the purposes of rule 47.4(1) the 'appropriate office' means

(1) the district registry or county court in which the case was being dealt with when the judgment or order was made or the event occurred which gave rise to the right to assessment, or to which it has subsequently been transferred;

(1A) where a tribunal, person or other body makes an order for the detailed assessment of costs, a county court (subject to paragraph 31.1A(1)); or

(2) in all other cases, including Court of Appeal cases, the Costs Office.

31.1A

(1) This paragraph applies where the appropriate office is any of the following county courts: Barnet, Bow, Brentford, Bromley, Central London, Clerkenwell and Shoreditch, Croydon, Edmonton, Ilford, Kingston, Lambeth, Mayors and City of London, Romford, Uxbridge, Wandsworth, West London, Willesden and Woolwich.

(2) Where this paragraph applies:–

(i) the receiving party must file any request for a detailed assessment hearing in the Costs Office and, for all purposes relating to that detailed assessment (other than the issue of default costs certificates and applications to set aside default costs certificates), the Costs Office will be treated as the appropriate office in that case;

(ii) default costs certificates should be issued and applications to set aside default costs certificates should be issued and heard in the relevant county court; and

(iii) unless an order is made under rule 47.4(2) directing that the Costs Office as part of the High Court shall be the appropriate office, an appeal from any decision made by a costs judge shall lie to the Designated Civil Judge for the London Group of County Courts or such judge as he shall nominate. The appeal notice and any other relevant papers should be lodged at the Central London Civil Justice Centre.

31.2

(1) A direction under rule 47.4(2) or (3) specifying a particular court, registry or office as the appropriate office may be given on application or on the court's own initiative.

(2) Before making such a direction on its own initiative the court will give the parties the opportunity to make representations.

(3) Unless the Costs Office is the appropriate office for the purposes of Rule 47.4(1) an order directing that an assessment is to take place at the Costs Office will be made only if it is appropriate to do so having regard to the size of the bill of

costs, the difficulty of the issues involved, the likely length of the hearing, the cost to the parties and any other relevant matter.

SECTION 32 COMMENCEMENT OF DETAILED ASSESSMENT PROCEEDINGS: RULE 47.6

32.1 * Precedents A, B, C and D in the Schedule of Costs Precedents annexed to this Practice Direction are model forms of bills of costs for detailed assessment. Further information about bills of costs is set out in Section 4.

32.2 A detailed assessment may be in respect of:

(1) base costs, where a claim for additional liability has not been made or has been agreed;

(2) a claim for additional liability only, base costs having been summarily assessed or agreed; or

(3) both base costs and additional liability.

32.3 If the detailed assessment is in respect of costs without any additional liability, the receiving party must serve on the paying party and all the other relevant persons the following documents:

(a) a notice of commencement;

(b) a copy of the bill of costs;

(c) copies of the fee notes of counsel and of any expert in respect of fees claimed in the bill;

(d) written evidence as to any other disbursement which is claimed and which exceeds £500;

(e) a statement giving the name and address for service of any person upon whom the receiving party intends to serve the notice of commencement.

32.4 If the detailed assessment is in respect of an additional liability only, the receiving party must serve on the paying party and all other relevant persons the following documents:

(a) a notice of commencement;

(b) a copy of the bill of costs;

(c) the relevant details of the additional liability;

(d) a statement giving the name and address of any person upon whom the receiving party intends to serve the notice of commencement.

32.5 The relevant details of an additional liability are as follows:

(1) In the case of a conditional fee agreement with a success fee:

(a) a statement showing the amount of costs which have been summarily assessed or agreed; and the percentage increase which has been claimed in respect of those costs;

(b) where the conditional fee agreement was entered into before 1st November 2005, a statement of the reasons for the percentage increase given in accordance with regulation 3(1)(a) of the Conditional Fee Agreements Regulations 2000 or regulation 5(1)(c) of the Collective Conditional Fee Agreements Regulations 2000 [Both sets of regulations were revoked by the Conditional Fee Agreements (Revocation) Regulations 2005 but continue to have effect in relation to conditional fee agreements and collective conditional fee agreements entered into before 1st November 2005.];

(c) where the conditional fee agreement was entered into on or after 1st November 2005 (except in cases where the percentage increase is fixed by CPR Part 45, sections II to V), either a statement of the reasons for the percentage increase or a copy of the risk assessment prepared at the time that the conditional fee agreement was entered into;

(d) if the conditional fee agreement is not disclosed (and the Court of Appeal has indicated that it should be the usual practice for a conditional fee agreement, redacted where appropriate, to be disclosed for the purpose of costs proceedings in which a success fee is claimed), a statement setting out the following information contained in the conditional fee agreement so as to enable the paying party and the court to determine the level of risk undertaken by the solicitor—

(i) the definition of 'win' and, if applicable, 'lose';

(ii) details of the receiving party's liability to pay costs if that party wins or loses; and

(iii) details of the receiving party's liability to pay costs if that party fails to obtain a judgment more advantageous than a Part 36 offer.

(2) If the additional liability is an insurance premium, a copy of the insurance certificate showing—

(a) whether the policy covers—

(i) the receiving party's own costs;

(ii) the receiving party's opponent's costs;

(iii) the receiving party's own costs and opponent's costs; and

(b) the maximum extent of that cover; and

(c) the amount of the premium paid or payable.

(3) If the receiving party claims an additional amount under section 30 of the Access to Justice Act 1999, a statement setting out the basis upon which the receiving party's liability for the additional amount is calculated.

32.6 Attention is drawn to the fact that the additional amount recoverable pursuant to section 30 of the Access to Justice Act 1999 in respect of a membership organisation must not exceed the likely cost of the premium of an insurance policy against the risk of incurring a liability to pay the costs of other parties to the proceedings as provided by the Access to Justice (Membership Organisation) Regulations 2000 Regulation 4 (for the purposes of arrangements entered into before 1st November 2005) and The Access to Justice (Membership Organisation) Regulations 2005 Regulation 5 (for the purposes of arrangements entered into on or after 1st November 2005).

32.7 If a detailed assessment is in respect of both base costs and an additional liability, the receiving party must serve on the paying party and all other relevant persons the documents listed in paragraph 32.3 and the documents giving relevant details of an additional liability listed in paragraph 32.5.

32.8

(1) The Notice of Commencement should be in Form N252.

(2) Before it is served, it must be completed to show as separate items;

(a) the total amount of the costs claimed in the bill;

(b) the extra sum which will be payable by way of fixed costs and court fees if a default costs certificate is obtained.

32.9

(1) This paragraph applies where the notice of commencement is to be served outside England and Wales.

(2) The date to be inserted in the notice of commencement for the paying party to send points of dispute is a date (not less than 21 days from the date of service of the notice) which must be calculated by reference to Section IV of Part 6 as if the notice were a claim form and as if the date to be inserted was the date for the filing of a defence.

32.10

(1) For the purposes of rule 47.6(2) a 'relevant person' means:

(a) any person who has taken part in the proceedings which gave rise to the assessment and who is directly liable under an order for costs made against him;

(b) any person who has given to the receiving party notice in writing that he has a financial interest in the outcome of the assessment and wishes to be a party accordingly;

(c) any other person whom the court orders to be treated as such.

(2) Where a party is unsure whether a person is or is not a relevant person, that party may apply to the appropriate office for directions.

(3) The court will generally not make an order that the person in respect of whom the application is made will be treated as a relevant person, unless within a specified time he applies to the court to be joined as a party to the assessment proceedings in accordance with Part 19 (Parties and Group Litigation).

32.11

(1) This paragraph applies in cases in which the bill of costs is capable of being copied onto a computer disk.

(2) If, before the detailed assessment hearing, a paying party requests a disk copy of a bill to which this paragraph applies, the receiving party must supply him with a copy free of charge not more than 7 days after the date on which he received the request.

SECTION 33 PERIOD FOR COMMENCING DETAILED ASSESSMENT PROCEEDINGS: RULE 47.7

33.1 The parties may agree under rule 2.11 (Time limits may be varied by parties) to extend or shorten the time specified by rule 47.7 for commencing the detailed assessment proceedings.

33.2 A party may apply to the appropriate office for an order under rule 3.1(2)(a) to extend or shorten that time.

33.3 Attention is drawn to rule 47.6(1). The detailed assessment proceedings are commenced by service of the documents referred to.

33.4 Permission to commence assessment proceedings out of time is not required.

SECTION 34 SANCTION FOR DELAY IN COMMENCING DETAILED ASSESSMENT PROCEEDINGS: RULE 47.8

34.1 (1) An application for an order under rule 47.8 must be made in writing and be issued in the appropriate office.

(2) The application notice must be served at least 7 days before the hearing.

SECTION 35 POINTS OF DISPUTE AND CONSEQUENCES OF NOT SERVING: RULE 47.9

35.1 The parties may agree under rule 2.11 (Time limits may be varied by parties) to extend or shorten the time specified by rule 47.9 for service of points of dispute. A party may apply to the appropriate office for an order under rule 3.1(2)(a) to extend or shorten that time.

35.2 Points of dispute should be short and to the point and should follow as closely as possible Precedent G of the Schedule of Costs Precedents annexed to this Practice Direction.

35.3 Points of dispute must—

(1) identify each item in the bill of costs which is disputed,

(2) in each case, state concisely the nature and grounds of dispute,

(3) where practicable suggest a figure to be allowed for each item in respect of which a reduction is sought, and

(4) be signed by the party serving them or his solicitor.

35.4

(1) The normal period for serving points of dispute is 21 days after the date of service of the notice of commencement.

(2) Where a notice of commencement is served on a party outside England and Wales the period within which that party should serve points of dispute is to be calculated by reference to Section IV of Part 6 as if the notice of commencement was a claim form and as if the period for serving points of dispute were the period for filing a defence.

35.5 A party who serves points of dispute on the receiving party must at the same time serve a copy on every other party to the detailed assessment proceedings, whose name and address for service appears on the statement served by the receiving party in accordance with paragraph 32.3 or 32.4 above.

35.6

(1) This paragraph applies in cases in which Points of Dispute are capable of being copied onto a computer disk.

(2) If, within 14 days of the receipt of the Points of Dispute, the receiving party requests a disk copy of them, the paying party must supply him with a copy free of charge not more than 7 days after the date on which he received the request.

35.7

(1) Where the receiving party claims an additional liability, a party who serves points of dispute on the receiving party may include a request for information about other methods of financing costs which were available to the receiving party.

(2) Part 18 (further information) and Practice Direction 18 apply to such a request.

SECTION 36 PROCEDURE WHERE COSTS ARE AGREED: RULE 47.10

36.1 Where the parties have agreed terms as to the issue of a costs certificate (either interim or final) they should apply under rule 40.6 (Consent judgments and orders) for an order that a certificate be issued in terms set out in the application. Such an application may be dealt with by a court officer, who may issue the certificate.

36.2 Where in the course of proceedings the receiving party claims that the paying party has agreed to pay costs but that he will neither pay those costs nor join in a consent application under paragraph 36.1, the receiving party may apply under Part 23 (General Rules about Applications for Court Orders) for a certificate either interim or final to be issued.

36.3 An application under paragraph 36.2 must be supported by evidence and will be heard by a costs judge or a district judge. The respondent to the application must file and serve any evidence he relies on at least two days before the hearing date.

36.4 Nothing in rule 47.10 prevents parties who seek a judgment or order by consent from including in the draft a term that a party shall pay to another party a specified sum in respect of costs.

36.5

(1) The receiving party may discontinue the detailed assessment proceedings in accordance with Part 38 (Discontinuance).

(2) Where the receiving party discontinues the detailed assessment proceedings before a detailed assessment hearing has been requested, the paying party may apply to the appropriate office for an order about the costs of the detailed assessment proceedings.

(3) Where a detailed assessment hearing has been requested the receiving party may not discontinue unless the court gives permission.

(4) A bill of costs may be withdrawn by consent whether or not a detailed assessment hearing has been requested.

SECTION 37 DEFAULT COSTS CERTIFICATE: RULE 47.11

37.1

(1) A request for the issue of a default costs certificate must be made in Form N254 and must be signed by the receiving party or his solicitor.

(2) The request must be accompanied by a copy of the document giving the right to detailed assessment. (Section 40.4 of the Costs Practice Direction identifies the appropriate documents).

37.2 The request must be filed at the appropriate office.

37.3 A default costs certificate will be in Form N255.

37.4 Attention is drawn to Rules 40.3 (Drawing up and Filing of Judgments and Orders) and 40.4 (Service of Judgments and Orders) which apply to the preparation and service of a default costs certificate. The receiving party will be treated as having permission to draw up a default costs certificate by virtue of this Practice Direction.

37.5 The issue of a default costs certificate does not prohibit, govern or affect any detailed assessment of the same costs which are payable out of the Community Legal Service Fund.

37.6 An application for an order staying enforcement of a default costs certificate may be made either—

(1) to a costs judge or district judge of the court office which issued the certificate; or

(2) to the court (if different) which has general jurisdiction to enforce the certificate.

37.7 Proceedings for enforcement of default costs certificates may not be issued in the Costs Office.

37.8 * The fixed costs payable in respect of solicitor's charges on the issue of the default costs certificate are £80.

SECTION 38 SETTING ASIDE DEFAULT COSTS CERTIFICATE: RULE 47.12

38.1

(1) A court officer may set aside a default costs certificate at the request of the receiving party under rule 47.12(3).

(2) A costs judge or a district judge will make any other order or give any directions under this rule.

38.2

(1) An application for an order under rule 47.12(2) to set aside or vary a default costs certificate must be supported by evidence.

(2) In deciding whether to set aside or vary a certificate under rule 47.12(2) the matters to which the court must have regard include whether the party seeking the order made the application promptly.

(3) As a general rule a default costs certificate will be set aside under rule 47.12(2) only if the applicant shows a good reason for the court to do so and if he files with his application a copy of the bill and a copy of the default costs certificate, and a draft of the points of dispute he proposes to serve if his application is granted.

38.3

(1) Attention is drawn to rule 3.1(3) (which enables the court when making an order to make it subject to conditions) and to rule 44.3(8) (which enables the court to order a party whom it has ordered to pay costs to pay an amount on account before the costs are assessed).

(2) A costs judge or a district judge may exercise the power of the court to make an order under rule 44.3(8) although he did not make the order about costs which led to the issue of the default costs certificate.

38.4 If a default costs certificate is set aside the court will give directions for the management of the detailed assessment proceedings.

SECTION 39 OPTIONAL REPLY: RULE 47.13

39.1

(1) A receiving party wishing to serve a reply to some or all of the points of dispute must also serve a copy on every other party to the detailed assessment proceedings. The time for doing so is within 21 days after service of the points of dispute.

(2) A reply means:

(a) a separate document prepared by the receiving party; or

(b) the receiving party's written comments added to the points of dispute.

(3) A reply must be signed by the party serving it or that party's solicitor.

39.2 Where there is a dispute about the insurance premium in a staged policy (which has the same meaning as in paragraph 19.4(3A)) it will normally be sufficient for the receiving party to set out in any reply the reasons for choosing the particular insurance policy and the basis on which the insurance premium is rated whether block rated or individually rated.

SECTION 40 DETAILED ASSESSMENT HEARING: RULE 47.14

40.1 The time for requesting a detailed assessment hearing is within 3 months of the expiry of the period for commencing detailed assessment proceedings.

40.2 The request for a detailed assessment hearing must be in Form N258. The request must be accompanied by:

(a) a copy of the notice of commencement of detailed assessment proceedings;

(b) a copy of the bill of costs,

(c) the document giving the right to detailed assessment (see paragraph 40.4 below);

(d) a copy of the points of dispute, annotated as necessary in order to show which items have been agreed and their value and to show which items remain in dispute and their value;

(e) as many copies of the points of dispute so annotated as there are persons who have served points of dispute;

(f) a copy of any replies served;

(g) a copy of all orders made by the court relating to the costs which are to be assessed;

(h) copies of the fee notes and other written evidence as served on the paying party in accordance with paragraph 32.3 above;

(i) where there is a dispute as to the receiving party's liability to pay costs to the solicitors who acted for the receiving party, any agreement, letter or other written information provided by the solicitor to his client explaining how the solicitor's charges are to be calculated;

(j) a statement signed by the receiving party or his solicitor giving the name, address for service, reference and telephone number and fax number, if any, of—

(i) the receiving party;

(ii) the paying party;

(iii) any other person who has served points of dispute or who has given notice to the receiving party under paragraph 32.10 (1) (b) above;

and giving an estimate of the length of time the detailed assessment hearing will take;

(k) where the application for a detailed assessment hearing is made by a party other than the receiving party, such of the documents set out in this paragraph as are in the possession of that party;

(l) where the court is to assess the costs of an assisted person or LSC funded client—

(i) the legal aid certificate, LSC certificate and relevant amendment certificates, any authorities and any certificates of discharge or revocation;

(ii) a certificate, in Precedent F(3) of the Schedule of Costs Precedents;

(iii) if the assisted person has a financial interest in the detailed assessment hearing and wishes to attend, the postal address of that person to which the court will send notice of any hearing;

(iv) if the rates payable out of the LSC fund are prescribed rates, a schedule to the bill of costs setting out all the items in the bill which are claimed against other parties calculated at the legal aid prescribed rates with or without any claim for enhancement: (further information as to this schedule is set out in Section 48 of this Practice Direction);

(v) a copy of any default costs certificate in respect of costs claimed in the bill of costs.

40.3

(1) This paragraph applies to any document described in paragraph 40.2(i) above which the receiving party has filed in the appropriate office. The document must be the latest relevant version and in any event have been filed not more than 2 years before filing the request for a detailed assessment hearing.

(2) In respect of any documents to which this paragraph applies, the receiving party may, instead of filing a copy of it, specify in the request for a detailed assessment hearing the case number under which a copy of the document was previously filed.

40.4 The document giving the right to detailed assessment' means such one or more of the following documents as are appropriate to the detailed assessment proceedings:

(a) a copy of the judgment or order of the court giving the right to detailed assessment;

(b) a copy of the notice served under rule 3.7 (sanctions for non-payment of certain fees) where a claim is struck out under that rule;

(c) a copy of the notice of acceptance where an offer to settle is accepted under Part 36 (Offers to settle);

(d) a copy of the notice of discontinuance in a case which is discontinued under Part 38 (Discontinuance);

(e) a copy of the award made on an arbitration under any Act or pursuant to an agreement, where no court has made an order for the enforcement of the award;

(f) a copy of the order, award or determination of a statutorily constituted tribunal or body;

(g) in a case under the Sheriffs Act 1887, the sheriff's bill of fees and charges, unless a court order giving the right to detailed assessment has been made;

(h) a notice of revocation or discharge under Regulation 82 of the Civil Legal Aid (General) Regulations 1989.

(j) In the county courts certain Acts and Regulations provide for costs incurred in proceedings under those Acts and Regulations to be assessed in the county court if so ordered on application. Where such an application is made, a copy of the order.

40.5 On receipt of the request for a detailed assessment hearing the court will fix a date for the hearing, or, if the costs officer so decides, will give directions or fix a date for a preliminary appointment.

40.6

(1) The court will give at least 14 days' notice of the time and place of the detailed assessment hearing to every person named in the statement referred to in paragraph 40.2(j) above.

(2) The court will when giving notice, give each person who has served points of dispute a copy of the points of dispute annotated by the receiving party in compliance with paragraph 40.2(d) above.

(3) Attention is drawn to rule 47.14(6)&(7): apart from the receiving party, only those who have served points of dispute may be heard on the detailed assessment unless the court gives permission, and only items specified in the points of dispute may be raised unless the court gives permission.

40.7

(1) If the receiving party does not file a request for a detailed assessment hearing within the prescribed time, the paying party may apply to the court to fix a time within which the receiving party must do so. The sanction, for failure to commence detailed assessment proceedings within the time specified by the court, is that all or part of the costs may be disallowed (see rule 47.8(2)).

(2) Where the receiving party commences detailed assessment proceedings after the time specified in the rules but before the paying party has made an application to the court to specify a time, the only sanction which the court may impose is to disallow all or part of the interest which would otherwise be payable for the period of delay, unless the court exercises its powers under rule 44.14 (court's powers in relation to misconduct).

40.8 If either party wishes to make an application in the detailed assessment proceedings the provisions of Part 23 (General Rules about Applications for Court Orders) apply.

40.9 (1) This paragraph deals with the procedure to be adopted where a date has been given by the court for a detailed assessment hearing and

(a) the detailed assessment proceedings are settled; or

(b) a party to the detailed assessment proceedings wishes to apply to vary the date which the court has fixed; or

(c) the parties to the detailed assessment proceedings agree about changes they wish to make to any direction given for the management of the detailed assessment proceedings.

(2) If detailed assessment proceedings are settled, the receiving party must give notice of that fact to the court immediately, preferably by fax.

(3) A party who wishes to apply to vary a direction must do so in accordance with Part 23 (General Rules about Applications for Court Orders).

(4) If the parties agree about changes they wish to make to any direction given for the management of the detailed assessment proceedings—

(a) they must apply to the court for an order by consent; and

(b) they must file a draft of the directions sought and an agreed statement of the reasons why the variation is sought; and

(c) the court may make an order in the agreed terms or in other terms without a hearing, but it may direct that a hearing is to be listed.

40.10 (1) If a party wishes to vary his bill of costs, points of dispute or a reply, an amended or supplementary document must be filed with the court and copies of it must be served on all other relevant parties.

(2) Permission is not required to vary a bill of costs, points of dispute or a reply but the court may disallow the variation or permit it only upon conditions, including conditions as to the payment of any costs caused or wasted by the variation.

40.11 Unless the court directs otherwise the receiving party must file with the court the papers in support of the bill not less than 7 days before the date for the detailed assessment hearing and not more than 14 days before that date.

40.12 The following provisions apply in respect of the papers to be filed in support of the bill;

(a) If the claim is for costs only without any additional liability the papers to be filed, and the order in which they are to be arranged are as follows:

- (i) instructions and briefs to counsel arranged in chronological order together with all advices, opinions and drafts received and response to such instructions;
- (ii) reports and opinions of medical and other experts;
- (iii) any other relevant papers;
- (iv) a full set of any relevant pleadings to the extent that they have not already been filed in court.
- (v) correspondence, files and attendance notes;

(b) where the claim is in respect of an additional liability only, such of the papers listed at (a) above, as are relevant to the issues raised by the claim for additional liability;

(c) where the claim is for both base costs and an additional liability, the papers listed at (a) above, together with any papers relevant to the issues raised by the claim for additional liability.

40.13 The provisions set out in Section 20 of this Practice Direction apply where the court disallows any amount of a legal representative's percentage increase, and the legal representative applies for an order that the disallowed amount should continue to be payable by the client in accordance with Rule 44.16.

40.14 The court may direct the receiving party to produce any document which in the opinion of the court is necessary to enable it to reach its decision. These documents will in the first instance be produced to the court, but the court may ask the receiving party to elect whether to disclose the particular document to the paying party in order to rely on the contents of the document, or whether to decline disclosure and instead rely on other evidence.

40.15 Costs assessed at a detailed assessment at the conclusion of proceedings may include an assessment of any additional liability in respect of the costs of a previous application or hearing.

40.16 Once the detailed assessment hearing has ended it is the responsibility of the legal representative appearing for the receiving party or, as the case may be, the receiving party in person to remove the papers filed in support of the bill.

SECTION 41 POWER TO ISSUE AN INTERIM CERTIFICATE: RULE 47.15

41.1 (1) A party wishing to apply for an interim certificate may do so by making an application in accordance with Part 23 (General Rules about Applications for Court Orders).

(2) Attention is drawn to the fact that the court's power to issue an interim certificate arises only after the receiving party has filed a request for a detailed assessment hearing.

SECTION 42 FINAL COSTS CERTIFICATE: RULE 47.16

42.1 At the detailed assessment hearing the court will indicate any disallowance or reduction in the sums claimed in the bill of costs by making an appropriate note on the bill.

42.2 The receiving party must, in order to complete the bill after the detailed assessment hearing make clear the correct figures agreed or allowed in respect of each item and must re-calculate the summary of the bill appropriately.

42.3 The completed bill of costs must be filed with the court no later than 14 days after the detailed assessment hearing.

42.4 At the same time as filing the completed bill of costs, the party whose bill it is must also produce receipted fee notes and receipted accounts in respect of all disbursements except those covered by a certificate in Precedent F(5) in the Schedule of Costs Precedents annexed to this Practice Direction.

42.5 No final costs certificate will be issued until all relevant court fees payable on the assessment of costs have been paid.

42.6 If the receiving party fails to file a completed bill in accordance with rule 47.16 the paying party may make an application under Part 23 (General Rules about Applications for Court Orders) seeking an appropriate order under rule 3.1 (The court's general powers of management).

42.7 A final costs certificate will show:

(a) the amount of any costs which have been agreed between the parties or which have been allowed on detailed assessment;

(b) where applicable the amount agreed or allowed in respect of VAT on the costs agreed or allowed.

This provision is subject to any contrary provision made by the statutory provisions relating to costs payable out of the Community Legal Service Fund.

42.8 A final costs certificate will include disbursements in respect of the fees of counsel only if receipted fee notes or accounts in respect of those disbursements have been produced to the court and only to the extent indicated by those receipts.

42.9 Where the certificate relates to costs payable between parties a separate certificate will be issued for each party entitled to costs.

42.10 Form N257 is a model form of interim costs certificate and Form N256 is a model form of final costs certificate.

42.11 An application for an order staying enforcement of an interim costs certificate or final costs certificate may be made either:

(1) to a costs judge or district judge of the court office which issued the certificate; or

(2) to the court (if different) which has general jurisdiction to enforce the certificate.

42.12 Proceedings for enforcement of interim costs certificates or final costs certificates may not be issued in the Costs Office.

SECTION 43 DETAILED ASSESSMENT PROCEDURE WHERE COSTS ARE PAYABLE OUT OF THE COMMUNITY LEGAL SERVICE FUND: RULE 47.17

43.1 The provisions of this section apply where the court is to assess costs which are payable only out of the community legal service fund. Paragraphs 39.1 to 40.16 and 49.1 to 49.8 apply in cases involving costs payable by another person as well as costs payable only out of the community legal service fund.

43.2 The time for requesting a detailed assessment under rule 47.17 is within 3 months after the date when the right to detailed assessment arose.

43.3 (1) The request for a detailed assessment of costs must be in Form N258A. The request must be accompanied by:

- (a) a copy of the bill of costs;
- (b) the document giving the right to detailed assessment (for further information as to this document, see paragraph 40.4 above);
- (c) a copy of all orders made by the court relating to the costs which are to be assessed;
- (d) copies of any fee notes of counsel and any expert in respect of fees claimed in the bill;
- (e) written evidence as to any other disbursement which is claimed and which exceeds £500;
- (f) the legal aid certificates, LSC certificates, any relevant amendment certificates, any authorities and any certificates of discharge or revocation and;
- (g) a statement signed by the solicitor giving the solicitor's name, address for service, reference, telephone number, fax number, e-mail address where available and, if the assisted person has a financial interest in the detailed assessment and wishes to attend, giving the postal address of that person, to which the court will send notice of any hearing.

(2) The relevant papers in support of the bill as described in paragraph 40.12 must only be lodged if requested by the costs officer.

43.4 Rule 47.17 provides that the court will hold a detailed assessment hearing if the assisted person has a financial interest in the detailed assessment and wishes to attend. The court may also hold a detailed assessment hearing in any other case, instead of provisionally assessing a bill of costs, where it considers that a hearing is necessary. Before deciding whether a hearing is necessary under this rule, the court may require the solicitor whose bill it is, to provide further information relating to the bill.

43.5 Where the court has provisionally assessed a bill of costs it will send to the solicitor a notice, in Form N253 annexed to this practice direction, of the amount of costs which the court proposes to allow together with the bill itself. The legal representative should, if the provisional assessment is to be accepted, then complete the bill.

43.6 The court will fix a date for a detailed assessment hearing if the solicitor informs the court within 14 days after he receives the notice of the amount allowed on the provisional assessment that he wants the court to hold such a hearing.

43.7The court will give at least 14 days notice of the time and place of the detailed assessment hearing to the solicitor and, if the assisted person has a financial interest in the detailed assessment and wishes to attend, to the assisted person.

43.8 If the solicitor whose bill it is, or any other party wishes to make an application in the detailed assessment proceedings, the provisions of Part 23 (General Rules about Applications for Court Orders) applies.

43.9 It is the responsibility of the legal representative to complete the bill by entering in the bill the correct figures allowed in respect of each item, recalculating the summary of the bill appropriately and completing the Community Legal Service assessment certificate (Form EX80A).

SECTION 44 COSTS OF DETAILED ASSESSMENT PROCEEDINGS WHERE COSTS ARE PAYABLE OUT OF A FUND OTHER THAN THE COMMUNITY LEGAL SERVICE FUND: RULE 47.17A

44.1 Rule 47.17A provides that the court will make a provisional assessment of a bill of costs payable out of a fund (other than the Community Legal Service Fund) unless it considers that a hearing is necessary. It also enables the court to direct under rule 47.17A(3) that the receiving party must serve a copy of the request for assessment and copies of the documents which accompany it, on any person who has a financial interest in the outcome of the assessment.

44.2 (a) A person has a financial interest in the outcome of the assessment if the assessment will or may affect the amount of money or property to which he is or may become entitled out of the fund.

(b) Where an interest in the fund is itself held by a trustee for the benefit of some other person, that trustee will be treated as the person having such a financial interest.

(c) 'Trustee' includes a personal representative, receiver or any other person acting in a fiduciary capacity.

44.3 The request for a detailed assessment of costs out of the fund should be in Form N258B, be accompanied by the documents set out at paragraph 43.3(a) to (e) and (g) above and the following;

(a) a statement signed by the receiving party giving his name, address for service, reference, telephone number, fax number and,

(b) a statement of the postal address of any person who has a financial interest in the outcome of the assessment, to which the court may send notice of any hearing; and

(c) in respect of each person stated to have such an interest if such person is a child or protected party, a statement to that effect.

44.4 The court will decide, having regard to the amount of the bill, the size of the fund and the number of persons who have a financial interest, which of those persons should be served. The court may dispense with service on all or some of them.

44.5 Where the court makes an order dispensing with service on all such persons it may proceed at once to make a provisional assessment, or, if it decides that a hearing is necessary, give appropriate directions. Before deciding whether a hearing is necessary under this rule, the court may require the receiving party to provide further information relating to the bill.

44.6

(1) Where the court has provisionally assessed a bill of costs, it will send to the receiving party, a notice in Form N253 of the amount of costs which the court proposes to allow together with the bill itself. If the receiving party is legally represented the legal representative should, if the provisional assessment is to be accepted, then complete the bill.

(2) The court will fix a date for a detailed assessment hearing, if the receiving party informs the court within 14 days after he receives the notice in Form N253 of the amount allowed on the provisional assessment, that he wants the court to hold such a hearing.

44.7 Where the court makes an order that a person who has a financial interest is to be served with a copy of the request for assessment, it may give directions about service and about the hearing.

44.8 The court will give at least 14 days notice of the time and place of the detailed assessment hearing to the receiving party and, to any person who has a financial interest in the outcome of the assessment and has been served with a copy of the request for assessment.

44.9 If the receiving party, or any other party or any person who has a financial interest in the outcome of assessment, wishes to make an application in the detailed assessment proceedings, the provisions of Part 23 (General Rules about Applications for Court Orders) applies.

44.10 If the receiving party is legally represented the legal representative must in order to complete the bill after the assessment make clear the correct figures allowed in respect of each item and must recalculate the summary of the bill if appropriate.

SECTION 45 LIABILITY FOR COSTS OF DETAILED ASSESSMENT PROCEEDINGS: RULE 47.18

45.1 As a general rule the court will assess the receiving party's costs of the detailed assessment proceedings and add them to the bill of costs.

45.2 If the costs of the detailed assessment proceedings are awarded to the paying party, the court will either assess those costs by summary assessment or make an order for them to be decided by detailed assessment.

45.3 No party should file or serve a statement of costs of the detailed assessment proceedings unless the court orders him to do so.

45.4 Attention is drawn to the fact that in deciding what order to make about the costs of detailed assessment proceedings the court must have regard to the conduct of all parties, the amount by which the bill of costs has been reduced and whether it was reasonable for a party to claim the costs of a particular item or to dispute that item.

45.5 (1) In respect of interest on the costs of detailed assessment proceedings, the interest shall begin to run from the date of the default, interim or final costs certificate as the case may be.

(2) This provision applies only to the costs of the detailed assessment proceedings themselves. The costs of the substantive proceedings are governed by rule 40.8(1).

SECTION 46 OFFERS TO SETTLE WITHOUT PREJUDICE SAVE AS TO THE COSTS OF THE DETAILED ASSESSMENT PROCEEDINGS: RULE 47.19

46.1 Rule 47.19 allows the court to take into account offers to settle, without prejudice save as to the costs of detailed assessment proceedings, when deciding who is liable for the costs of those proceedings. The rule does not specify a time within which such an offer should be made. An offer made by the paying party should usually be made within 14 days after service of the notice of commencement on that party. If the offer is made by the receiving party, it should normally be made within 14 days after the service of points of dispute by the paying party. Offers made after these periods are likely to be given less weight by the court in deciding what order as to costs to make unless there is good reason for the offer not being made until the later time.

46.2 Where an offer to settle is made it should specify whether or not it is intended to be inclusive of the cost of preparation of the bill, interest and value added tax (VAT). The offer may include or exclude some or all of these items but the position must be made clear on the face of the offer so that the offeree is clear about the terms of the offer when it is being considered. Unless the offer states otherwise, the offer will be treated as being inclusive of all these items.

46.3 Where an offer to settle is accepted, an application may be made for a certificate in agreed terms, or the bill of costs may be withdrawn, in accordance with rule 47.10 (Procedure where costs are agreed).

46.4 Where the receiving party is an assisted person or an LSC funded client, an offer to settle without prejudice save as to the costs of the detailed assessment proceedings will not have the consequences specified under rule 47.19 unless the court so orders.

SECTION 47 APPEALS FROM AUTHORISED COURT OFFICERS IN DETAILED ASSESSMENT PROCEEDINGS – RIGHT TO APPEAL: RULE 47.20

47.1 This Section and the next Section of this Practice Direction relate only to appeals from authorised court officers in detailed assessment proceedings. All other appeals arising out of detailed assessment proceedings (and arising out of summary assessments) are dealt with in accordance with Part 52 and Practice Direction 52. The destination of appeals is dealt with in accordance with the Access to Justice Act 1999 (Destination of Appeals) Order 2000.

47.2 In respect of appeals from authorised court officers, there is no requirement to obtain permission, or to seek written reasons.

SECTION 48 PROCEDURE ON APPEAL FROM AUTHORISED COURT OFFICERS: RULE 47.22

48.1 The appellant must file a notice which should be in Form N161 (an appellant's notice).

48.2 The appeal will be heard by a costs judge or a district judge of the High Court, and is a re-hearing.

48.3 The appellant's notice should, if possible, be accompanied by a suitable record of the judgment appealed against. Where reasons given for the decision have been officially recorded by the court an approved transcript of that record should accompany the notice. Photocopies will not be accepted for this purpose. Where there is no official record the following documents will be acceptable:

(1) The officer's comments written on the bill.

(2) Advocates' notes of the reasons agreed by the respondent if possible and approved by the authorised court officer.

When the appellant was unrepresented before the authorised court officer, it is the duty of any advocate for the respondent to make his own note of the reasons promptly available, free of charge to the appellant where there is no official record or if the court so directs. Where the appellant was represented before the authorised court officer, it is the duty of his/her own former advocate to make his/her notes available. The appellant should submit the note of the reasons to the costs judge or district judge hearing the appeal.

48.4 The appellant may not be able to obtain a suitable record of the authorised court officer's decision within the time in which the appellant's notice must be filed. In such cases, the appellant's notice must still be completed to the best of the appellant's ability. It may however be amended subsequently with the permission of the costs judge or district judge hearing the appeal.

SECTION 49 COSTS PAYABLE BY THE LSC AT PRESCRIBED RATES

49.1 This section applies to a bill of costs of an assisted person or LSC funded client which is payable by another person where the costs which can be claimed against the LSC are restricted to prescribed rates (with or without enhancement).

49.2 Where this section applies, the solicitor of the assisted person or LSC funded client must file a legal aid/ LSC schedule in accordance with Paragraph 40.2(l) above. The schedule should follow as closely as possible Precedent E of the Schedule of Costs Precedents annexed to this Practice Direction.

49.3 The schedule must set out by reference to the item numbers in the bill of costs, all the costs claimed as payable by another person, but the arithmetic in the schedule should claim those items at prescribed rates only (with or without any claim for enhancement).

49.4 Where there has been a change in the prescribed rates during the period covered by the bill of costs, the schedule (as opposed to the bill) should be divided into separate parts, so as to deal separately with each change of rate. The schedule must also be divided so as to correspond with any divisions in the bill of costs.

49.5 If the bill of costs contains additional columns setting out costs claimed against the LSC only, the schedule may be set out in a separate document or, alternatively, may be included in the additional columns of the bill.

49.6 The detailed assessment of the legal aid/ LSC schedule will take place immediately after the detailed assessment of the bill of costs.

49.7 Attention is drawn to the possibility that, on occasions, the court may decide to conduct the detailed assessment of the legal aid/ LSC schedule separately from any detailed assessment of the bill of costs. This will occur, for example, where a default costs certificate is obtained as between the parties but that certificate is not set aside at the time of the detailed assessment pursuant to the Legal Aid Act 1988 or regulations thereunder.

49.8 Where costs have been assessed at prescribed rates it is the responsibility of the legal representative to enter the correct figures allowed in respect of each item and to recalculate the summary of the legal aid/ LSC schedule.

SECTION 49A COSTS PAYABLE BY THE TRUSTEE FOR CIVIL RECOVERY UNDER A RECOVERY ORDER

49A.1 In this section—

'the Act' means the Proceeds of Crime Act 2002;

'the Order in Council' means the Proceeds of Crime Act 2002 (External Requests and Orders) Order 2005; and

'the Regulations' means the Proceeds of Crime Act 2002 (Legal Expenses in Civil Recovery Proceedings) Regulations 2005.

49A.2 This section applies to the assessment of costs where the court has made a recovery order which provides for the payment by the trustee for civil recovery of a person's reasonable legal costs in respect of civil recovery proceedings. Such an order may be made under section 266(8A) of the Act or article 177(10) of the Order in Council. The procedure for obtaining a recovery order is set out in the Act and Order in Council, together with the Civil Recovery Proceedings Practice Direction.

49A.3 Where this section applies, costs are to be assessed in accordance with the procedure for detailed assessment under Part 47, subject to the modifications set out in Parts 4 and 5 of the Regulations.

49A.4 The detailed assessment will normally be made by a costs judge, even if the costs are within the authorised amounts specified in paragraph 30.1(1). The appropriate office for the purpose of rule 47.4(1) is the Costs Office.

49A.5 In detailed assessment proceedings to which this section applies—

(1) the paying party is the trustee for civil recovery;

(2) the receiving party is the person whose reasonable legal costs are payable pursuant to provision made in the recovery order under section 266(8A) of the Act or article 177(10) of the Order in Council; and

(3) the relevant persons for the purpose of rule 47.6(2) include the enforcement authority or the appropriate officer as defined in paragraph 1.5 of the Practice Direction – Civil Recovery Proceedings in addition to the persons referred to in paragraph 32.10.

49A.6 On commencing detailed assessment proceedings, the receiving party must, in addition to serving the documents listed in paragraph 32.3 on the paying party and all other relevant persons, serve a statement giving the date, amount and source of all interim payments which have been released in respect of any of those costs under Part 3 of the Regulations.

49A.7 By virtue of regulation 13(2) of the Regulations, detailed assessment proceedings must be commenced not later than 2 months after the date of the recovery order, and a request for a detailed assessment hearing must be filed not later than 2 months after the expiry of the period for commencing the detailed assessment proceedings.

49A.8 The documents which must accompany the request for a detailed assessment hearing shall include copies of all exclusions from property freezing orders or interim receiving orders made by the court for the purpose of enabling the receiving party to meet the costs which are to be assessed, and of every estimate of costs filed by the receiving party in support of an application for such an exclusion.

49A.9 The receiving party's costs will be assessed on the standard basis, subject to Part 5 of the Regulations (and in particular regulation 17, which specifies the hourly rates which may be allowed). Attention is also drawn to regulation 14, which provides that the amounts of any interim payments released in respect of the receiving party's costs will be deducted from the costs allowed in accordance with Part 5 of the Regulations.

DIRECTIONS RELATING TO PART 48 COSTS – SPECIAL CASES

SECTION 50 AMOUNT OF COSTS WHERE COSTS ARE PAYABLE PURSUANT TO CONTRACT: RULE 48.3

50.1 Where the court is assessing costs payable under a contract, it may make an order that all or part of the costs payable under the contract shall be disallowed if it is satisfied by the paying party that costs have been unreasonably incurred or are unreasonable in amount.

50.2 Rule 48.3 only applies if the court is assessing costs payable under a contract. It does not

(1) require the court to make an assessment of such costs; or

(2) require a mortgagee to apply for an order for those costs that he has a contractual right to recover out of the mortgage funds.

50.3 The following principles apply to costs relating to a mortgage—

(1) An order for the payment of costs of proceedings by one party to another is always a discretionary order: section 51 of the Senior Courts Act 1981.

(2) Where there is a contractual right to the costs the discretion should ordinarily be exercised so as to reflect that contractual right.

(3) The power of the court to disallow a mortgagee's costs sought to be added to the mortgage security is a power that does not derive from section 51, but from the power of the courts of equity to fix the terms on which redemption will be allowed.

(4) A decision by a court to refuse costs in whole or in part to a mortgagee litigant may be—

(a) a decision in the exercise of the section 51 discretion;

(b) a decision in the exercise of the power to fix the terms on which redemption will be allowed;

(c) a decision as to the extent of a mortgagee's contractual right to add his costs to the security;

or

(d) a combination of two or more of these things.

The statements of case in the proceedings or the submissions made to the court may indicate which of the decisions has been made.

(5) A mortgagee is not to be deprived of a contractual or equitable right to add costs to the security merely by reason of an order for payment of costs made without reference to the mortgagee's contractual or equitable rights, and without any adjudication as to whether or not the mortgagee should be deprived of those costs.

50.4 (1) Where the contract entitles a mortgagee to—

(a) add the costs of litigation relating to the mortgage to the sum secured by it;

(b) require a mortgagor to pay those costs, or

(c) both,

the mortgagor may make an application for the court to direct that an account of the mortgagee's costs be taken.

(Rule 25.1(1)(n) provides that the court may direct that a party file an account)

(2) The mortgagor may then dispute an amount in the mortgagee's account on the basis that it has been unreasonably incurred or is unreasonable in amount.

(3) Where a mortgagor disputes an amount, the court may make an order that the disputed costs are assessed under rule 48.3.

SECTION 50A – LIMITATION ON COURT'S POWER TO AWARD COSTS IN FAVOUR OF TRUSTEE OR PERSONAL REPRESENTATIVE: RULE 48.4

50A.1 A trustee or personal representative is entitled to an indemnity out of the relevant trust fund or estate for costs properly incurred, which may include costs awarded against the trustee or personal representative in favour of another party.

50A.2 Whether costs were properly incurred depends on all the circumstances of the case, and may, for example, depend on—

(1) whether the trustee or personal representative obtained directions from the court before bringing or defending the proceedings;

(2) whether the trustee or personal representative acted in the interests of the fund or estate or in substance for a benefit other than that of the estate, including his own; and

(3) whether the trustee or personal representative acted in some way unreasonably in bringing or defending, or in the conduct of, the proceedings.

50A.3 The trustee or personal representative is not to be taken to have acted in substance for a benefit other than that of the fund by reason only that he has defended a claim in which relief is sought against him personally.

SECTION 51 COSTS WHERE MONEY IS PAYABLE BY OR TO A CHILD OR PROTECTED PARTY: RULE 48.5

51.1 The circumstances in which the court need not order the assessment of costs under rule 48.5(3) are as follows:

(a) where there is no need to do so to protect the interests of the child or protected party or his estate;

(b) where another party has agreed to pay a specified sum in respect of the costs of the child or protected party and the solicitor acting for the child or protected party has waived the right to claim further costs;

(c) where the court has decided the costs payable to the child or protected party by way of summary assessment and the solicitor acting for the child or protected party has waived the right to claim further costs;

(d) where an insurer or other person is liable to discharge the costs which the child or protected party would otherwise be liable to pay to his solicitor and the court is satisfied that the insurer or other person is financially able to discharge those costs.

SECTION 52 LITIGANTS IN PERSON: RULE 48.6

52.1 In order to qualify as an expert for the purpose of rule 48.6(3)(c) (expert assistance in connection with assessing the claim for costs), the person in question must be a

(1) barrister,

(2) solicitor,

(3) Fellow of the Institute of Legal Executives,

(4) Fellow of the Association of Law Costs Draftsmen,

(5) law costs draftsman who is a member of the Academy of Experts,

(6) law costs draftsman who is a member of the Expert Witness Institute.

52.2 Where a litigant in person wishes to prove that he has suffered financial loss he should produce to the court any written evidence he relies on to support that claim, and serve a copy of that evidence on any party against whom he seeks costs at least 24 hours before the hearing at which the question may be decided.

52.3 Where a litigant in person commences detailed assessment proceedings under rule 47.6 he should serve copies of that written evidence with the notice of commencement.

52.4 The amount, which may be allowed to a litigant in person under rule 46.3(5)(b) and rule 48.6(4), is £9.25 per hour.

52.5 Attention is drawn to rule 48.6(6)(b). A solicitor who, instead of acting for himself, is represented in the proceedings by his firm or by himself in his firm name, is not, for the purpose of the Civil Procedure Rules, a litigant in person.

SECTION 53 PERSONAL LIABILITY OF LEGAL REPRESENTATIVE FOR COSTS – WASTED COSTS ORDERS: RULE 48.7

53.1 Rule 48.7 deals with wasted costs orders against legal representatives. Such orders can be made at any stage in the proceedings up to and including the proceedings relating to the detailed assessment of costs. In general, applications for wasted costs are best left until after the end of the trial.

53.2 The court may make a wasted costs order against a legal representative on its own initiative.

53.3 A party may apply for a wasted costs order—

(1) by filing an application notice in accordance with Part 23; or

(2) by making an application orally in the course of any hearing.

53.4 It is appropriate for the court to make a wasted costs order against a legal representative, only if—

(1) the legal representative has acted improperly, unreasonably or negligently;

(2) his conduct has caused a party to incur unnecessary costs, and

(3) it is just in all the circumstances to order him to compensate that party for the whole or part of those costs.

53.5 The court will give directions about the procedure that will be followed in each case in order to ensure that the issues are dealt with in a way which is fair and as simple and summary as the circumstances permit.

53.6 As a general rule the court will consider whether to make a wasted costs order in two stages—

(1) in the first stage, the court must be satisfied—

(a) that it has before it evidence or other material which, if unanswered, would be likely to lead to a wasted costs order being made; and

(b) the wasted costs proceedings are justified notwithstanding the likely costs involved.

(2) at the second stage (even if the court is satisfied under paragraph (1)) the court will consider, after giving the legal representative an opportunity to give reasons why the court should not make a wasted costs order, whether it is appropriate to make a wasted costs order in accordance with paragraph 53.4 above.

53.7 On an application for a wasted costs order under Part 23 the court may proceed to the second stage described in paragraph 53.6 without first adjourning the hearing if it is satisfied that the legal representative has already had a reasonable opportunity to give reasons why the court should not make a wasted costs order. In other cases the court will adjourn the hearing before proceeding to the second stage.

53.8 On an application for a wasted costs order under Part 23 the application notice and any evidence in support must identify—

(1) what the legal representative is alleged to have done or failed to do; and

(2) the costs that he may be ordered to pay or which are sought against him.

53.9 A wasted costs order is an order—

(1) that the legal representative pay a specified sum in respect of costs to a party; or

(2) for costs relating to a specified sum or items of work to be disallowed.

53.10 Attention is drawn to rule 44.3A(1) and (2) which respectively prevent the court from assessing any additional liability until the conclusion of the proceedings (or the part of the proceedings) to which the funding arrangement relates, and set out the orders the court may make at the conclusion of the proceedings.

SECTION 54 BASIS OF DETAILED ASSESSMENT OF SOLICITOR AND CLIENT COSTS: RULE 48.8

54.1 A client and his solicitor may agree whatever terms they consider appropriate about the payment of the solicitor's charges for his services. If however, the costs are of an unusual nature (either in amount or in the type of costs incurred) those costs will be presumed to have been unreasonably incurred unless the solicitor satisfies the court that he informed the client that they were unusual and, where the costs relate to litigation, that he informed the client they might not be allowed on an assessment of costs between the parties. That information must have been given to the client before the costs were incurred.

54.2 (1) Costs as between a solicitor and client are assessed on the indemnity basis as defined by rule 44.4.

(2) Attention is drawn to the presumptions set out in rule 48.8(2). These presumptions may be rebutted by evidence to the contrary.

54.3 Rule 48.10 and Section 56 of this Practice Direction deal with the procedure to be followed for obtaining the assessment of a solicitor's bill pursuant to an order under Part III of the Solicitors Act 1974.

54.4 If a party fails to comply with the requirements of rule 48.10 concerning the service of a breakdown of costs or points of dispute, any other party may apply to the court in which the detailed assessment hearing should take place for an order requiring compliance with rule 48.10. If the court makes such an order, it may –

(a) make it subject to conditions including a condition to pay a sum of money into court; and

(b) specify the consequence of failure to comply with the order or a condition.

54.5

(1) A client who has entered into a conditional fee agreement with a solicitor may apply for assessment of the base costs (which is carried out in accordance with rule 48.8(2) as if there were no conditional fee agreement) or for assessment of the percentage increase (success fee) or both.

(2) Where the court is to assess the percentage increase the court will have regard to all the relevant factors as they appeared to the solicitor or counsel when the conditional fee agreement was entered into.

54.6 Where the client applies to the court to reduce the percentage increase which the solicitor has charged the client under the conditional fee agreement, the client must set out in his application notice:

(a) the reasons why the percentage increase should be reduced; and

(b) what the percentage increase should be.

54.7 The factors relevant to assessing the percentage increase include—

(a) the risk that the circumstances in which the fees or expenses would be payable might not occur;

(b) the disadvantages relating to the absence of payment on account;

(c) whether there is a conditional fee agreement between the solicitor and counsel;

(d) the solicitor's liability for any disbursements.

54.8 When the court is considering the factors to be taken into account, it will have regard to the circumstances as they reasonably appeared to the solicitor or counsel when the conditional fee agreement was entered into.

SECTION 56 PROCEDURE ON ASSESSMENT OF SOLICITOR AND CLIENT COSTS: RULE 48.10

56.1 The paragraphs in this section apply to orders made under Part III of the Solicitors Act 1974 for the assessment of costs. In these paragraphs 'client' includes any person entitled to make an application under Part III of that Act.

56.2 The procedure for obtaining an order under Part III of the Solicitors Act 1974 is by the alternative procedure for claims under Part 8, as modified by rule 67.3 and Practice Direction 67. Precedent J of the Schedule of Costs Precedents annexed to this Practice Direction is a model form of claim form. The application must be accompanied by the bill or bills in respect of which assessment is sought, and, if the claim concerns a conditional fee agreement, a copy of that agreement. If the original bill is not available a copy will suffice.

56.3 Model forms of order, which the court may make, are set out in Precedents K, L and M of the Schedule of Costs Precedents annexed to this Practice Direction.

56.4 Attention is drawn to the time limits within which the required steps must be taken: i.e. the solicitor must serve a breakdown of costs within 28 days of the order for costs to be assessed, the client must serve points of dispute within 14 days after service on him of the breakdown, and any reply must be served within 14 days of service of the points of dispute.

56.5 The breakdown of costs referred to in rule 48.10 is a document which contains the following information:

(a) details of the work done under each of the bills sent for assessment; and

(b) in applications under Section 70 of the Solicitors Act 1974, an account showing money received by the solicitor to the credit of the client and sums paid out of that money on behalf of the client but not payments out which were made in satisfaction of the bill or of any items which are claimed in the bill.

56.6 Precedent P of the Schedule of Costs Precedents annexed to this Practice Direction is a model form of breakdown of costs. A party who is required to serve a breakdown of costs must also serve—

(1) copies of the fee notes of counsel and of any expert in respect of fees claimed in the breakdown, and

(2) written evidence as to any other disbursement which is claimed in the breakdown and which exceeds £250.

56.7 The provisions relating to default costs certificates (rule 47.11) do not apply to cases to which rule 48.10 applies.

56.8 Points of dispute should, as far as practicable, be in the form complying with paragraphs 35.1 to 35.7.

56.9 The time for requesting a detailed assessment hearing is within 3 months after the date of the order for the costs to be assessed.

56.10 The form of request for a hearing date must be in Form N258C. The request must be accompanied by copies of—

(a) the order sending the bill or bills for assessment;

(b) the bill or bills sent for assessment;

(c) the solicitor's breakdown of costs and any invoices or accounts served with that breakdown;

(d) a copy of the points of dispute, annotated as necessary in order to show which items have been agreed and their value and to show which items remain in dispute;

(e) as many copies of the points of dispute so annotated as there are other parties to the proceedings to whom the court should give details of the assessment hearing requested;

(f) a copy of any replies served;

(g) a statement signed by the party filing the request or his legal representative giving the names and addresses for service of all parties to the proceedings.

56.11 The request must include an estimate of the length of time the detailed assessment hearing will take.

56.12 On receipt of the request for a detailed assessment hearing the court will fix a date for the hearing or if the costs judge or district judge so decides, will give directions or fix a date for a preliminary appointment.

56.13

(1) The court will give at least 14 days notice of the time and place of the detailed assessment hearing to every person named in the statement referred to in paragraph 56.10(g) above.

(2) The court will when giving notice, give all parties other than the party who requested the hearing a copy of the points of dispute annotated by the party requesting the hearing in compliance with paragraph 56.10(e) above.

(3) Attention is drawn to rule 47.14(6) and (7): apart from the solicitor whose bill it is, only those parties who have served points of dispute may be heard on the detailed assessment unless the court gives permission, and only items specified in the points of dispute may be raised unless the court gives permission.

56.14

(1) If a party wishes to vary his breakdown of costs, points of dispute or reply, an amended or supplementary document must be filed with the court and copies of it must be served on all other relevant parties.

(2) Permission is not required to vary a breakdown of costs, points of dispute or a reply but the court may disallow the variation or permit it only upon conditions, including conditions as to the payment of any costs caused or wasted by the variation.

56.15 Unless the court directs otherwise the solicitor must file with the court the papers in support of the bill not less than 7 days before the date for the detailed assessment hearing and not more than 14 days before that date.

56.16 Once the detailed assessment hearing has ended it is the responsibility of the legal representative appearing for the solicitor or, as the case may be, the solicitor in person to remove the papers filed in support of the bill.

56.17

(1) Attention is drawn to rule 47.15 (power to issue an interim certificate).

(2) If, in the course of a detailed assessment hearing of a solicitor's bill to his client, it appears to the costs judge or district judge that in any event the solicitor will be liable in connection with that bill to pay money to the client, he may issue an interim certificate specifying an amount which in his opinion is payable by the solicitor to his client. Such a certificate will include an order to pay the sum it certifies unless the court orders otherwise.

56.18

(1) Attention is drawn to rule 47.16 which requires the solicitor to file a completed bill within 14 days after the end of the detailed assessment hearing. The court may dispense with the requirement to file a completed bill.

(2) After the detailed assessment hearing is concluded the court will—

   (a) complete the court copy of the bill so as to show the amount allowed;

   (b) determine the result of the cash account;

   (c) award the costs of the detailed assessment hearing in accordance with Section 70(8) of the Solicitors Act 1974; and

   (d) issue a final costs certificate showing the amount due following the detailed assessment hearing.

56.19 A final costs certificate will include an order to pay the sum it certifies unless the court orders otherwise.

SECTION 57 TRANSITIONAL ARRANGEMENTS

Not herein printed: relates to bills etc lodged pre 26th April 1999

SCHEDULE OF COSTS PRECEDENTS

A: Model form of bill of costs (receiving party's solicitor and counsel on CFA terms)

B: Model form of bill of costs (detailed assessment of additional liability only)

C: Model form of bill of costs (payable by Defendant and the LSC)

D: Model form of bill of costs (alternative form, single column for amounts claimed, separate parts for costs payable by the LSC only)

E: Legal Aid/ LSC Schedule of Costs

F: Certificates for inclusion in bill of costs

G: Points of Dispute

H: Estimate of costs served on other parties

J: Solicitors Act 1974: Part 8 claim form under Part III of the Act

K: Solicitors Act 1974: order for delivery of bill

L: Solicitors Act 1974: order for detailed assessment (client)

M: Solicitors Act 1974: order for detailed assessment (solicitors)

N: Solicitors Act 1974: breakdown of costs

PART 36

Rule 36.A1 Scope of this Part

(1) This Part contains rules about-

(a) offers to settle; and

(b) the consequences where an offer to settle is made in accordance with this Part.

(2) Section I of this Part contains rules about offers to settle other than where Section II applies.

(3) Section II of this Part contains rules about offers to settle where the parties have followed the Pre-Action Protocol for Low Value Personal Injury Claims in Road Traffic Accidents ("the RTA Protocol") and have started proceedings under Part 8 in accordance with Practice Direction 8B.

Rule 36.1 Scope of this Section

(1) This Section does not apply to an offer to settle to which Section II of this Part applies.

(2) Nothing in this Section prevents a party making an offer to settle in whatever way he chooses, but if the offer is not made in accordance with rule 36.2, it will not have the consequences specified in rules 36.10, 36.11 and 36.14.

(Rule 44.3 requires the court to consider an offer to settle that does not have the costs consequences set out in this Section in deciding what order to make about costs)

Rule 36.2 Form and content of a Part 36 offer

(1) An offer to settle which is made in accordance with this rule is called a Part 36 offer.

(2) A Part 36 offer must-

(a) be in writing;

(b) state on its face that it is intended to have the consequences of Section I of Part 36;

(c) specify a period of not less than 21 days within which the defendant will be liable for the claimant's costs in accordance with rule 36.10 if the offer is accepted;

(d) state whether it relates to the whole of the claim or to part of it or to an issue that arises in it and if so to which part or issue; and

(e) state whether it takes into account any counterclaim.

(Rule 36.7 makes provision for when a Part 36 offer is made)

(3) Rule 36.2(2)(c) does not apply if the offer is made less than 21 days before the start of the trial.

(4) In appropriate cases, a Part 36 offer must contain such further information as is required by rule 36.5 (Personal injury

claims for future pecuniary loss), rule 36.6 (Offer to settle a claim for provisional damages), and rule 36.15 (Deduction of benefits).

(5) An offeror may make a Part 36 offer solely in relation to liability.

Rule 36.3 Part 36 offers-general provisions]

(1) In this Part-

(a) the party who makes an offer is the "offeror";

(b) the party to whom an offer is made is the "offeree"; and

(c) "the relevant period" means-

(i) in the case of an offer made not less than 21 days before trial, the period stated under rule 36.2(2)(c) or such longer period as the parties agree;

(ii) otherwise, the period up to end of the trial or such other period as the court has determined.

(2) A Part 36 offer-

(a) may be made at any time, including before the commencement of proceedings; and

(b) may be made in appeal proceedings.

(3) A Part 36 offer which offers to pay or offers to accept a sum of money will be treated as inclusive of all interest until-

(a) the date on which the period stated under rule 36.2(2)(c) expires; or

(b) if rule 36.2(3) applies, a date 21 days after the date the offer was made.

(4) A Part 36 offer shall have the consequences set out [in this Section] only in relation to the costs of the proceedings in respect of which it is made, and not in relation to the costs of any appeal from the final decision in those proceedings.

(5) Before expiry of the relevant period, a Part 36 offer may be withdrawn or its terms changed to be less advantageous to the offeree, only if the court gives permission.

(6) After expiry of the relevant period and provided that the offeree has not previously served notice of acceptance, the offeror may withdraw the offer or change its terms to be less advantageous to the offeree without the permission of the court.

(7) The offeror does so by serving written notice of the withdrawal or change of terms on the offeree.

(Rule 36.14(6) deals with the costs consequences following judgment of an offer that is withdrawn)

Rule 36.4 Part 36 offers-defendants' offers

(1) Subject to rule 36.5(3) and rule 36.6(1), a Part 36 offer by a defendant to pay a sum of money in settlement of a claim must be an offer to pay a single sum of money.

(2) But, an offer that includes an offer to pay all or part of the sum, if accepted, at a date later than 14 days following the date of acceptance will not be treated as a Part 36 offer unless the offeree accepts the offer.

* * * * *

Rule 36.7 Time when a Part 36 offer is made

(1) A Part 36 offer is made when it is served on the offeree.

(2) A change in the terms of a Part 36 offer will be effective when notice of the change is served on the offeree.

(Rule 36.3 makes provision about when permission is required to change the terms of an offer to make it less advantageous to the offeree).

Rule 36.8 Clarification of a Part 36 offer

(1) The offeree may, within 7 days of a Part 36 offer being made, request the offeror to clarify the offer.

(2) If the offeror does not give the clarification requested under paragraph (1) within 7 days of receiving the request, the offeree may, unless the trial has started, apply for an order that he does so.

(Part 23 contains provisions about making an application to the court)

(3) If the court makes an order under paragraph (2), it must specify the date when the Part 36 offer is to be treated as having been made.

Rule 36.9 Acceptance of a Part 36 offer

(1) A Part 36 offer is accepted by serving written notice of the acceptance on the offeror.

(2) Subject to rule 36.9(3), a Part 36 offer may be accepted at any time (whether or not the offeree has subsequently made a different offer) unless the offeror serves notice of withdrawal on the offeree.

(Rule 21.10 deals with compromise etc by or on behalf of a child or protected party)

(3) The court's permission is required to accept a Part 36 offer where-

(a) rule 36.12(4) applies;

(b) rule 36.15(3)(b) applies, the relevant period has expired and further deductible [amounts] have been paid to the claimant since the date of the offer;

(c) an apportionment is required under rule 41.3A; or

(d) the trial has started.

(Rule 36.12 deals with offers by some but not all of multiple defendants)

(Rule 36.15 defines "deductible amounts".)

(Rule 41.3A requires an apportionment in proceedings under the Fatal Accidents Act 1976 and Law Reform (Miscellaneous Provisions) Act 1934)

(4) Where the court gives permission under paragraph (3), unless all the parties have agreed costs, the court will make an order dealing with costs, and may order that the costs consequences set out in rule 36.10 will apply.

(5) Unless the parties agree, a Part 36 offer may not be accepted after the end of the trial but before judgment is handed down.

Rule 36.10 Costs consequences of acceptance of a Part 36 offer

(1) Subject to paragraph (2) and paragraph (4)(a), where a Part 36 offer is accepted within the relevant period the claimant will be entitled to [the] costs of the proceedings up to the date on which notice of acceptance was served on the offeror.

(2) Where-

(a) a defendant's Part 36 offer relates to part only of the claim; and

(b) at the time of serving notice of acceptance within the relevant period the claimant abandons the balance of the claim,

the claimant will be entitled to the costs of the proceedings up to the date of serving notice of acceptance unless the court orders otherwise.

(3) Costs under paragraphs (1) and (2) of this rule will be assessed on the standard basis if the amount of costs is not agreed.

(Rule 44.4(2) explains the standard basis for assessment of costs)

(Rule 44.12 contains provisions about when a costs order is deemed to have been made and applying for an order under section 194(3) of the Legal Services Act 2007.)

(4) Where-

(a) a Part 36 offer that was made less than 21 days before the start of trial is accepted; or

(b) a Part 36 offer is accepted after expiry of the relevant period,

if the parties do not agree the liability for costs, the court will make an order as to costs.

(5) Where paragraph (4)(b) applies, unless the court orders otherwise-

(a) the claimant will be entitled to the costs of the proceedings up to the date on which the relevant period expired; and

(b) the offeree will be liable for the offeror's costs for the period from the date of expiry of the relevant period to the date of acceptance.

(6) The claimant's costs include any costs incurred in dealing with the defendant's counterclaim if the Part 36 offer states that it takes into account the counterclaim.

Rule 36.11 The effect of acceptance of a Part 36 offer

(1) If a Part 36 offer is accepted, the claim will be stayed (GL).

(2) In the case of acceptance of a Part 36 offer which relates to the whole claim the stay (GL) will be upon the terms of the offer.

(3) If a Part 36 offer which relates to part only of the claim is accepted-

(a) the claim will be stayed (GL) as to that part upon the terms of the offer; and

(b) subject to rule 36.10(2), unless the parties have agreed costs, the liability for costs shall be decided by the court.

(4) If the approval of the court is required before a settlement can be binding, any stay (GL) which would otherwise arise on the acceptance of a Part 36 offer will take effect only when that approval has been given.

(5) Any stay (GL) arising under this rule will not affect the power of the court-

(a) to enforce the terms of a Part 36 offer;

(b) to deal with any question of costs (including interest on costs) relating to the proceedings.

(6) Unless the parties agree otherwise in writing, where a Part 36 offer by a defendant that is or that includes an offer to pay a single sum of money is accepted, that sum must be paid to the offeree within 14 days of the date of-

(a) acceptance; or

(b) the order when the court makes an order under rule 41.2 (order for an award of provisional damages) or rule 41.8 (order for an award of periodical payments), unless the court orders otherwise.

(7) If the accepted sum is not paid within 14 days or such other period as has been agreed the offeree may enter judgment for the unpaid sum.

(8) Where-

(a) a Part 36 offer (or part of a Part 36 offer) which is not an offer to which paragraph (6) applies is accepted; and

(b) a party alleges that the other party has not honoured the terms of the offer,

that party may apply to enforce the terms of the offer without the need for a new claim.

Rule 36.12 Acceptance of a Part 36 offer made by one or more, but not all, defendants

(1) This rule applies where the claimant wishes to accept a Part 36 offer made by one or more, but not all, of a number of defendants.

(2) If the defendants are sued jointly or in the alternative, the claimant may accept the offer if-

(a) he discontinues his claim against those defendants who have not made the offer; and

(b) those defendants give written consent to the acceptance of the offer.

(3) If the claimant alleges that the defendants have a several liability (GL) to him, the claimant may-

(a) accept the offer; and

(b) continue with his claims against the other defendants if he is entitled to do so.

(4) In all other cases the claimant must apply to the court for an order permitting him to accept the Part 36 offer.

Rule 36.13 Restriction on disclosure of a Part 36 offer

(1) A Part 36 offer will be treated as "without prejudice (GL) except as to costs".

(2) The fact that a Part 36 offer has been made must not be communicated to the trial judge or to the judge (if any) allocated in advance to conduct the trial until the case has been decided.

(3) Paragraph (2) does not apply-

(a) where the defence of tender before claim (GL) has been raised;

(b) where the proceedings have been stayed (GL) under rule 36.11 following acceptance of a Part 36 offer; or

(c) where the offeror and the offeree agree in writing that it should not apply.

Rule 36.14 Costs consequences following judgment

(1) This rule applies where upon judgment being entered-

(a) a claimant fails to obtain a judgment more advantageous than a defendant's Part 36 offer; or

(b) judgment against the defendant is at least as advantageous to the claimant as the proposals contained in a claimant's Part 36 offer.

(2) Subject to paragraph (6), where rule 36.14(1)(a) applies, the court will, unless it considers it unjust to do so, order that the defendant is entitled to-

(a) his costs from the date on which the relevant period expired; and

(b) interest on those costs.

(3) Subject to paragraph (6), where rule 36.14(1)(b) applies, the court will, unless it considers it unjust to do so, order that the claimant is entitled to-

(a) interest on the whole or part of any sum of money (excluding interest) awarded at a rate not exceeding 10% above base rate (GL) for some or all of the period starting with the date on which the relevant period expired;

(b) his costs on the indemnity basis from the date on which the relevant period expired; and

(c) interest on those costs at a rate not exceeding 10% above base rate (GL).

(4) In considering whether it would be unjust to make the orders referred to in paragraphs (2) and (3) above, the court will take into account all the circumstances of the case including-

(a) the terms of any Part 36 offer;

(b) the stage in the proceedings when any Part 36 offer was made, including in particular how long before the trial started the offer was made;

(c) the information available to the parties at the time when the Part 36 offer was made; and

(d) the conduct of the parties with regard to the giving or refusing to give information for the purposes of enabling the offer to be made or evaluated.

(5) Where the court awards interest under this rule and also awards interest on the same sum and for the same period under any other power, the total rate of interest may not exceed 10% above base rate (GL).

(6) Paragraphs (2) and (3) of this rule do not apply to a Part 36 offer-

(a) that has been withdrawn;

(b) that has been changed so that its terms are less advantageous to the offeree, and the offeree has beaten the less advantageous offer;

(c) made less than 21 days before trial, unless the court has abridged the relevant period.

(Rule 44.3 requires the court to consider an offer to settle that does not have the costs consequences set out in this Section in deciding what order to make about costs)

* * * * *

2. Fixed Costs

Court of Protection

The fixed costs that may be claimed by solicitors and public authorities acting in Court of Protection proceedings and the fixed amounts of remuneration that may be claimed by solicitors and office holders in public authorities appointed to act as a deputy are set out below. The amounts are prescribed by the Court of Protection Rules 2007(SI2007/1744) Practice Direction and apply where the period covered by the category of fixed costs or remuneration ends on or after 1 May 2009.

The fixed costs are as follows:

Solicitors' costs in court proceedings

Category I

Work up to and including the date upon which the court makes an order appointing a deputy for property and affairs £825 (plus VAT)

Category II

Applications under sections 36 (9) or 54 of the Trustee Act 1925 or section 20 of the Trusts of Land and Appointment of Trustees Act 1996 for the appointment of a new trustee in the place of 'P' and applications under section 18(1) (j) of the Mental Capacity Act 2005 for authority to exercise any power vested in P, whether beneficially, or as trustee, or otherwise.....£370 (plus VAT)

The categories of fixed costs above will apply as follows:

- *Category I to all orders appointing a deputy for property and affairs made on or after 1 May 2009.*
- *Category II to all applications for the appointment of a new trustee made on or after 1 May 2009.*

Remuneration of solicitors appointed as deputy for P

Category III

Annual management fee where the court appoints a professional deputy for property and affairs, payable on the anniversary of the court order

a. For the first year £1,440 (plus VAT)

b. For the second and subsequent years £1,140 (plus VAT)

c. Provided that, where the net assets of P are below £16,000, the professional deputy for property and affairs may take an annual management fee not exceeding 4.5% of P's net assets on the anniversary of the court order appointing the professional as deputy.

Category IV

Where the court appoints a professional deputy for health and welfare, the deputy may take an annual management fee not exceeding 2.5% of P's net assets on the anniversary of the court order appointing the professional as deputy for health and welfare up to a maximum of £500.

Category V

Preparation and lodgement of the annual report or annual account to the Public Guardian £225 (plus VAT)

Category VI

Preparation of an HMRC income tax return on behalf of P £225 (plus VAT)

The categories of remuneration, above will apply as follows:

- *Category III and IV to all annual management fees for anniversaries falling on or after 1 May 2009.*
- *Category V to reports or accounts lodged on or after 1 May 2009.*
- *Category VI to all HMRC returns made on or after 1 May 2009.*

Where the period for which an annual management fee claimed is less than one year, for example where the deputyship comes to an end before the anniversary of appointment, then the amount claimed must be the same proportion of the applicable fee as the period bears to one year.

Remuneration of public authority deputies

Where an office holder in a public authority is appointed to act as deputy for P, he may claim the following fixed costs:

Category I

Work up to and including the date upon which the court makes an order appointing a deputy for property and affairs £645 (plus VAT)

Category II

Annual management fee where the court appoints a local authority deputy for property and affairs, payable on the anniversary of the court order:

a. for the first year £670 (plus VAT)

b. for the second and subsequent years £565 (plus VAT)

c. Provided that, where the net assets of P are below £16,000, the local authority deputy for property and affairs may take an annual management fee not exceeding 3% of P's net assets on the anniversary of the court order appointing the local authority as deputy

d. Where the court appoints a local authority deputy for health and welfare, the local authority may take an annual management fee not exceeding 2.5% of P's net assets on the anniversary of the court order appointing the local authority as deputy for health and welfare up to a maximum of £500.

Category III

Annual property management fee to include work involved in preparing property for sale, instructing agents, conveyancers, etc or the ongoing maintenance of property including management and letting of a rental property £260 (plus VAT)

Category IV

Preparation and lodgement of an annual report or account to the Public Guardian £185 (plus VAT)

The categories of remuneration, above will apply as follows:

- *Category I to all orders appointing a deputy for property and affairs made on or after 1 May 2009.*
- *Category II to all annual management fees for anniversaries falling on or after 1 May 2009.*

- *Category III on the anniversary of appointment as deputy where the anniversary falls on or after 1 May 2009; or upon completion of the sale of a property, where the transaction was concluded on or after 1 May 2009.*
- *Category V to reports or accounts lodged on or after 1 May 2009.*

Where the period for which the annual management fee ends before an anniversary, for example where the deputyship comes to an end before the anniversary of appointment, then the amount claimed must be the same proportion of the applicable fee as the period bears to one year.

3. Guideline Hourly Rates for Summary Assessment

There are four grades of fee earner:

A. Solicitors with over 8 years post qualification experience including at least 8 years litigation experience.

B. Solicitors and legal executives with over 4 years post qualification experience including at least 4 years litigation experience.

London 1 (City of London: EC1, EC2, EC3, EC4)						
Grade	2010	2009	2008	2007	2005–6	2003–4
A	£409	£402	£396	£380	£359	£342
B	£296	£291	£285	£274	£259	£247
C	£226	£222	£219	£210	£198	£189
D	£138	£136	£134	£129	£122	£116

London 2 (W1, WC1, WC2, SW1)						
Grade	2010	2009	2008	2007	2005–6	2003–4
A	£317	£312	£304	£292	£276	£263
B	£242	£238	£231	£222	£210	£200
C	£196	£193	£189	£181	£171	£163
D	£126	£124	£121	£116	£110	£105

London 3 (All other London post codes: W, NW, N, E, SE, SW and Bromley, Croydon, Dartford, Gravesend and Uxbridge)						
Grade	2010	2009	2008	2007	2005–6	2003–4
A	£229–267	£225–263	£219–256	£210–246	£198–232	£189–221
B	£172–229	£169–225	£165–219	£158–210	£149–198	£142–189
C	£165	£162	£158	£152	£144	£137
D	£121	£119	£116	£111	£105	£100

Guideline rates for outside the London Area

Guideline Hourly Rates for 2010				
National Band 1	£217	£192	£161	£118
National Bands 2/3	£201	£17	£146	£111

Guideline rates for 2009				
National Band 1	£213	£189	£158	£116
National 2/3	£198	£174	£144	£109

For the locations to which these rates apply see the Guideline rates for 2008 below.

Guideline Rates for 2008

Band One Grade*	A**	B	C	D
Guideline Rates	£203	£180	£151	£110
Aldershot, Farnham, Bournemouth (including Poole). Birmingham Inner, Bristol, Cambridge City, Harlow. Canterbury, Maidstone, Medway & Tunbridge Wells. Cardiff (Inner), Chelmsford South, Essex & East Suffolk. Chester, Fareham, Winchester. Hampshire, Dorset, Wiltshire, Isle of Wight. Kingston, Guildford, Reigate, Epsom. Leeds Inner (within 2 km radius of the City Art Gallery). Lewes. Liverpool, Birkenhead. Manchester Central. Newcastle – City Centre (within a 2 mile radius of St Nicholas Cathedral). Norwich City, Nottingham City, Oxford, Thames Valley. Southampton, Portsmouth Swindon, Basingstoke, Watford.				

Band Two Grade*	A**	B	C	D
Guideline Rates	£191	£168	£139	£105
Bath, Cheltenham and Gloucester, Taunton, Yeovil. Bury Chelmsford North, Cambridge County, Peterborough, Bury St E,Norfolk, Lowestoft Cheshire & North Wales, Coventry, Rugby, Nuneaton, Stratford and Warwick, Exeter, Plymouth, Hull (City). Leeds Outer, Wakefield & Pontefract, Leigh, Lincoln Luton, Bedford. St Albans, Hitchin, Hertford, Manchester Outer, Oldham, Bolton, Tameside, Newcastle (other than City Centre), Nottingham & Derbyshire. Sheffield, Doncaster and South Yorkshire, Southport, St Helens. Stockport, Altrincham, Salford, Swansea, Newport, Cardiff (Outer). Wigan, Wolverhampton, Walsall, Dudley & Stourbridge. York, Harrogate.				

Band Three Grade*	A**	B	C	D
Guideline Rates	£174	£156	£133	£99
Birmingham Outer, Bradford (Dewsbury, Halifax, Huddersfield Keighley & Skipton), Cumbria, Devon, Cornwall, Grimsby, Skegness. Hull Outer, Kidderminster, Northampton & Leicester, Preston, Lancaster, Blackpool, Chorley, Accrington, Burnley, Blackburn. Rawtenstall & Nelson, Scarborough & Ripon, Stafford, Stoke, Tamworth. Teesside, Worcester, Hereford, Evesham and Redditch. Shrewsbury, Telford, Ludlow, Oswestry, South & West Wales.				

London Bands

Table of Counsel's Fees		
Queens Bench	1 hour hearing	½ day hearing
Junior up to 5 years call	£259	£450
Junior 5 – 10 years call	£386	£767
Junior 10+ years call	£582	£1,164
Chancery Division		
Junior up to 5 years call	£291	£556
Junior 5 – 10 years call	£497	£931
Junior 10+ years call	£757	£1,397
Administrative Court		
Junior up to 5 years call	£381	£582
Junior 5 – 10 years call	£698	£1,164
Junior 10+ years call	£989	£1,746

4. Community Legal Service Funding (Prescribed Rates)

The following Tables are extracted from Schedule 1 to the Community Legal Services (Funding Order 2007 (SI 2007/2441) (as amended). The prescribed rates apply to work done on or after the 14th October 2010.

1. Legal Help and Help at Court

Table 1

The fees in this Table for Housing do not apply to the Housing Possession Court Duty Scheme—see Table 6.

Category	Schedule Authorisation Fixed fee	*Schedule Authorisation Exceptional Thresholds*	Tolerance Fixed Fee	*Tolerance Exceptional Thresholds*
Actions against the Police	£266	£798	£154	£462
Clinical Negligence	£217	£651	—	—
Community Care	£296	£888	£179	£537
Consumer General Contract	£177	£531	£149	£447
Debt	£200	£600	£123	£369
Education	£302	£906	£152	£456
Employment	£230	£690	£150	£450
Housing	£174	£522	£138	£414
Miscellaneous	£88	£264	—	—
Personal Injury	£226	£678	£154	£462
Public Law	£288	£864	£207	£621
Welfare Benefits	£167	£501	£136	£408

2. Family Public Law

Table 2(a): Legal Help

National	£147

Table 2(b): Family Help (Lower)—section 31 Children Act 1989 Care or Supervision Proceedings only

National	£405

Table 2(c): Legal Representation—section 31 Children Act 1989 Care or Supervision Proceedings only

Party	Court	*Number of Clients*	Midlands	*North*	London and South	*Wales*
Child	Other	1	£2,165	£1,775	£2,485	£2,426
Child	Other	2 or more	£3,247	£2,662	£3,728	£3,639
Child	High	1	£2,879	£2,361	£3,305	£3,226
Child	High	2 or more	£4,319	£3,542	£4,957	£4,838
Joined Party	Other	—	£1,148	£887	£1,334	£1,445
Joined Party	High	—	£1,527	£1,180	£1,774	£1,922
Parent	Other	1	£2,840	£2,359	£3,230	£2,925
Parent	Other	2	£3,551	£2,948	£4,037	£3,657
Parent	High	1	£3,777	£3,137	£4,296	£3,891
Parent	High	2	£4,721	£3,922	£5,369	£4,864

3. Family Private Law

Table 3(a): Legal Help

National	£96

Table 3(b): Legal Help—Divorce Petition only

National	£162

Table 3(c): Family Help (Lower)—Children

	Fee	*Settlement Fee*
London	£256	£153
Non-London	£221	£132

Table 3(d): Family Help (Lower)—Finance

	Fee	*Settlement Fee*
London	£268	£161
Non-London	£231	£139

Table 3(e): Higher Standard Fee Schemes—Children

	Court	Family Help (Higher) Standard fee	Legal Representation Standard Fee
London	Other	£471	£335
	High Court	£565	£402
Non-London	Other	£392	£279
	High Court	£471	£335

Table 3(f): Higher Standard Fee Schemes—Finance

	Court	Family Help (Higher) Standard Fee	Family Help (Higher) Settlement Fee	Legal Representation Standard Fee
London	Other	£523	£105	£416
	High Court	£628	£125	£499
Non-London	Other	£436	£87	£346
	High Court	£523	£105	£416

Table 3(g): Higher Standard Fee Schemes—Domestic Abuse Proceedings

	Court	*Legal Representation Standard Fee*
London	Other	£675
	High Court	£810
Non-London	Other	£563
	High Court	£675

4. Immigration

Table 4(a): Immigration standard fees

	Stage 1 (Legal Help)	*Stage 2a (Controlled Legal Representation)*	Stage 2b (Controlled Legal Representation)
Asylum	£459	£252	£630
Immigration Non-asylum	£260	£252	£504

Table 4(b) Additional payment—Home Office interview

Representation at Home Office interview	£296

Table 4(c): Additional payments—advocacy services

	Additional Payment
Oral Case Management Review Hearing	£184
Telephone Case Management Review Hearing	£100
Representation at a substantive hearing in the Immigration and Asylum Chamber of the First-tier Tribunal	£336 Asylum, £263 Immigration
Additional day substantive hearing	£179 Asylum, £179 Immigration

Table 4(d): Immigration removal centres standard fees (for exclusive schedule holders only)

On-site surgery—advising five or more clients	£400
On-site surgery—advising four clients or fewer	£200
Fast-track standby payment	£37.80

5. Mental Health

Table 5(a): Basic Fees

	Basic Fees
Mental Health—non-Tribunal	£281
Level 1 (Mental Health Proceedings)	£143
Level 2 (Mental Health Proceedings)	£357
Level 3 (Mental Health Proceedings)	£327

Table 5(b): Additional Fees

	Additional Fees
Adjourned Hearing Fee	£130
Remote Travel payment Level 1 (Mental Health Proceedings)	£77
Remote Travel payment: Mental Health—non-Tribunal, Level 2 (Mental Health Proceedings), Level 3 (Mental Health Proceedings)	£153

6. Housing Possession Court Duty Scheme

Table 6: Standard Fee

London	£84
Non-London	£79.50

7. Legal Help, Help at Court and Family Help (Lower)

Table 7(a): Immigration exceptional cases, Mental Health, Actions against the Police etc, Public Law, Education and Community Care

Activity	London Rate	*Non-London Rate*
Preparation, attendance and advocacy	£58.50 per hour	£53.60 per hour
Travel and waiting time	£30.90 per hour	£30.00 per hour
Routine letters out and telephone calls	£4.50 per item	£4.20 per item

Table 7(b): Family and Housing (except as in Table 7(c)) and Employment

Activity	London Rate	*Non-London Rate*
Preparation, attendance and advocacy	£54.15 per hour	£51.05 per hour
Travel and waiting time	£28.60 per hour	£28.60 per hour
Routine letters out and telephone calls	£4.20 per item	£4.05 per item

Table 7(c): Legal Help or Help at Court provided in relation to a review under section 202 of the Housing Act 1996 and to a defendant to a possession claim in the county court; Family Help (Lower) and related Legal Help in relation to care or supervision proceedings under section 31 of the Children Act 1989

Activity	London Rate	*Non-London Rate*
Preparation, attendance and advocacy	£62.40 per hour	£58.40 per hour
Travel and waiting time	£30.90 per hour	£30.05 per hour
Routine letters out and telephone calls	£4.50 per item	£4.20 per item

Table 7(d): Immigration hourly rates cases

Activity	London Rate	*Non-London Rate*
Preparation, attendance and advocacy	£57.35 per hour	£52.55 per hour
Travel and waiting time	£30.30 per hour	£29.45 per hour
Routine letters out and telephone calls	£4.40 per item	£4.10 per item

Table 7(e): All other categories and all tolerance work

Activity	London Rate	*Non-London Rate*
Preparation, attendance and advocacy	£51.70 per hour	£48.75 per hour
Travel and waiting time	£27.35 per hour	£27.35 per hour
Routine letters out and telephone calls	£4.00 per item	£3.85 per item

8. Controlled Legal Representation

Table 8(a): Immigration—exceptional cases

Activity	London Rate	*Non-London Rate*
Preparation and attendance	£64.25 per hour	£60.10 per hour
Travel and waiting time	£31.80 per hour	£30.90 per hour
Routine letters out and telephone calls	£4.60 per item	£4.30 per item
Advocacy	£73.10 per hour	£73.10 per hour

Table 8(b): Immigration—Upper Tribunal cases where permission granted to client (non-Fast-track)

Activity	London Rate	*Non-London Rate*
Preparation and attendance	£82.62 per hour	£77.29 per hour
Travel and waiting time	£40.91 per hour	£39.76 per hour
Routine letters out and telephone calls	£5.94 per item	£5.54 per item
Advocacy	£93.96 per hour	£93.96 per hour

Table 8(c): Immigration—other hourly rates cases

Activity	London Rate	*Non-London Rate*
Preparation and attendance	£61.20 per hour	£57.25 per hour
Travel and waiting time	£30.30 per hour	£29.45 per hour
Routine letters out and telephone calls	£4.40 per item	£4.10 per item
Advocacy	£69.60 per hour	£69.60 per hour

Table 8(d): Representation in Mental Health proceedings

Activity	London Rate	*Non London Rate*
Preparation and attendance	£64.25 per hour	£60.10 per hour
Travel and waiting time	£31.80 per hour	£30.90 per hour
Letters and telephone calls	£4.60 per item	£4.30 per item
Advocacy	£73.10 per hour	£73.10 per hour
Attending tribunal with counsel	£34.20 per hour	£34.20 per hour

9. Family Prescribed Rates: Licensed work

Table 9(a): Care Proceedings

Activity	Higher Courts	*County court and family proceedings court*
Writing routine letters	£4.70 per item	£4.10 per item
Receiving routine letters	£2.35 per item	£2.05 per item
Routine telephone calls	£4.70 per item	£4.10 per item
Preparation and attendance	£77.85 per hour (London Rate)	£68.20 per hour (London Rate)
	£73.15 per hour (non-London Rate)	£64.90 per hour (non-London Rate)
Attending at court or conference with counsel	£41.25 per hour	£36.30 per hour
Advocacy	£77.85 per hour (London Rate)	£71.50 per hour
	£73.15 per hour (non-London Rate)	
Travelling and waiting time	£35.75 per hour	£32.45 per hour

Table 9(b): Other Family Proceedings

Activity	Higher Courts	*County court and family proceedings court*
Writing routine letters	£7.05 per item	£6.00 per item
Receiving routine letters	£3.50 per item	£3.00 per item
Routine telephone calls	£7.05 per item	£6.00 per item
Preparation and attendance	£78.40 per hour (London Rate)	£66.00 per hour (London Rate)
	£73.05 per hour (non-London Rate)	£61.00 per hour (non-London Rate)
Attending at court or conference with counsel	£41.25 per hour	£36.00 per hour
Advocacy	£78.40 per hour (London Rate)	£66.00 per hour (London Rate)
	£73.05 per hour (non-London Rate)	£63.00 per hour (non-London Rate)
Travelling and waiting time	£35.75 per hour	£32.00 per hour (London Rate)
		£31.00 per hour (non-London Rate)

10. Non Family Prescribed Rates

Table 10(a): Higher Courts, county courts and magistrates' courts for work carried out with Schedule authorisation

Activity	Higher Courts	*County court and magistrates' court*
Writing routine letters	£7.50 per item	£6.60 per item
Routine telephone calls	£4.15 per item	£3.65 per item
Preparation and attendance	£79.50 per hour (London Rate)	£70.00 per hour (London Rate)
	£75.00 per hour (non-London Rate)	£66.00 per hour (non-London Rate)
Attending at court or conference with counsel	£37.00 per hour	£32.50 per hour
Advocacy	£75.00 per hour	£66.00 per hour
Travelling and waiting time	£33.25 per hour	£29.20 per hour

Table 10(b): Higher Courts, county court and magistrates' court for work not carried out with Schedule authorisation

Activity	Higher Courts	*County court and magistrates' court*
Writing routine letters	£7.40 per item	£6.50 per item
Routine telephone calls	£4.10 per item	£3.60 per item
Preparation and attendance	£78.50 per hour (London Rate)	£69.00 per hour (London Rate)
	£74.00 per hour (non-London Rate)	£65.00 per hour (non-London Rate)
Attending at court or conference with counsel	£36.40 per hour	£32.00 per hour
Advocacy	£74.00 per hour	£65.00 per hour
Travelling and waiting time	£32.70 per hour	£28.75 per hour

Table 10(c): First-tier Tribunal

Activity	London Rate	*Non-London Rate*
Preparation and attendance	£61.20 per hour	£57.25 per hour
Routine letters out and telephone calls	£4.40 per item	£4.10 per item
Advocacy	£69.60 per hour	£69.60 per hour
Attending tribunal or conference with counsel	£32.55 per hour	£32.55 per hour
Travelling and waiting time	£30.30 per hour	£29.45 per hour

11. Family Mediation

Table 11(a): Willingness Test

Category of Work	*Fee*
Willingness Test	£25

Table 11(b): Assessment Meetings

Activity	
Assessment alone	£87
Assessment separate	£87
Assessment together	£130

Table 11(c): Mediation Fees

Category of Work	Single Session	*Multi Session*	Agreed Proposal
All Issues Sole Mediation	£168	£756	£252
All Issues Co-Mediation	£230	£1,064	£252
Property and Finance Sole Mediation	£168	£588	£189
Property and Finance Co-Mediation	£230	£834	£189
Child Sole Mediation	£168	£462	£126
Child Co-Mediation	£230	£647	£126

PART 2 COSTS IN CRIMINAL PROCEEDINGS

Graduated Fees for Trial

Calculation of Graduated Fees

The following text and tables are extracted from the Criminal Defence Service (Funding) Order 2007 (SI 2007/1174) (as amended).

(1) The amount of the graduated fee for a single trial advocate representing one assisted person being tried on one indictment in the Crown Court in a trial lasting one to 40 days must be calculated in accordance with the following formula—

$$G = B + (d \times D) + (e \times E) + (w \times W)$$

(2) In the formula in sub-paragraph (1)—

G is the amount of the graduated fee;

B is the basic fee specified in the Table following paragraph 5 as appropriate to the offence for which the assisted person is tried and the category of trial advocate;

d is the number of days or parts of a day on which the advocate attends at court by which the trial exceeds 2 days but does not exceed 40 days;

D is the fee payable in respect of daily attendance at court for the number of days by which the trial exceeds two days but does not exceed 40 days, as appropriate to the offence for which the assisted person is tried and the category of trial advocate;

e is the number of pages of prosecution evidence excluding the first 50, up to a maximum of 10,000;

E is the evidence uplift specified in the Table following paragraph 5 as appropriate to the offence for which the assisted person is tried and the category of trial advocate;

w is the number of prosecution witnesses excluding the first 10;

W is the witness uplift specified in the Table following paragraph 5 as appropriate to the offence for which the assisted person is tried and the category of trial advocate.

Table of fees

For the purposes of this paragraph the basic fee (B), the daily attendance fee (D), the evidence uplift (E) and the witness uplift (W) appropriate to any offence will be those specified in the Table following this paragraph in accordance with the Class within which that offence falls.

Table of Fees and Uplifts in force from 27 April 2010 to 1 April 2011				
Class of Offence	*Basic Fee (B)*	*Daily attendance fee (D)*	*Evidence Uplift (E)*	*Witness Uplift (W)*
	(£)	*(£)*	*(£)*	*(£)*
QC				
A	4,234	1,262	1.80	7.21
B	2,792	946	1.80	7.21
C	2,173	901	1.80	7.21
D	2,522	901	1.80	7.21
E	1,671	676	1.80	7.21
F	1,671	676	1.80	7.21
G	2,101	901	1.80	7.21

Table of Fees and Uplifts in force from 1 April 2011 to 1 April 2012				
Class of Offence	*Basic Fee (B)*	*Daily attendance fee (D)*	*Evidence Uplift (E)*	*Witness (W) Uplift*
	(£)	*(£)*	*(£)*	*(£)*
QC				
A	4,035	1,202	1.72	6.87
B	2,661	902	1.72	6.87
C	2,070	858	1.72	6.87
D	2,403	858	1.72	6.87
E	1,593	644	1.72	6.87
F	1,593	644	1.72	6.87
G	2,002	858	1.72	6.87
H	2,002	858	1.72	6.87
I	2,232	858	1.72	6.87
J	3,005	1,030	1.72	6.87
K	3,005	1,030	1.72	6.87
Leading Junior				
A	3,026	902	1.29	5.15
B	1,996	676	1.29	5.15
C	1,552	644	1.29	5.15
D	1,803	644	1.29	5.15
E	1,195	483	1.29	5.15
F	1,195	483	1.29	5.15
G	1,502	644	1.29	5.15
H	1,502	644	1.29	5.15
I	1,674	644	1.29	5.15
J	2,253	773	1.29	5.15
K	2,253	773	1.29	5.15
Led Junior				
A	2,017	601	0.86	3.43
B	1,330	450	0.86	3.43
C	945	430	0.86	3.43
D	1,183	430	0.86	3.43
E	730	322	0.86	3.43
F	730	322	0.86	3.43
G	1,001	430	0.86	3.43
H	858	430	0.86	3.43
I	1,030	430	0.86	3.43
J	1,717	515	0.86	3.43
K	1,502	515	0.86	3.43

Table of Fees and Uplifts in force from 27 April 2010 to 1 April 2011 (cont.)				
Class of Offence	*Basic Fee (B)*	*Daily attendance fee (D)*	*Evidence Uplift (E)*	*Witness Uplift (W)*
	(£)	*(£)*	*(£)*	*(£)*
H	2,101	901	1.80	7.21
I	2,343	901	1.80	7.21
J	3,153	1,081	1.80	7.21
K	3,153	1,081	1.80	7.21
Leading Junior				
A	3,175	946	1.36	5.41
B	2,094	710	1.36	5.41
C	1,629	676	1.36	5.41
D	1,892	676	1.36	5.41
E	1,254	507	1.36	5.41
F	1,254	507	1.36	5.41
G	1,576	676	1.36	5.41
H	1,576	676	1.36	5.41
I	1,757	676	1.36	5.41
J	2,365	811	1.36	5.41
K	2,365	811	1.36	5.41
Led Junior				
A	2,177	630	0.90	3.60
B	1,396	473	0.90	3.60
C	991	451	0.90	3.60
D	1,242	451	0.90	3.60
E	766	338	0.90	3.60
F	766	338	0.90	3.60
G	1,051	451	0.90	3.60
H	901	451	0.90	3.60
I	1,081	451	0.90	3.60
J	1,802	541	0.90	3.60
K	1,577	541	0.90	3.60
Junior alone				
A	2,432	743	1.08	5.41
B	1,441	518	1.08	5.41
C	991	451	1.08	5.41
D	1,242	451	1.08	5.41
E	721	360	1.08	5.41
F	766	360	1.08	5.41
G	1,351	451	1.08	5.41
H	901	451	1.08	5.41
I	1,081	451	1.08	5.41
J	1,802	585	1.08	5.41
K	1,802	585	1.08	5.41

Table of Fees and Uplifts in force from 1 April 2011 to 1 April 2012 (cont.)				
Class of Offence	*Basic Fee (B)*	*Daily attendance fee (D)*	*Evidence Uplift (E)*	*Witness (W) Uplift*
	(£)	*(£)*	*(£)*	*(£)*
Junior alone				
A	2,318	708	1.03	5.15
B	1,373	493	1.03	5.15
C	945	430	1.03	5.15
D	1,183	430	1.03	5.15
E	687	343	1.03	5.15
F	730	343	1.03	5.15
G	1,288	430	1.03	5.15
H	858	430	1.03	5.15
I	1,030	430	1.03	5.15
J	1,717	558	1.03	5.15
K	1,717	558	1.03	5.15

Graduated Fees for Guilty Pleas and Cracked Trials

Calculation of graduated fees in guilty pleas and cracked trials—

The amount of the graduated fee for a single trial advocate representing one assisted person in a guilty plea or cracked trial is—

(a) the basic fee specified in the table following as appropriate to the offence with which the assisted person is charged, the category of trial advocate and whether the case is a guilty plea or a cracked trial; and

(b) the evidence uplift, as appropriate to the number of pages of prosecution evidence, calculated in accordance with the table following

Tables of fees

(1) Subject to sub-paragraphs (2) and (3), for the purposes of this paragraph the basic fee and evidence uplift appropriate to any offence are specified in the Tables following this paragraph in accordance with the class within which that offence falls.

(2) Where—

(a) the trial of a case does not commence on the date first fixed; or

(b) the case is not taken and disposed of from the first warned list in which it is entered,

the basic fee and evidence uplift for the offence are specified for the last third in the Table referred to in sub-paragraph (1).

(3) In this paragraph, and in the Tables following this paragraph, references to the first, second and last third are references to the first, second and last third—

(a) where a case is first listed for trial on a fixed date, of the period of time beginning after the date on which the case is so listed and ending before the date so fixed,

(b) where the case is first placed in a warned list, of the period of time beginning after the date on which the case is so placed and ending before the date of the start of that warned list, and

where the number of days in this period of time cannot be divided by three equally, any days remaining after such division must be added to the last third.

(4) Where a graduated fee is calculated in accordance with this Part for the purposes of paragraph 2(4), the fee must be calculated as if the trial had cracked in the final third.

Table A—Fees and uplifts in guilty pleas and trials which crack in the first third in force from 27th April 2010 to 1 April 2011 (cont.)			
Class of Offence	*Basic Fee*	*Evidence uplift per page of prosecution evidence (pages 1 to 1,000)*	*Evidence uplift per page of prosecution evidence (1,001 to 10,000)*
Junior Alone			
A	1,253	1.03	0.52
B	766	0.90	0.45
C	496	0.66	0.33
D	766	1.31	0.65
E	451	0.39	0.19
F	451	0.60	0.30
G	721	1.13	0.56
H	541	0.60	0.31
I	630	0.47	0.24
J	1,081	1.31	0.65
K	1,081	1.13	0.56

Table A—Fees and uplifts in guilty pleas and trials which crack in the first third in force from 27 April 2010 to 1 April 2011			
Class of Offence	*Basic Fee*	*Evidence uplift per page of prosecution evidence (pages 1 to 1,000)*	*Evidence uplift per page of prosecution evidence (1,001 to 10,000)*
QC			
A	2,146	2.30	1.06
B	1,373	1.89	0.95
C	1,288	1.35	0.67
D	1,373	3.00	1.50
E	1,138	0.96	0.48
F	1,138	1.26	0.64
G	1,288	1.67	0.84
H	1,288	1.74	0.86
I	1,288	1.69	0.84
J	1,803	3.00	1.50
K	1,803	1.67	0.84
Leading Junior			
A	1,609	1.73	0.80
B	1,030	1.42	0.71
C	966	1.01	0.51
D	1,030	2.26	1.13
E	853	0.73	0.36
F	853	0.95	0.48
G	966	1.26	0.63
H	966	1.30	0.65
I	966	1.27	0.63

Table A—Fees and uplifts in guilty pleas and trials which crack in the first third in force from 27th April 2010 to 1 April 2011			
Class of Offence	*Basic Fee*	*Evidence uplift per page of prosecution evidence (pages 1 to 1,000)*	*Evidence uplift per page of prosecution evidence (1,001 to 10,000)*
QC			
A	2,252	2.42	1.12
B	1,441	1.99	0.99
C	1,351	1.41	0.71
D	1,441	3.15	1.58
E	1,194	1.01	0.51
F	1,194	1.33	0.67
G	1,351	1.76	0.88
H	1,351	1.82	0.91
I	1,351	1.78	0.88
J	1,892	3.15	1.58
K	1,892	1.76	0.88
Leading Junior			
A	1,689	1.81	0.84
B	1,081	1.49	0.74
C	1,013	1.06	0.53
D	1,081	2.37	1.18
E	895	0.76	0.38
F	895	0.99	0.51
G	1,013	1.32	0.66
H	1,013	1.37	0.68
I	1,013	1.34	0.66
J	1,419	2.37	1.18
K	1,419	1.32	0.66
Led Junior			
A	1,126	1.21	0.56
B	721	0.99	0.50
C	676	0.71	0.35
D	721	1.58	0.79
E	597	0.51	0.26
F	597	0.67	0.33
G	676	0.88	0.44]
H	676	0.92	0.46
I	676	0.89	0.44
J	946	1.58	0.79
K	946	0.88	0.44

Table A—Fees and uplifts in guilty pleas and trials which crack in the first third in force from 27 April 2010 to 1 April 2011 (cont.)			
Class of Offence	*Basic Fee*	*Evidence uplift per page of prosecution evidence (pages 1 to 1,000)*	*Evidence uplift per page of prosecution evidence (1,001 to 10,000)*
J	1,352	2.26	1.13
K	1,352	1.26	0.63
Led Junior			
A	1,073	1.16	0.54
B	687	0.95	0.47
C	644	0.67	0.34
D	687	1.50	0.76
E	569	0.48	0.25
F	569	0.64	0.32
G	644	0.84	0.42]
H	644	0.87	0.44
I	644	0.85	0.42
J	901	1.50	0.76
K	901	0.84	0.42
Junior Alone			
A	1,194	0.98	0.49
B	730	0.86	0.43
C	472	0.63	0.32
D	730	1.25	0.62
E	430	0.37	0.18
F	430	0.57	0.28
G	687	1.07	0.54
H	515	0.57	0.29
I	601	0.45	0.23
J	1,030	1.25	0.62
K	1,030	1.07	0.54

Table B—Fees and uplifts in trials which crack in the second or final third in force from 1 April 2011 to 1 April 2012

Class of Offence	*Basic Fee*	*Evidence uplift per page of prosecution evidence (pages 1 to 250)*	*Evidence uplift per page of prosecution evidence (pages 251 to 1,000)*	*A case that cracks in the second third: Evidence uplift per page of prosecution evidence (pages 1,001 to 10,000)*	*A case that cracks in the final third: Evidence uplift per page of prosecution evidence (pages 1,001 to 10,000)*
QC					
A	3,424	4.49	1.12	1.48	4.49
B	2,162	3.97	0.99	1.32	3.97
C	1,886	2.82	0.71	0.93	2.82
D	2,162	6.29	1.58	2.08	6.29
E	1,528	2.02	0.51	0.67	2.02
F	1,528	2.65	0.67	0.88	2.65
G	1,910	3.51	0.88	1.17	3.51
H	1,910	3.63	0.91	1.19	3.63
I	1,982	3.55	0.88	1.17	3.55
J	2,883	6.29	1.58	2.08	6.29
K	2,883	3.51	0.88	1.17	3.51
Leading Junior					
A	2,568	3.37	0.84	1.11	3.37
B	1,622	2.98	0.74	0.99	2.98
C	1,415	2.11	0.53	0.70	2.11
D	1,622	4.72	1.18	1.57	4.72
E	1,146	1.51	0.38	0.51	1.51
F	1,146	1.99	0.51	0.66	1.99
G	1,433	2.64	0.66	0.88	2.64
H	1,433	2.72	0.68	0.90	2.72
I	1,486	2.66	0.66	0.88	2.66
J	2,162	4.72	1.18	1.57	4.72
K	2,162	2.64	0.66	0.88	2.64
Led Junior					
A	1,712	2.24	0.56	0.74	2.24
B	1,081	1.99	0.50	0.66	1.99
C	943	1.41	0.35	0.47	1.41
D	1,081	3.15	0.79	1.04	3.15
E	764	1.01	0.26	0.33	1.01
F	764	1.33	0.33	0.44	1.33
G	955	1.76	0.44	0.58	1.76
H	955	1.81	0.46	0.60	1.81
I	991	1.78	0.44	0.59	1.78
J	1,442	3.15	0.79	1.04	3.15
K	1,442	1.76	0.44	0.58	1.76

Table B—Fees and uplifts in trials which crack in the second or final third in force from 1 April 2011 to 1 April 2012					
Class of Offence	*Basic Fee*	*Evidence uplift per page of prosecution evidence (pages 1 to 250)*	*Evidence uplift per page of prosecution evidence (pages 251 to 1,000)*	*A case that cracks in the second third: Evidence uplift per page of prosecution evidence (pages 1,001 to 10,000)*	*A case that cracks in the final third: Evidence uplift per page of prosecution evidence (pages 1,001 to 10,000)*
QC					
A	3,262	4.28	1.06	1.41	4.28
B	2,060	3.79	0.95	1.26	3.79
C	1,797	2.68	0.67	0.88	2.68
D	2,060	6.00	1.50	1.98	6.00
E	1,456	1.92	0.48	0.64	1.92
F	1,456	2.52	0.64	0.84	2.52
G	1,820	3.35	0.84	1.11	3.35
H	1,820	3.46	0.86	1.14	3.46
I	1,888	3.39	0.84	1.12	3.39
J	2,747	6.00	1.50	1.98	6.00
K	2,747	3.35	0.84	1.11	3.35
Leading Junior					
A	2,447	3.21	0.80	1.06	3.21
B	1,545	2.84	0.71	0.95	2.84
C	1,348	2.01	0.51	0.66	2.01
D	1,545	4.50	1.13	1.49	4.50
E	1,092	1.44	0.36	0.48	1.44
F	1,092	1.89	0.48	0.63	1.89
Junior alone					
A	1,892	4.42	2.05	0.68	2.05
B	1,126	3.85	1.80	0.59	1.80
C	721	2.86	1.33	0.44	1.33
D	1,003	5.61	2.61	0.86	2.61
E	630	1.67	0.78	0.26	0.78
F	630	2.58	1.19	0.40	1.19
G	1,081	4.85	2.26	0.74	2.26
H	766	2.59	1.20	0.40	1.20
I	901	2.02	0.94	0.31	0.94
J	1,622	5.61	2.61	0.86	2.61
K	1,532	4.85	2.26	0.74	2.26

Fixed Fees

General provisions

Except as provided, all work undertaken by an advocate is included within the basic fee (B) specified in the Table below] as appropriate to—

(a) the offence for which the assisted person is tried;

(b) the category of advocate; and

(c) whether the case is a cracked trial, guilty plea or trial.

Fees for plea and case management hearings and standard appearances

(1) The fee payable in respect of—

(a) an appearance by the trial advocate or substitute advocate at the first plea and case management hearing or pre-trial review; and

(b) up to four standard appearances by the trial advocate or substitute advocate,

is included within the basic fee (B) specified above as appropriate to the offence for which the assisted person is tried and the category of trial advocate.

(2) The fee payable in respect of an appearance by the trial advocate or substitute advocate at a plea and case management hearing or standard appearance not included in sub-paragraph (1) is specified in the Table headed Noting brief fees as appropriate to the category of trial advocate or substitute advocate.

(3) The fee payable for preparing and filing the plea and case management questionnaire where no oral hearing takes place is specified in the Table headed Noting brief fees as appropriate to the category of trial advocate or substitute advocate.

(4) This paragraph does not apply to a standard appearance which is or forms part of the main hearing in a case or to a hearing for which a fee is payable elsewhere under this Schedule.

Fees for abuse of process, disclosure, admissibility and withdrawal of plea hearings

(1) This paragraph applies to—

(a) the hearing of an application to stay the case on indictment or any count on the ground that the proceedings constitute an abuse of the process of the court;

(b) any hearing relating to the question of whether any material should be disclosed by the prosecution to the defence or the defence to the prosecution (whether or not any claim to public interest immunity is made);

(c) the hearing of an application under section 2(1) of the Criminal Procedure (Attendance of Witnesses) Act 1965 (issue of witness summons on application to Crown Court) for disclosure of material held by third parties;

(d) any hearing relating to the question of the admissibility as evidence of any material; and

(e) the hearing of an application to withdraw a plea of guilty where the application is—

(i) made by an advocate other than the advocate who appeared at the hearing at which the plea of guilty was entered; and

(ii) unsuccessful.

(2) Where a hearing to which this paragraph applies is held on any day of the main hearing of a case on indictment, no separate fee is payable in respect of attendance at the hearing, but the hearing is included in the length of the main hearing for the purpose of calculating the fees payable.

(3) Where a hearing to which this paragraph applies is held prior to the first or only day of the main hearing, it is not included in the length of the main hearing for the purpose of calculating the fees payable and the trial advocate or substitute advocate must be remunerated for attendance at such a hearing—

(a) in respect of any day where the hearing begins before and ends after the luncheon adjournment, at the daily rate set out in the Table headed Noting brief fees as appropriate to the category of trial advocate or substitute advocate; or

(b) in respect of any day where the hearing begins and ends before the luncheon adjournment, or begins after the luncheon adjournment, at the half-daily rate set out in the Table headed Noting brief fees as appropriate to the category of trial advocate or substitute advocate.

Fees for confiscation hearings

(1) This paragraph applies to—

Table B—Fees and uplifts in trials which crack in the second or final third in force from 1 April 2011 to 1 April 2012 (cont.)

Class of Offence	*Basic Fee*	*Evidence uplift per page of prosecution evidence (pages 1 to 250)*	*Evidence uplift per page of prosecution evidence (pages 251 to 1,000)*	*A case that cracks in the second third: Evidence uplift per page of prosecution evidence (pages 1,001 to 10,000)*	*A case that cracks in the final third: Evidence uplift per page of prosecution evidence (pages 1,001 to 10,000)*
G	1,365	2.51	0.63	0.84	2.51
H	1,365	2.59	0.65	0.86	2.59
I	1,416	2.54	0.63	0.84	2.54
J	2,060	4.50	1.13	1.49	4.50
K	2,060	2.51	0.63	0.84	2.51
Led Junior					
A	1,631	2.14	0.54	0.71	2.14
B	1,030	1.89	0.47	0.63	1.89
C	899	1.35	0.34	0.45	1.35
D	1,030	3.00	0.76	0.99	3.00
E	728	0.96	0.25	0.32	0.96
F	728	1.26	0.32	0.42	1.26
G	910	1.67	0.42	0.56	1.67
H	910	1.73	0.44	0.57	1.73
I	944	1.69	0.42	0.56	1.69
J	1,374	3.00	0.76	0.99	3.00
K	1,374	1.67	0.42	0.56	1.67
Junior alone					
A	1,803	4.21	1.96	0.65	1.96
B	1,073	3.67	1.71	0.56	1.71
C	687	2.72	1.26	0.42	1.26
D	956	5.34	2.48	0.82	2.48
E	601	1.59	0.75	0.25	0.75
F	601	2.46	1.14	0.38	1.14
G	1,030	4.62	2.16	0.71	2.16
H	730	2.47	1.15	0.38	1.15
I	858	1.92	0.89	0.29	0.89
J	1,545	5.34	2.48	0.82	2.48
K	1,460	4.62	2.16	0.71	2.16

(a) a hearing under Part 2 of the Proceeds of Crime Act 2002 (confiscation: England and Wales);

(b) a hearing under section 2 of the Drug Trafficking Act 1994; (confiscation orders) and

(c) a hearing under section 71 of the Criminal Justice Act 1988 (confiscation orders).

(2) A hearing to which this paragraph applies is not included in the length of the main hearing or of any sentencing hearing for the purpose of calculating the fees payable, and the trial advocate or substitute advocate must be remunerated in respect of such a hearing—

(a) where the number of pages of evidence is fewer than 51, for attendance—

(i) in respect of any day when the hearing begins before and ends after the luncheon adjournment, at the daily rate set out in the first section of the table following this sub-paragraph; or

(ii) in respect of any day when the hearing begins and ends before the luncheon adjournment, or begins after the luncheon adjournment, at the half-daily rate set out in the first section of that table,

as appropriate to the category of trial advocate or substitute advocate;

(b) where the number of pages of evidence is between 51 and 1000—

(i) at the rates for the relevant number of pages set out in the second section of the table following this sub-paragraph; and

(ii) where the hearing lasts for more than one day, for attendance on subsequent days or half-days at the daily rate or half-daily rate set out in the first section of that table,

as appropriate to the category of trial advocate or substitute advocate; or

(c) where the number of pages of evidence exceeds 1000—

(i) at the rates for 751 to 1000 pages set out in the second section of the table following this sub-paragraph;

(ii) with such fee as the appropriate officer considers reasonable for preparation in respect of the pages in excess of 1000, at the hourly rates for preparation set out in the third section of that table; and

(iii) where the hearing lasts for more than one day, for attendance on subsequent days or half-days at the daily rate or half-daily rate set out in the first section of that table, as appropriate to the category of trial advocate or substitute advocate.

Fees for confiscation hearings (£) in force from 27 April 2010 to 1April 2011

	Fee for QC	Fee for leading junior	Fee for junior alone	Fee for led junior
1—Daily and half-daily rates				
Half-daily rate	287	215	143	143
Daily rate	549	382	263	263
2—Pages of evidence				
51–250	716	597	478	358
251–500	1,074	896	716	537
501–750	1,433	1,194	955	716
751–1000	2,149	1,791	1,433	1,074
3—Preparation				
Hourly rates	81	62	43	43

Fees for confiscation hearings (£) in force from 1 April 2011 to 1 April 2012

	Fee for QC	Fee for leading junior	Fee for junior alone	Fee for led junior
1—Daily and half-daily rates				
Half-daily rate	273	205	137	137
Daily rate	523	364	250	250
2—Pages of evidence				
51–250	683	569	455	341
251–500	1,024	854	683	511
501–750	1,365	1,138	910	683
751–1000	2,048	1,706	1,365	1,024
3— Preparation				
Hourly rates	77	59	41	41

(3) In sub-paragraph (2) "evidence" means—

(a) the statement of information served under section 16 of the Proceeds of Crime Act 2002 and relied on by the prosecution for the purposes of a hearing under Part 2 of that Act, or a similar statement served and so relied on for the purposes of a hearing under section 2 of the Drug Trafficking Act 1994 or under section 71 of the Criminal Justice Act 1988 and, in each case, any attached annexes and exhibits;

(b) any other document which—

(i) is served as a statement or an exhibit for the purposes of the trial;

(ii) is specifically referred to in, but not served with, a statement mentioned in paragraph (a); and

(iii) the prosecution state that they intend to rely on in the hearing; and

(c) any written report of an expert obtained with the prior authority of the Commission under CDS Regulations or allowed by the appropriate officer under this Order, and any attached annexes and exhibits, other than documents contained in such annexes or exhibits which have also been served under paragraph (a) or (b) or which consist of financial records or similar data.

Fees for sentencing hearings

(1) This paragraph applies to—

(a) a sentencing hearing following a case on indictment to which this Schedule applies, where sentence has been deferred under section 1 of the Powers of Criminal Courts (Sentencing) Act 2000 (deferment of sentence); or

(b) a sentencing hearing following a case on indictment to which this Schedule applies, other than a hearing within paragraph (a) or a sentencing hearing forming part of the main hearing.

(2) The fee payable to an advocate for appearing at a hearing to which this paragraph applies is that set out in the Table following paragraph 19 as appropriate to the category of trial advocate or substitute advocate and the circumstances of the hearing.

Fees for ineffective trials

The fee set out in the Table headed Noting Brief Fees as appropriate to the category of trial advocate will be payable in respect of each day on which the case was listed for trial but did not proceed on the day for which it was listed, for whatever reason.

Fees for special preparation

(1) This paragraph applies where, in any case on indictment in the Crown Court in respect of which a graduated fee is payable under Part 2 or Part 3—

(a) it has been necessary for an advocate to do work by way of preparation substantially in excess of the amount normally done for cases of the same type because the case involves a very unusual or novel point of law or factual issue;

(b) the number of pages of prosecution evidence, as defined in paragraph 1(2), exceeds 10,000 and the appropriate officer considers it reasonable to make a payment in excess of the graduated fee payable under this Schedule; or

(c) any or all of the prosecution evidence, as defined in paragraph 1(2), is served in electronic form only, and the appropriate officer considers it reasonable to make a payment in excess of the graduated fee payable under this Schedule.

(2) Where this paragraph applies, a special preparation fee may be paid, in addition to the graduated fee payable under Part 2 or Part 3.

(3) The amount of the special preparation fee must be calculated—

(a) where sub-paragraph (1)(a) applies, from the number of hours preparation in excess of the amount the appropriate officer considers reasonable for cases of the same type;

(b) where sub-paragraph (1)(b) applies, from the number of hours which the appropriate officer considers reasonable to read the excess pages; and

(c) where sub-paragraph (1)(c) applies, from the number of hours which the appropriate officer considers reasonable to view the prosecution evidence,

and in each case using the rates of hourly fees set out in the table following paragraph 19 as appropriate to the category of trial advocate.

(4) Any claim for a special preparation fee under this paragraph must be made by an instructed advocate, whether or not he did the work claimed for.

(5) An instructed advocate claiming a special preparation fee must supply such information and documents as may be required by the appropriate officer in support of the claim.

(6) In determining a claim under this paragraph, the appropriate officer must take into account all the relevant circumstances of the case, including, where special preparation work has been undertaken by more than one advocate, the benefit of such work to the trial advocate.

Fees for wasted preparation

(1) A wasted preparation fee may be claimed where a trial advocate in any case to which this paragraph applies is prevented from representing the assisted person in the main hearing by any of the following circumstances—

(a) the trial advocate is instructed to appear in other proceedings at the same time as the main hearing in the case and has been unable to secure a change of date for either the main hearing or the other proceedings;

(b) the date fixed for the main hearing is changed by the court despite the trial advocate's objection;

(c) the trial advocate has withdrawn from the case with the leave of the court because of his professional code of conduct or to avoid embarrassment in the exercise of his profession;

(d) the trial advocate has been dismissed by the assisted person or the litigator; or

(e) the trial advocate is obliged to attend at any place by reason of a judicial office held by him or other public duty.

(2) This paragraph applies to every case on indictment to which this Schedule applies provided that—

(a) the case goes to trial, and the trial lasts for five days or more; or

(b) the case is a cracked trial, and the number of pages of prosecution evidence exceeds 150.

(3) The amount of the wasted preparation fee must be calculated from the number of hours of preparation reasonably carried out by the trial advocate, using the rates for hourly fees set out in the Table Headed Noting Brief fees as appropriate to the category of trial advocate, but no such fee is payable unless the number of hours of preparation is eight or more.

(4) Any claim for a wasted preparation fee under this paragraph must be made by an instructed advocate, whether or not he did the work claimed for.

(5) An instructed advocate claiming a wasted preparation fee must supply such information and documents as may be required by the appropriate officer as proof of the circumstances in which he was prevented from representing the assisted person and of the number of hours of preparation.

Fees for conferences and views

(1) This paragraph applies to the following types of work—

(a) attendance by the trial advocate at pre-trial conferences with prospective or actual expert witnesses not held at court;

(b) attendance by the trial advocate at views at the scene of the alleged offence;

(c) attendance by the trial advocate at pre-trial conferences with the assisted person not held at court;

(d) reasonable travelling time by the trial advocate for the purpose of attending a view at the scene of the alleged offence; or

(e) reasonable travelling time by the trial advocate for the purpose of attending a pre-trial conference with the assisted person or prospective or actual expert witness, where the appropriate officer is satisfied that the assisted person or prospective or actual expert witness was unable or could not reasonably have been expected to attend a conference at the trial advocate's chambers or office.

(2) The fees payable in respect of attendance at the first three pre-trial conferences or views, as set out in sub-paragraph (1)(a) to (c), are included in the basic fee (B) specified in the Tables headed Table of Fees and Uplifts as appropriate to the offence for which the assisted person is tried, the category of trial advocate and whether the case is a guilty plea, cracked trial or trial, provided that the trial advocate satisfies the appropriate officer that the work was reasonably necessary.

(3) The fee specified in the Table headed Noting Brief Fees as appropriate to the category of trial advocate will be payable in the following circumstances, provided that the trial advocate satisfies the appropriate officer that the work was reasonably necessary—

(a) for trials lasting not less than 21 and not more than 25 days, and cracked trials where it was accepted by the court at the plea and case management hearing that the trial would last not less than 21 days and not more than 25 days, one further pre-trial conference or view not exceeding two hours;

(b) for trials lasting not less than 26 and not more than 35 days, and cracked trials where it was accepted by the court at the plea and case management hearing that the trial would last not less than 26 days and not more than 35 days, two further pre-trial conferences or views each not exceeding two hours; and

(c) for trials lasting not less than 36 days, and cracked trials where it was accepted by the court at the plea and case management hearing that the trial would last not less than 36 days and not more than 40 days, three further pre-trial conferences or views each not exceeding two hours.

(4) Travel expenses must be paid for all conferences and views set out in sub-paragraph (1)(a) to (c), provided that the trial advocate satisfies the appropriate officer that they were reasonably incurred.

(5) Travelling time must be paid for all conferences and views set out in sub-paragraph (1)(a) to (c), provided that the trial advocate satisfies the appropriate officer that it was reasonable.

Fees for appeals, committals for sentence and breach hearings

(1) Subject to sub-paragraphs (4) and (5) and paragraph 21 the fee payable to a trial advocate in any of the hearings referred to in paragraph 2(1)(b) is the fixed fee specified in the Table following paragraph 19.

(2) Where a hearing referred to in paragraph 2(1)(b) is listed but cannot proceed because of the failure of the assisted person or a witness to attend, the unavailability of a pre-sentence report, or other good reason, the fee payable to the advocate is the fixed fee specified in the Table headed Noting Brief Fees.

(3) Where—

(a) a bail application;

(b) a mention hearing; or

(c) any other application

takes place in the course of a hearing referred to in paragraph 2(1)(b), the fee payable to the advocate is the fixed fee specified in the Table headed Noting Brief Fees.

(4) Where it appears to the appropriate officer that the fixed fee allowed under sub-paragraph (1) would be inappropriate taking into account all of the relevant circumstances of the case he may instead allow fees in such amounts as appear to him to be reasonable remuneration for the relevant work in accordance with sub-paragraph (5).

(5) The appropriate officer may allow any of the following classes of fees to an advocate in respect of work allowed by him under this paragraph—

(a) a fee for preparation including, where appropriate, the first day of the hearing including, where they took place on that day—

(i) short conferences;

(ii) consultations;

(iii) applications and appearances (including bail applications);

(iv) views at the scene of the alleged offence; and

(v) any other preparation;

(b) a refresher fee for any day or part of a day for which a hearing continued, including, where they took place on that day—

(i) short conferences;

(ii) consultations;

(iii) applications and appearances (including bail applications);

(iv) views at the scene of the alleged offence; and

(v) any other preparation; and

(c) subsidiary fees for—

(i) attendance at conferences, consultations and views at the scene of the alleged offence not covered by paragraph (a) or (b);

(ii) written advice on evidence, plea, appeal, case stated or other written work; and

(iii) attendance at applications and appearances (including bail applications and adjournments for sentence) not covered by paragraph (a) or (b)

Fees for contempt proceedings

(1) Subject to sub-paragraph (2), remuneration for advocates in proceedings referred to in section 12(2)(f) of the Act in the Crown Court must be at the rates specified in the table below.

In force from 27 April to 1 April 2010	
Category of advocate	*Payment rates (£ per day)*
QC	300
Leading Junior	225
Led junior or junior acting alone	150

(2) Where an advocate and a litigator are instructed in proceedings referred to in section 12(2)(f) of the Act, remuneration must be at the rates specified in the table below, as appropriate to the category of advocate.

In force from 1 April 2011 to 1 April 2012	
Category of advocate	*Payment rates (£ per day)*
QC	175
Leading Junior	125
Led junior or junior acting alone	100

Discontinuance or dismissal of sent or transferred proceedings

(1) This paragraph applies to proceedings which are—

(a) sent for trial to the Crown Court under section 51 of the Crime and Disorder Act 1998 (no committal proceedings for indictable-only offences); or

(b) transferred to the Crown Court under—

(i) section 4 of the Criminal Justice Act 1987 (transfer of serious fraud cases); or

(ii) section 53 of the Criminal Justice Act 1991 (transfer of certain cases involving children).

(2) Where proceedings referred to in sub-paragraph (1) are discontinued by a notice served under section 23A of the Prosecution of Offences Act 1985 (discontinuance of proceedings after accused has been sent for trial) at any time before the prosecution serves its evidence in accordance with the Crime and Disorder Act 1998 (Service of Prosecution Evidence) Regulations 2005 the advocate must be paid 50 percent of the Basic fee (B) for a guilty plea, as specified in the Table following paragraph 7 as appropriate to the offence for which the assisted person is charged and the category of advocate.

(3) Where proceedings referred to in sub-paragraph (1) are discontinued by a notice served under section 23A of the Prosecution of Offences Act 1985 (discontinuance of proceedings after accused has been sent for trial) at any time after the prosecution serves its evidence in accordance with the Crime and Disorder Act 1998 (Service of Prosecution Evidence) Regulations 2005, the advocate must be paid a graduated fee calculated in accordance with paragraph 6, as appropriate for representing an assisted person in a guilty plea.

(4) Sub-paragraph (4A) applies to—

(a) a plea and case management hearing that takes place after the prosecution serves its evidence; and

(b) any other hearing that takes place before a plea and case management hearing has taken place but after the prosecution has served its evidence.

(4A) Where, at a hearing to which this sub-paragraph applies—

(a) the prosecution offers no evidence and the assisted person is discharged; or

(b) the assisted person is charged on an indictment which includes no offence that is triable only on indictment and the case is remitted to the magistrates' court in accordance with paragraph 10(3)(a) of Schedule 3 to the Crime and Disorder Act 1998 (procedure where no indictable offence remains), the advocate instructed in the proceedings must be paid a graduated fee calculated in accordance with paragraph 6, as appropriate for representing an assisted person in a guilty plea.]

(5) Where an application for dismissal is made under paragraph 2 of Schedule 3 to the Crime and Disorder Act 1998 (applications for dismissal), section 6 of the Criminal Justice Act 1987 (applications for dismissal) or paragraph 5 of Schedule 6 to the Criminal Justice Act 1991 (applications for dismissal), the advocate must be remunerated for attendance at the hearing of the application for dismissal—

(a) in respect of any day where the hearing begins before and ends after the luncheon adjournment, at the daily rate set out in the Table following paragraph 19 as appropriate to the category of advocate; or

(b) in respect of any day where the hearing begins and ends before the luncheon adjournment, or begins after the luncheon adjournment, at the half-daily rate set out in that Table as appropriate to the category of advocate, provided that a fee is not payable elsewhere under this Schedule in respect of any day of the hearing.

(6) Where an application for dismissal is made under paragraph 2 of Schedule 3 to the Crime and Disorder Act 1998, section 6 of the Criminal Justice Act 1987 or paragraph 5 of Schedule 6 to the Criminal Justice Act 1991, and—

(a) the charge, or charges, are dismissed and the assisted person is discharged; or

(b) the charge, or charges, of an offence triable only on indictment are dismissed and the case is remitted to the magistrates' court in accordance with paragraph 10(3)(a) of Schedule 3 to the Crime and Disorder Act 1998,

in respect of the first day of the hearing of the application to dismiss, the advocate instructed in the proceedings must be paid a graduated fee calculated in accordance with paragraph 6, as appropriate for representing an assisted person in a guilty plea.

(7) Where an advocate represents more than one assisted person in proceedings referred to in sub-paragraph (1), the advocate must be paid a fixed fee of 20 percent of—

(a) the fee specified in sub-paragraph (2) where that sub-paragraph applies; or

(b) the Basic fee (B) specified in the Table following paragraph 7 where sub-paragraph (3), (4) or (5) applies, as appropriate for the circumstances set out in the relevant sub-paragraph, in respect of each additional assisted person he represents.

Noting brief fees

The fee payable to an advocate retained solely for the purpose of making a note of any hearing must be the daily fee set out in the table below

Fixed Fees in force from 27 April 2010 to 1 April 2011				
Category of work	*Paragraph providing for fee*	*Fee for QC(£)*	*Fee for leading junior (£)*	*Fee for led junior or junior alone (£)*
Standard appearance	9(2)	191 per day	143 per day	96 per day
Paper plea and case management hearing	9(3)	29 per case	29 per case	29 per case
Abuse of process hearing	10(1)(a)	287 Half day	215 Half day	143 Half day
		549 Full day	382 Full day	263 Full day
Hearings relating to disclosure	10(1)(b) and (c)	287 Half day	215 Half day	143 Half day
		549 Full day	382 Full day	263 Full day
Hearings relating to the admissibility of evidence	10(1)(d)	287 Half day	215 Half day	143 Half day
		549 Full day	382 Full day	263 Full day
Hearings on withdrawal of guilty plea	10(1)(e)	287 Half day	215 Half day	143 Half day
		549 Full day	382 Full day	263 Full day
Deferred sentencing hearing	12(1)(a)	358 per day	263 per day	191 per day
Sentencing hearing	12(1)(b)	287 per day	191 per day	119 per day
Ineffective trial payment	13	310 per day	215 per day	143 per day
Special preparation	14	81 per hour	62 per hour	43 per hour
Wasted preparation	15	81 per hour	62 per hour	43 per hour
Conferences and views	16	81 per hour	62 per hour	43 per hour
Appeals to the Crown Court against conviction	17(1)	287 per day	215 per day	143 per day
Appeals to the Crown Court against sentence	17(1)	239 per day	167 per day	119 per day
Proceedings relating to breach of an order of the Crown Court	17(1)	239 per day	167 per day	119 per day
Committal for sentence	17(1)	287 per day	215 per day	143 per day

Adjourned appeals, committals for sentence and breach hearings	17(2)	191 per day	143 per day	96 per day
Bail applications, mentions and other applications in appeals, committals for sentence and breach hearings	17(3)	191 per day	143 per day	96 per day
Second and subsequent days of an application to dismiss	18(6)	287 Half day	215 Half day	143 Half day
		549 Full day	382 Full day	263 Full day
Noting brief	19	—	—	119 per day

Fixed Fees in force from 1 April 2011 to 1 April 2012				
Category of work	*Paragraph providing for fee*	*Fee for QC(£)*	*Fee for leading junior (£)*	*Fee for led junior or junior alone (£)*
Standard appearance	9(2)	182 per day	137 per day	91 per day
Paper plea and case management hearing	9(3)	27 per case	27 per case	27 per case
Abuse of process hearing	10(1)(a)	273 Half day	205 Half day	137 Half day
		523 Full day	364 Full day	250 Full day
Hearings relating to disclosure	10(1)(b) and (c)	273 Half day	205 Half day	137 Half day
		523 Full day	364 Full day	250 Full day
Hearings relating to the admissibility of evidence	10(1)(d)	273 Half day	205 Half day	137 Half day
		523 Full day	364 Full day	250 Full day
Hearings on withdrawal of guilty plea	10(1)(e)	273 Half day	205 Half day	137 Half day
		523 Full day	364 Full day	250 Full day
Deferred sentencing hearing	12(1)(a)	341 per day	250 per day	182 per day
Sentencing hearing	12(1)(b)	273 per day	182 per day	114 per day
Ineffective trial payment	13	296 per day	205 per day	137 per day
Special preparation	14	77 per hour	59 per hour	41 per hour
Wasted preparation	15	77 per hour	59 per hour	41 per hour
Conferences and views	16	77 per hour	59 per hour	41 per hour
Appeals to the Crown Court against conviction	17(1)	273 per day	205 per day	137 per day
Appeals to the Crown Court against sentence	17(1)	228 per day	159 per day	114 per day
Proceedings relating to breach of an order of the Crown Court	17(1)	228 per day	159 per day	114 per day
Committal for sentence	17(1)	273 per day	205 per day	137 per day
Adjourned appeals, committals for sentence and breach hearings	17(2)	182 per day	137 per day	91 per day
Bail applications, mentions and other applications in appeals, committals for sentence and breach hearings	17(3)	182 per day	137 per day	91 per day
Second and subsequent days of an application to dismiss	18(6)	273 Half day	205 Half day	137 Half day
		523 Full day	364 Full day	250 Full day
Noting brief	19	—	—	114 per day

Fixed Fees in force from 1 April 2011 to 1 April 2012				
Category of work	*Paragraph providing for fee*	*Fee for QC(£)*	*Fee for leading junior (£)*	*Fee for led junior or junior alone (£)*
Standard appearance	9(2)	182 per day	137 per day	91 per day
Paper plea and case management hearing	9(3)	27 per case	27 per case	27 per case
Abuse of process hearing	10(1)(a)	273 Half day	205 Half day	137 Half day
		523 Full day	364 Full day	250 Full day
Hearings relating to disclosure	10(1)(b) and (c)	273 Half day	205 Half day	137 Half day
		523 Full day	364 Full day	250 Full day
Hearings relating to the admissibility of evidence	10(1)(d)	273 Half day	205 Half day	137 Half day
		523 Full day	364 Full day	250 Full day
Hearings on withdrawal of guilty plea	10(1)(e)	273 Half day	205 Half day	137 Half day
		523 Full day	364 Full day	250 Full day
Deferred sentencing hearing	12(1)(a)	341 per day	250 per day	182 per day
Sentencing hearing	12(1)(b)	273 per day	182 per day	114 per day
Ineffective trial payment	13	296 per day	205 per day	137 per day
Special preparation	14	77 per hour	59 per hour	41 per hour
Wasted preparation	15	77 per hour	59 per hour	41 per hour
Conferences and views	16	77 per hour	59 per hour	41 per hour
Appeals to the Crown Court against conviction	17(1)	273 per day	205 per day	137 per day
Appeals to the Crown Court against sentence	17(1)	228 per day	159 per day	114 per day
Proceedings relating to breach of an order of the Crown Court	17(1)	228 per day	159 per day	114 per day
Committal for sentence	17(1)	273 per day	205 per day	137 per day
Adjourned appeals, committals for sentence and breach hearings	17(2)	182 per day	137 per day	91 per day
Bail applications, mentions and other applications in appeals, committals for sentence and breach hearings	17(3)	182 per day	137 per day	91 per day
Second and subsequent days of an application to dismiss	18(6)	273 Half day	205 Half day	137 Half day
		523 Full day	364 Full day	250 Full day
Noting brief	19	—	—	114 per day

Trials lasting over 40 days

Where a trial exceeds 40 days, the trial advocate must be paid a fee as set out in the Table below, as appropriate to the category of trial advocate and the class of offence, for each day by which the trial exceeds 40 days on which the trial advocate attends at court.

Daily rates payable where a trial lasts over 40 days

Daily rates payable where a trial lasts over 40 days in force from 27 April 2010 to 1 April 2011					
Class of Offence	*Daily rate payable for days 41–50 (£)*	*Daily rate payable for days 51 and over (£)*	*Class of Offence*	*Daily rate payable for days 41–50 (£)*	*Daily rate payable for days 51 and over (£)*
QC			**Led Junior**		
A	606	649	A	347	371
B	427	457	B	244	262
C	427	457	C	244	262
D	427	457	D	244	262
E	427	457	E	244	262
F	427	457	F	244	262
G	427	457	G	244	262
H	427	457	H	244	262
I	427	457	I	244	262
J	427	457	J	244	262
K	427	457	K	244	262
Leading Junior			**Junior Acting Alone**		
A	520	557	A	415	446
B	366	393	B	273	292
C	366	393	C	273	292
D	366	393	D	293	314
E	366	393	E	248	266
F	366	393	F	248	266
G	366	393	G	293	314
H	366	393	H	273	292
I	366	393	I	273	292
J	366	393	J	293	314
K	366	393	K	293	314

Daily rates payable where a trial lasts over 40 days in force from 1 April 2011 to 1 April 2012					
Class of Offence	*Daily rate payable for days 41–50 (£)*	*Daily rate payable for days 51 and over (£)*	*Class of Offence*	*Daily rate payable for days 41–50 (£)*	*Daily rate payable for days 51 and over (£)*
QC			**Led Junior**		
A	578	619	A	330	354
B	407	436	B	233	249
C	407	436	C	233	249
D	407	436	D	233	249
E	407	436	E	233	249
F	407	436	F	233	249
G	407	436	G	233	249
H	407	436	H	233	249
I	407	436	I	233	249
J	407	436	J	233	249
K	407	436	K	233	249
Leading Junior			**Junior Acting Alone**		
A	495	531	A	396	425
B	349	374	B	260	278
C	349	374	C	260	278
D	349	374	D	279	299
E	349	374	E	237	254
F	349	374	F	237	254
G	349	374	G	279	299
H	349	374	H	260	278
I	349	374	I	260	278
J	349	374	J	279	299
K	349	374	K	279	299

Litigators' Fees in the Crown Court

Graduated Fees for Guilty Pleas, Cracked Trials and Trials

(1) For the purposes of this Part, the Pages of Prosecution Evidence (PPE) Cut-off figures in a cracked trial or guilty plea are specified in the table below as appropriate to the offence with which the assisted person is charged.

PPE Cut-off figures in cracked trials and guilty pleas

	Class of offence										
Type of case	A	B	C	D	E	F	G	H	I	J	K
Cracked trial or guilty plea	150	70	40	80	40	50	120	40	40	80	120

(2) For the purposes of this Part, the PPE Cut-off figures in a trial are specified in the table following this sub-paragraph, as appropriate to the offence for which the assisted person is tried, and the length of trial.

PPE Cut-off figures in trials

Trial length in days	PPE Cut off A	*PPE Cut off B*	PPE Cut off C	*PPE Cut off D*	PPE Cut off E	*PPE Cut off F*	PPE Cut off G	*PPE Cut off H*	PPE Cut off I	*PPE Cut off J*	PPE Cut off K
1	150	70	40	80	40	50	120	40	40	80	120
2	150	70	40	80	40	50	120	40	40	80	120
3	246	105	81	95	120	138	186	122	134	95	186
4	341	139	120	126	158	173	252	157	185	126	252
5	431	170	157	156	195	206	314	191	232	156	314
6	523	203	193	186	229	240	372	225	281	186	372
7	615	238	230	218	265	276	433	260	329	218	433
8	716	274	267	257	301	310	495	301	376	257	495
9	807	306	301	293	333	342	550	338	420	293	550
10	898	338	339	330	365	373	606	374	464	330	606
11	991	370	378	367	399	405	663	412	509	367	663
12	1,084	402	417	404	433	437	721	449	554	404	721
13	1,184	434	455	440	467	470	779	486	598	440	779
14	1,286	465	493	477	500	501	836	523	642	477	836
15	1,389	497	531	514	532	533	894	559	686	514	894
16	1,491	535	569	551	565	564	951	596	730	551	951
17	1,594	573	607	587	598	596	1,007	637	774	587	1,007
18	1,696	611	646	624	646	627	1,063	687	818	624	1,063
19	1,798	649	684	661	696	659	1,119	736	862	661	1,119
20	1,901	687	722	697	746	690	1,174	786	907	697	1,174
21	2,017	722	753	742	787	720	1,230	826	943	742	1,230
22	2,132	757	785	786	828	752	1,286	867	980	786	1,286
23	2,247	792	819	830	868	784	1,341	908	1,017	830	1,341
24	2,362	826	857	874	908	816	1,396	948	1,053	874	1,396
25	2,477	860	894	917	948	848	1,451	988	1,088	917	1,451
26	2,593	895	931	961	988	880	1,505	1,028	1,124	961	1,505
27	2,708	935	967	1,005	1,802	912	1,560	1,068	1,160	1,005	1,560
28	2,823	975	1,004	1,049	1,068	944	1,615	1,107	1,196	1,049	1,615
29	2,938	1,601	1,041	1,099	1,108	976	1,670	1,147	1,231	1,099	1,670
30	3,053	1,705	1,077	1,150	1,148	1,700	1,725	1,187	1,267	1,150	1,725
31	3,168	1,809	1,114	1,200	1,188	1,903	1,780	1,226	1,303	1,200	1,780
32	3,284	1,813	1,151	1,251	1,228	1,007	1,835	1,266	1,349	1,251	1,835
33	3,399	1,917	1,187	1,301	1,268	1,210	1,889	1,307	1,394	1,301	1,889
34	3,514	1,022	1,224	1,352	1,308	1,313	1,944	1,357	1,439	1,352	1,944
35	3,629	1,126	1,262	1,402	1,347	1,516	1,999	1,407	1,485	1,402	1,999
36	3,744	1,230	1,303	1,453	1,435	1,619	2,054	1,457	1,530	1,453	2,054
37	3,859	1,834	1,345	1,503	1,526	1,822	2,109	1,507	1,575	1,503	2,109
38	3,975	1,539	1,386	1,554	1,617	1,925	2,164	1,557	1,621	1,554	2,164
39	4,090	1,144	1,428	1,604	1,708	1,129	2,219	1,607	1,666	1,604	2,219
40	4,178	1,448	1,444	1,652	1,745	1,431	2,271	1,629	1,704	1,652	2,271

Trial length in days	PPE Cut off A	*PPE Cut off B*	PPE Cut off C	*PPE Cut off D*	PPE Cut off E	*PPE Cut off F*	PPE Cut off G	*PPE Cut off H*	PPE Cut off I	*PPE Cut off J*	PPE Cut off K
41	4,266	1,752	1,461	1,700	1,782	1,833	2,324	1,651	1,742	1,700	2,324
42	4,355	1,057	1,477	1,748	1,820	1,136	2,377	1,673	1,780	1,748	2,377
43	4,443	1,361	1,494	1,796	1,857	1,438	2,430	1,695	1,818	1,796	2,430
44	4,532	1,665	1,511	1,844	1,895	1,041	2,483	1,716	1,856	1,844	2,483
45	4,621	1,969	1,527	1,892	1,932	1,044	2,536	1,738	1,894	1,892	2,536
46	4,709	1,274	1,544	1,939	1,970	1,047	2,589	1,760	1,932	1,939	2,589
47	4,798	1,578	1,560	1,987	2,007	1,150	2,642	1,782	1,970	1,987	2,642
48	4,887	1,882	1,577	2,039	2,045	1,153	2,695	1,804	2,008	2,039	2,695
49	4,975	1,187	1,594	2,091	2,082	1,156	2,749	1,826	2,046	2,091	2,749
50	5,064	1,491	1,610	2,144	2,120	1,159	2,802	1,848	2,084	2,144	2,802
51	5,153	1,795	1,627	2,196	2,158	1,262	2,855	1,870	2,122	2,196	2,855
52	5,242	2,000	1,644	2,249	2,195	1,265	2,908	1,892	2,160	2,249	2,908
53	5,330	2,043	1,066	2,130	2,233	1,268	2,962	1,914	2,198	2,301	2,962
54	5,419	2,086	1,677	2,354	2,271	1,271	3,015	1,936	2,236	2,354	3,015
55	5,508	2,129	1,694	2,406	2,308	1,374	3,068	1,958	2,275	2,406	3,068
56	5,597	2,172	1,710	2,459	2,346	1,773	3,112	1,980	2,313	2,459	3,121
57	5,686	2,215	1,772	2,512	2,384	1,380	3,175	2,002	2,351	2,512	3,175
58	5,775	2,258	1,744	2,564	2,422	1,833	3,228	2,024	2,389	2,564	3,228
59	5,863	2,301	1,760	2,617	2,459	1,864	3,281	2,046	2,427	2,617	3,281
60	5,952	2,345	1,777	2,669	2,497	1,894	3,335	2,068	2,465	2,669	3,335
61	6,041	2,388	1,794	2,722	2,535	1,924	3,388	2,090	2,503	2,722	3,388
62	6,130	2,431	1,811	2,775	2,572	1,959	3,442	2,112	2,542	2,775	3,442
63	6,219	2,474	1,827	2,827	2,610	2,020	3,495	2,134	2,580	2,827	3,495
64	6,308	2,517	1,844	2,880	2,648	2,081	3,549	2,156	2,618	2,880	3,549
65	6,397	2,561	1,861	2,933	2,686	2,141	3,602	2,178	2,656	2,933	3,602
66	6,486	2,604	1,877	2,985	2,723	2,202	3,656	2,200	2,694	2,985	3,656
67	6,575	2,647	1,894	3,038	2,761	2,263	3,709	2,222	2,776	3,038	3,709
68	6,664	2,690	1,911	3,091	2,799	2,323	3,763	2,244	2,865	3,091	3,763
69	6,754	2,734	1,927	3,144	2,836	2,384	3,816	2,266	2,954	3,144	3,816
70	6,843	2,777	1,944	3,196	2,874	2,445	3,870	2,288	3,043	3,196	3,870
71	6,932	2,820	1,961	3,249	2,912	2,506	3,923	2,310	3,132	3,249	3,923
72	7,021	2,864	1,978	3,302	2,950	2,566	3,977	2,332	3,221	3,302	3,977
73	7,110	2,907	1,994	3,355	2,987	2,627	4,031	2,354	3,310	3,355	4,031
74	7,199	2,950	2,016	3,407	3,025	2,688	4,084	2,376	3,399	3,407	4,084
75	7,289	2,994	2,040	3,460	3,063	2,749	4,138	2,398	3,488	3,460	4,138
76	7,378	3,037	2,064	3,513	3,101	2,809	4,192	2,420	3,577	3,513	4,192
77	7,467	3,080	2,089	3,566	3,138	2,870	4,245	2,442	3,666	3,566	4,245
78	7,556	3,124	2,113	3,619	3,176	2,931	4,299	2,464	3,755	3,619	4,299
79	7,646	3,167	2,137	3,672	3,214	2,992	4,353	2,486	3,844	3,672	4,353
80	7,735	3,211	2,161	3,724	3,251	3,052	4,406	2,508	3,933	3,724	4,406

Trial length in days	PPE Cut off A	*PPE Cut off B*	PPE Cut off C	*PPE Cut off D*	PPE Cut off E	*PPE Cut off F*	PPE Cut off G	*PPE Cut off H*	PPE Cut off I	*PPE Cut off J*	PPE Cut off K
81	7,824	3,254	2,185	3,777	3,289	3,113	4,460	2,530	4,023	3,777	4,460
82	7,914	3,297	2,210	3,830	3,327	3,174	4,514	2,552	4,112	3,830	4,514
83	8,003	3,341	2,234	3,883	3,365	3,235	4,568	2,575	4,201	3,883	4,568
84	8,093	3,384	2,258	3,936	3,402	3,295	4,622	2,597	4,290	3,936	4,622
85	8,182	3,428	2,228	3,989	3,044	3,356	4,675	2,961	4,379	3,989	4,675
86	8,271	3,471	2,307	4,042	3,478	3,417	4,729	2,641	4,469	4,042	4,729
87	8,361	3,515	2,331	4,095	3,516	3,478	4,783	2,663	4,558	4,095	4,783
88	8,450	3,558	2,355	4,148	3,553	3,539	4,837	2,685	4,647	4,148	4,837
89	8,540	3,602	2,379	4,201	3,591	3,599	4,891	2,707	4,737	4,201	4,891
90	8,629	3,645	2,404	4,254	3,629	3,660	4,945	2,729	4,826	4,254	4,945
91	8,719	3,689	2,428	4,307	3,666	3,721	4,999	2,751	4,915	4,307	4,999
92	8,809	3,733	2,452	4,360	3,704	3,782	5,053	2,774	5,005	4,360	5,053
93	8,898	3,776	2,477	4,413	3,742	3,843	5,107	2,796	5,094	4,413	5,107
94	8,988	3,820	2,501	4,466	3,780	3,903	5,161	2,818	5,183	4,466	5,161
95	9,077	3,863	2,525	4,519	3,817	3,964	5,215	2,840	5,273	4,519	5,215
96	9,167	3,907	2,549	4,572	3,855	4,025	5,269	2,862	5,362	4,572	5,269
97	9,257	3,951	2,574	4,625	3,893	4,086	5,323	2,884	5,452	4,625	5,323
98	9,346	3,994	2,598	4,679	3,930	4,147	5,377	2,906	5,541	4,679	5,377
99	9,436	4,038	2,622	4,732	3,968	4,207	5,431	2,929	5,631	4,732	5,431
100	9,526	4,082	2,647	4,785	4,006	4,268	5,485	2,951	5,720	4,785	5,485
101	9,616	4,125	2,671	4,838	4,044	4,329	5,539	2,973	5,810	4,838	5,539
102	9,705	4,169	2,695	4,891	4,081	4,390	5,593	2,995	5,899	4,891	5,593
103	9,795	4,213	2,720	4,944	4,119	4,451	5,647	3,032	5,989	4,944	5,647
104	9,885	4,257	2,744	4,997	4,157	4,512	5,702	3,073	6,079	4,997	5,702
105	9,975	4,300	2,768	5,051	4,195	4,573	5,756	3,114	6,168	5,051	5,756
106	10,506	4,344	2,793	5,104	4,232	4,633	5,810	3,155	6,258	5,104	5,810
107	10,515	4,838	2,817	5,157	4,270	4,694	5,864	3,196	6,348	5,157	5,864
108	10,524	4,432	2,841	5,210	4,308	4,755	5,918	3,237	6,437	5,210	5,918
109	10,334	4,475	2,866	5,264	4,345	4,816	5,973	3,278	6,527	5,264	5,973
110	10,424	4,519	2,890	5,317	4,383	4,877	6,027	3,319	6,617	5,317	6,027
111	10,514	4,563	2,914	5,370	4,421	4,938	6,081	3,361	6,706	5,370	6,081
112	10,604	4,607	2,939	5,423	4,459	4,999	6,135	3,402	6,796	5,423	6,135
113	10,694	4,650	2,963	5,477	4,496	5,059	6,189	3,443	6,886	5,477	6,189
114	10,784	4,694	2,987	5,530	4,534	5,120	6,244	3,484	6,976	5,530	6,244
115	10,874	4,738	3,012	5,583	4,572	5,181	6,298	3,525	7,066	5,583	6,298
116	10,964	4,782	3,036	5,637	4,610	5,242	6,352	3,566	7,155	5,637	6,352
117	11,054	4,826	3,060	5,690	4,647	5,303	6,406	3,607	7,245	5,690	6,406
118	11,145	4,869	3,085	5,743	4,685	5,364	6,460	3,648	7,335	5,743	6,460
119	11,235	4,913	3,109	5,797	4,723	5,425	6,514	3,689	7,425	5,797	6,514
120	11,325	4,957	3,133	5,850	4,760	5,486	6,569	3,730	7,515	5,850	6,569

Trial length in days	PPE Cut off A	*PPE Cut off B*	PPE Cut off C	*PPE Cut off D*	PPE Cut off E	*PPE Cut off F*	PPE Cut off G	*PPE Cut off H*	PPE Cut off I	*PPE Cut off J*	PPE Cut off K
121	11,415	5,001	3,158	5,904	4,798	5,527	6,623	3,771	7,605	5,904	6,623
122	11,504	5,044	3,182	5,956	4,836	5,607	6,677	3,812	7,693	5,956	6,677
123	11,593	5,088	3,206	6,009	4,874	5,668	6,731	3,853	7,782	6,009	6,731
124	11,681	5,131	3,230	6,061	4,911	5,729	6,785	3,895	7,871	6,061	6,785
125	11,770	5,175	3,254	6,114	4,949	5,789	6,839	3,936	7,959	6,114	6,839
126	11,859	5,218	3,278	6,167	4,987	5,850	6,892	3,977	8,048	6,167	6,892
127	11,948	5,261	3,302	6,219	5,025	5,911	6,945	4,017	8,137	6,219	6,945
128	12,037	5,304	3,326	6,272	5,062	5,971	6,999	4,058	8,225	6,272	6,999
129	12,125	5,347	3,350	6,324	5,100	6,032	7,052	4,098	8,314	6,324	7,052
130	12,214	5,390	3,374	6,377	5,138	6,093	7,106	4,139	8,403	6,377	7,106
131	12,303	5,433	3,398	6,430	5,175	6,153	7,159	4,179	8,491	6,430	7,159
132	12,392	5,476	3,422	6,482	5,213	6,214	7,212	4,219	8,580	6,482	7,212
133	12,481	5,520	3,446	6,535	5,251	6,274	7,266	4,260	8,669	6,535	7,266
134	12,570	5,563	3,470	6,588	5,289	6,335	7,319	4,300	8,757	6,588	7,319
135	12,658	5,606	3,494	6,640	5,326	6,396	7,373	4,341	8,846	6,640	7,373
136	12,747	5,649	3,518	6,693	5,364	6,456	7,426	4,381	8,935	6,693	7,426
137	12,836	5,692	3,542	6,745	5,402	6,517	7,479	4,422	9,023	6,745	7,479
138	12,925	5,735	3,566	6,798	5,439	6,578	7,533	4,462	9,112	6,798	7,533
139	13,014	5,778	3,590	6,851	5,477	6,638	7,586	4,503	9,201	6,851	7,586
140	13,102	5,821	3,614	6,903	5,515	6,699	7,639	4,543	9,289	6,903	7,639
141	13,191	5,864	3,638	6,956	5,553	6,760	7,693	4,584	9,378	6,956	7,693
142	13,280	5,908	3,662	7,008	5,590	6,820	7,746	4,624	9,467	7,008	7,746
143	13,369	5,951	3,686	7,061	5,628	6,881	7,800	4,664	9,555	7,061	7,800
144	13,458	5,994	3,709	7,114	5,666	6,942	7,853	4,705	9,644	7,114	7,853
145	13,546	6,037	3,733	7,166	5,704	7,002	7,906	4,745	9,733	7,166	7,906
146	13,635	6,080	3,757	7,219	5,741	7,063	7,960	4,786	9,821	7,219	7,960
147	13,724	6,123	3,781	7,272	5,779	7,124	8,013	4,826	9,910	7,272	8,013
148	13,813	6,166	3,805	7,324	5,817	7,184	8,067	4,867	9,999	7,324	8,067
149	13,902	6,209	3,829	7,377	5,854	7,245	8,120	4,907	10,087	7,377	8,120
150	13,990	6,252	3,853	7,429	5,892	7,305	8,173	4,948	10,176	7,429	8,173
151	14,079	6,296	3,877	7,482	5,930	7,366	8,227	4,988	10,265	7,482	8,227
152	14,168	6,339	3,901	7,535	5,968	7,427	8,280	5,029	10,353	7,535	8,280
153	14,257	6,382	3,925	7,587	6,005	7,487	8,333	5,069	10,442	7,587	8,333
154	14,346	6,425	3,949	7,640	6,043	7,548	8,387	5,110	10,531	7,640	8,387
155	14,435	6,468	3,973	7,692	6,081	7,609	8,440	5,150	10,619	7,692	8,440
156	14,523	6,511	3,997	7,745	6,119	7,669	8,494	5,190	10,708	7,745	8,494
157	14,612	6,554	4,021	7,798	6,156	7,730	8,547	5,231	10,797	7,798	8,547
158	14,701	6,597	4,045	7,850	6,194	7,791	8,600	5,271	10,885	7,850	8,600
159	14,790	6,641	4,069	7,903	6,232	7,851	8,654	5,312	10,974	7,903	8,654
160	14,879	6,684	4,093	7,956	6,269	7,912	8,707	5,352	11,063	7,956	8,707

Trial length in days	PPE Cut off A	*PPE Cut off B*	PPE Cut off C	*PPE Cut off D*	PPE Cut off E	*PPE Cut off F*	PPE Cut off G	*PPE Cut off H*	PPE Cut off I	*PPE Cut off J*	PPE Cut off K
161	14,967	6,727	4,117	8,008	6,307	7,973	8,760	5,393	11,151	8,008	8,760
162	15,056	6,770	4,141	8,061	6,345	8,033	8,814	5,433	11,240	8,061	8,814
163	15,145	6,813	4,165	8,113	6,383	8,094	8,867	5,474	11,329	8,113	8,867
164	15,234	6,856	4,189	8,166	6,420	8,155	8,921	5,514	11,417	8,166	8,921
165	15,323	6,899	4,213	8,219	6,458	8,215	8,974	5,555	11,506	8,219	8,974
166	15,411	6,942	4,237	8,271	6,496	8,276	9,027	5,595	11,595	8,271	9,027
167	15,500	6,985	4,261	8,324	6,534	8,337	9,081	5,636	11,683	8,324	9,081
168	15,589	7,029	4,285	8,376	6,571	8,397	9,134	5,676	11,772	8,376	9,134
169	15,678	7,072	4,309	8,429	6,609	8,458	9,188	5,716	11,861	8,429	9,188
170	15,767	7,115	4,333	8,482	6,647	8,518	9,241	5,757	11,949	8,482	9,241
171	15,855	7,158	4,357	8,534	6,684	8,579	9,294	5,797	12,038	8,534	9,294
172	15,944	7,201	4,380	8,587	6,722	8,640	9,348	5,838	12,127	8,587	9,348
173	16,033	7,244	4,404	8,639	6,760	8,700	9,401	5,878	12,215	8,639	9,401
174	16,122	7,287	4,428	8,692	6,798	8,761	9,454	5,919	12,304	8,692	9,454
175	16,211	7,330	4,452	8,745	6,835	8,822	9,508	5,959	12,393	8,745	9,508
176	16,300	7,373	4,476	8,797	6,873	8,882	9,561	6,000	12,481	8,797	9,561
177	16,388	7,417	4,500	8,850	6,911	8,943	9,615	6,040	12,570	8,850	9,615
178	16,477	7,460	4,524	8,903	6,948	9,004	9,668	6,081	12,659	8,903	9,668
179	16,566	7,503	4,548	8,955	6,986	9,064	9,721	6,121	12,747	8,955	9,721
180	16,655	7,546	4,572	9,008	7,024	9,125	9,775	6,162	12,836	9,008	9,775
181	16,744	7,589	4,596	9,060	7,062	9,186	9,828	6,202	12,925	9,060	9,828
182	16,832	7,632	4,620	9,113	7,099	9,246	9,881	6,242	13,013	9,113	9,881
183	16,921	7,675	4,644	9,166	7,137	9,307	9,935	6,283	13,102	9,166	9,935
184	17,010	7,718	4,668	9,218	7,174	9,368	9,988	6,323	13,191	9,218	9,988
185	17,099	7,762	4,692	9,271	7,211	9,428	10,042	6,364	13,279	9,271	10,042
186	17,188	7,805	4,716	9,323	7,248	9,489	10,095	6,404	13,368	9,323	10,095
187	17,276	7,848	4,740	9,376	7,285	9,549	10,148	6,445	13,457	9,376	10,148
188	17,365	7,891	4,764	9,429	7,322	9,610	10,202	6,485	13,545	9,429	10,202
189	17,454	7,934	4,788	9,481	7,360	9,671	10,255	6,526	13,634	9,481	10,255
190	17,543	7,977	4,812	9,534	7,397	9,731	10,309	6,566	13,723	9,534	10,309
191	17,632	8,020	4,836	9,587	7,434	9,792	10,362	6,607	13,811	9,587	10,362
192	17,720	8,063	4,860	9,639	7,471	9,853	10,415	6,647	13,900	9,639	10,415
193	17,809	8,106	4,884	9,692	7,508	9,913	10,469	6,687	13,988	9,692	10,469
194	17,898	8,150	4,908	9,744	7,545	9,974	10,522	6,728	14,077	9,744	10,522
195	17,987	8,193	4,932	9,797	7,582	10,035	10,575	6,768	14,166	9,797	10,575
196	18,076	8,236	4,956	9,850	7,620	10,095	10,629	6,809	14,254	9,850	10,629
197	18,165	8,279	4,980	9,902	7,657	10,156	10,682	6,849	14,343	9,902	10,682
198	18,253	8,322	5,004	9,955	7,694	10,217	10,736	6,890	14,432	9,955	10,736
199	18,342	8,365	5,028	10,007	7,731	10,277	10,789	6,930	14,520	10,007	10,789
200	18,431	8,408	5,051	10,060	7,768	10,338	10,842	6,971	14,609	10,060	10,842

Cracked trial or guilty plea where the number of pages of prosecution evidence is less than or equal to the PPE Cut-off

(1) Where in a cracked trial or guilty plea the number of pages of prosecution evidence is less than or equal to the PPE Cut-off specified in the table following paragraph 4(1) as appropriate to the class of offence with which the assisted person is charged, the total fee payable to the litigator will be—

(a) the basic fee, calculated in accordance with the table following sub-paragraph (2) of this paragraph;

(b) the defendant uplift, if any, calculated in accordance with the table headed Uplifts; and

(c) the adjustment for transfers and retrials, if any, calculated in accordance with the paragraph headed "transfers and retrials"

(2) For the purposes of sub-paragraph (1), the basic fee appropriate to a cracked trial or a guilty plea is specified in the table following this sub-paragraph, in accordance with the type of case and Class of offence with which the assisted person is charged.

	Class of Offence										
Type of case	A	B	C	D	E	F	G	H	I	J	K
Cracked trial	2785.18	1036.20	766.89	1255.67	340.50	327.63	1074.22	346.31	370.66	1321.76	1130.76
Guilty plea	1907.11	609.44	485.38	708.34	202.41	214.59	667.17	209.28	191.34	745.63	702.29

Trial where the number of pages of prosecution evidence is less than or equal to the PPE Cut-off

(1) Where in a trial the number of pages of prosecution evidence is less than or equal to the PPE Cut-off specified in the table following paragraph 4(2) as appropriate to the offence for which the assisted person is tried and the length of trial, the total fee payable to the litigator will be—

(a) the basic fee, calculated in accordance with the table following sub-paragraph (2) of this paragraph;

(b) the length of trial proxy, if any, calculated in accordance with the table following sub-paragraph (3);

(c) the defendant uplift, if any, calculated in accordance with the table headed Uplifts; and

(d) the adjustment for transfers and retrials, if any, calculated in accordance with the paragraph headed transfers and retrials.

(2) For the purposes of sub-paragraph (1), the basic fee appropriate to a trial is specified in the table following this sub-paragraph, in accordance with the offence for which the assisted person is tried.

Basic Fees for trials (£)											
Type of case	*Class of Offence*										
	A	*B*	*C*	*D*	*E*	*F*	*G*	*H*	*I*	*J*	*K*
Trial	2785.18	1202.92	810.51	1527.89	386.54	391.89	1074.22	392.05	391.72	1608.31	1130.76

Cracked trials and guilty pleas where the number of pages of prosecution evidence exceeds the PPE Cut-off

(1) Where in a cracked trial or guilty plea the number of pages of prosecution evidence exceeds the PPE Cut-off specified in the tables following paragraph 4(1) as appropriate to the offence with which the assisted person is charged, the total fee payable to the litigator will be—

(a) the final fee, calculated in accordance with sub-paragraph (2) of this paragraph;

(b) the defendant uplift, if any, calculated in accordance with the table following paragraph 9; and

(c) the adjustment for transfers and retrials, if any, calculated in accordance with paragraph 10.

(2) For the purposes of sub-paragraph (1), the final fee payable to a litigator in a cracked trial or guilty plea will be calculated in accordance with the following formula—

F = I + (D x i)

(3) In the formula in sub-paragraph (2)—

F is the amount of the final fee;

I is the initial fee specified in the tables following this paragraph, as appropriate to the type of case, the offence with which the assisted person is charged and the number of pages of prosecution evidence;

D is the difference between—

(a) the number of pages of prosecution evidence in the case; and

(b) the lower number in the PPE range as specified in the tables following this paragraph, as appropriate to the type of case, the offence with which the assisted person is charged and the number of pages of prosecution evidence in the case;

i is the incremental fee per page of prosecution evidence specified in the tables following this paragraph, as appropriate to the type of case, the offence with which the assisted person is charged and the number of pages of prosecution evidence in the case.

Table of final fees in cracked trials

Class of Offence	PPE Range	Initial Fee (£)	Incremental fee per page of prosecution evidence (£)
A	0–149	2,785.18	0
A	150–249	2,785.18	16.5771
A	250–499	4,442.89	16.2953
A	500–999	8,516.71	8.9555
A	1000–2799	12,994.44	5.7143
A	2800–4599	23,280.20	5.7143
A	4600–6399	33,565.95	5.7143
A	6400–8199	43,851.70	5.7143
A	8200–9999	54,137.46	5.7143
A	10000	64,417.49	0
B	0–69	1,036.20	0
B	70–249	1,036.20	11.4339
B	250–999	3,094.31	5.3516
B	1000–2799	7,108.03	3.5644
B	2800–4599	13,524.03	3.5644
B	4600–6399	19,940.03	2.9971
B	6400–8199	25,334.77	2.9971
B	8200–9999	30,729.49	2.9971
B	10000	36,121.23	0
C	0–39	766.89	0
C	40–249	766.89	5.7329
C	250–999	1,970.80	3.2811
C	1000–2799	4,431.86	2.0898
C	2800–4599	8,193.57	2.0898
C	4600–6399	11,955.28	2.0898
C	6400–8199	15,716.99	2.0898
C	8200–9999	19,478.70	2.0898
C	10000	23,238.32	0
D	0–79	1,255.67	0
D	80–249	1,255.67	14.8109
D	250–999	3,773.52	8.9254
D	1000–2799	10,467.60	5.27
D	2800–4599	19,953.59	5.27
D	4600–6399	29,439.57	4.3244
D	6400–8199	37,223.44	4.3244
D	8200–9999	45,007.29	4.3244
D	10000	52,786.83	0
E	0–39	340.5	0
E	40–249	340.5	6.7242
E	250–999	1,752.59	2.1277
E	1000–2799	3,348.37	0.8919
E	2800–4599	4,953.80	0.8919
F	2800–4599	5,413.21	1.0182
F	4600–6399	7,245.94	1.0182
F	6400–8199	9,078.67	1.0182
F	8200–9999	10,911.40	1.0182
F	10000	12,743.11	0
G	0–119	1,074.22	0
G	120–249	1,074.22	9.0709
G	250–999	2,253.44	6.8647
G	1000–2799	7,401.94	6.053
G	2800–4599	18,297.33	6.053
G	4600–6399	29,192.73	5.2019
G	6400–8199	38,556.20	5.2019
G	8200–[9999]	47,919.68	5.2019
G	10000	57,277.96	0
H	0–39	346.31	0
H	40–249	346.31	6.2247
H	250–999	1,653.49	2.2728
H	1000–2799	3,358.10	1.0168
H	2800–4599	5,188.37	1.0168
H	4600–6399	7,018.63	1.0168
H	6400–8199	8,848.89	1.0168
H	8200–9999	10,679.16	1.0168
H	10000	12,508.40	0
I	0–39	370.66	0
I	40–249	370.66	8.6497
I	250–999	2,187.10	3.3804
I	1000–2799	4,722.43	1.3114
I	2800–4599	7,082.89	1.3114
I	4600–6399	9,443.34	1.3114
I	6400–8199	11,803.80	1.3114
I	8200–9999	14,164.26	1.3114
I	10000	16,523.40	0
J	0–79	1,321.76	0
J	80–249	1,321.76	15.6288
J	250–999	3,978.65	9.8095
J	1000–2799	11,335.74	5.7334
J	2800–4599	21,655.89	5.7334
J	4600–6399	31,976.05	4.5514
J	6400–8199	40,168.54	4.5514
J	8200–9999	48,361.04	4.5514
J	10000	56,548.99	0
K	0–119	1,130.76	0

Table of final fees in cracked trials (cont.)

Class of Offence	PPE Range	Initial Fee (£)	Incremental fee per page of prosecution evidence (£)	Class of Offence	PPE Range	Initial Fee (£)	Incremental fee per page of prosecution evidence (£)
E	4600–6399	6,559.23	0.8919	K	120–249	1,130.76	9.565
E	6400–8199	8,164.66	0.8919	K	250–999	2,374.21	7.3335
E	8200–9999	9,770.09	0.8919	K	1000–2799	7,874.30	6.4212
E	10000	11,374.63	0	K	2800–4599	19,432.39	6.4212
F	0–49	327.63	0	K	4600–6399	30,990.49	5.4755
F	50–249	327.63	6.4534	K	6400–8199	40,846.45	5.4755
F	250–999	1,618.30	2.6162	K	8200–9999	50,702.41	5.4755
F	1000–2799	3,580.48	1.0182	K	10000	60,552.89	0

Table of final fees in guilty pleas

Class of offence	PPE Range	Initial fee(£)	Incremental fee per page of prosecution evidence (£)	Class of offence	PPE Range	Initial fee(£)	Incremental fee per page of prosecution evidence (£)
A	0–149	1,907.11	0	F	4600–6399	3,207.59	0.3488
A	150–399	1,907.11	9.2742	F	6400–8199	3,835.38	0.3488
A	400–999	4,225.66	5.3634	F	8200–9999	4,463.17	0.3488
A	1000–2799	7,443.69	3.8	F	10000	5,090.61	0
A	2800–4599	14,283.77	3.8001	G	0–119	667.17	0
A	4600–6399	21,123.86	3.8001	G	120–399	667.17	4.7216
A	6400–8199	27,963.96	3.8001	G	400–999	1,989.23	3.0953
A	8200–9999	34,804.05	3.8001	G	1000–2799	3,846.43	2.7317
A	10000	41,640.34	0	G	2800–4599	8,763.51	2.7317
B	0–69	609.44	0	G	4600–6399	13,680.59	2.1643
B	70–399	609.44	4.9497	G	6400–8199	17,576.39	2.1643
B	400–999	2,242.84	2.4934	G	8200–9999	21,472.20	2.1643
B	1000–2799	3,738.90	1.5916	G	10000	25,365.84	0
B	2800–4599	6,603.75	1.5916	H	0–39	209.28	0
B	4600–6399	9,468.61	1.1661	H	40–399	209.28	3.0613
B	6400–8199	11,567.51	1.1661	H	400–999	1,311.33	1.0852
B	8200–9999	13,666.41	1.1661	H	1000–2799	1,962.46	0.3465
B	10000	15,764.14	0	H	2800–4599	2,586.14	0.3465
C	0–39	485.38	0	H	4600–6399	3,209.84	0.3465
C	40–399	485.38	2.9193	H	6400–8199	3,833.53	0.3465
C	400–999	1,536.31	1.5971	H	8200–9999	4,457.23	0.3465
C	1000–2799	2,494.54	0.8668	H	10000	5,080.55	0
C	2800–4599	4,054.72	0.8668	I	0–39	191.34	0
C	4600–6399	5,614.91	0.8668	I	40–399	191.34	3.4214
C	6400–8199	7,175.10	0.8668	I	400–999	1,423.04	1.4936
C	8200–9999	8,735.29	0.8668	I	1000–2799	2,319.22	0.5581
C	10000	10,294.60	0	I	2800–4599	3,323.86	0.5581
D	0–79	708.34	0	I	4600–6399	4,328.49	0.5581
D	80–399	708.34	5.7339	I	6400–8199	5,333.13	0.5581
D	400–999	2,543.19	3.0095	I	8200–9999	6,337.78	0.5581
D	1000–2799	4,348.90	1.8739	I	10000	7,341.86	0
D	2800–4599	7,721.86	1.8739	J	0–79	745.63	0
D	4600–6399	11,094.83	1.1647	J	80–399	745.63	6.1572
D	6400–8199	13,191.21	1.1646	J	400–999	2,715.93	3.2471
D	8200–9999	15,287.57	1.1647	J	1000–2799	4,664.21	2.0766
D	10000	17,382.78	0	J	2800–4599	8,402.07	2.0766

Table of final fees in guilty pleas (cont.)			
Class of offence	PPE Range	Initial fee(£)	Incremental fee per page of prosecution evidence (£)
E	0–39	202.41	0
E	40–399	202.41	3.2041
E	400–999	1,355.88	1.3732
E	1000–2799	2,179.80	0.5057
E	2800–4599	3,090.08	0.5057
E	4600–6399	4,000.36	0.5057
E	6400–8199	4,910.64	0.5057
E	8200–9999	5,820.92	0.5057
E	10000	6,730.69	0
F	0–49	214.59	0
F	50–399	214.59	3.1058
F	400–999	1,301.62	1.084
F	1000–2799	1,952.01	0.3488
F	2800–4599	2,579.80	0.3488
J	4600–6399	12,139.92	1.2255
J	6400–8199	14,345.86	1.2255
J	8200–9999	16,551.81	1.2255
J	1000o	18,756.53	0
K	0–119	702.29	0
K	120–399	702.29	5.7624
K	400–999	2,315.76	3.2075
K	1000–2799	4,240.26	2.9871
K	2800–4599	9,617.04	2.9871
K	4600–6399	14,993.82	2.2779
K	6400–8199	19,094.01	2.2779
K	8200–9999	23,194.20	2.2779
K	10000	27,292.10	0

Defendant uplifts

(1) The defendant uplift payable to a litigator will be calculated in accordance with the table following sub-paragraph (3).

(2) Only one defendant uplift will be payable in each case.

(3) In the table following this paragraph, the total fee means—

(a) in a cracked trial or guilty plea where the number of pages of prosecution evidence does not exceed the PPE Cut-off specified in the table following paragraph 4(1), the basic fee specified in the table headed "Cracked trial or guilty plea where the number of pages of prosecution evidence is less than or equal to the PPE Cut-off"

(b) in a trial where the number of pages of prosecution evidence does not exceed the PPE Cut-off specified in the table following paragraph 4(2), the basic fee specified in the table headed "Basic Fees for trial" plus the length of trial proxy specified in the table following paragraph 6(3);

(c) in a cracked trial or guilty plea where the number of pages of prosecution evidence exceeds the PPE Cut-off specified in the table following paragraph 4(1), the final fee, as calculated in accordance with paragraph 7(2); and

(d) in a trial where the number of pages of prosecution evidence exceeds the PPE Cut-off specified in the table following paragraph 4(2), the final fee, as calculated in accordance with paragraph 8(2).

Defendant uplifts	
Total number of defendants represented by litigator	Percentage uplift to total fee
2–4	20%
5+	30%

Retrials and Transfers

Where following a trial an order is made for a retrial and the same litigator acts for the assisted person at both trials that litigator will receive—

(a) in respect of the first trial, a fee calculated in accordance with the provisions of this Schedule; and

(b) in respect of the retrial, 25% of the fee, as appropriate to the circumstances and timing of the retrial, in accordance with the provisions of this Schedule.

Where—

(a) a case is transferred to a new litigator; or

(b) a retrial is ordered and a new litigator acts for the assisted person at the retrial;

the original litigator and the new litigator must receive a percentage of the total fee, in accordance with the table following sub-paragraph (6), as appropriate to the circumstances and timing of the retrial, transfer or withdrawal of the representation order.

In the table following this paragraph, the total fee means—

(a) in a cracked trial or guilty plea where the number of pages of prosecution evidence is less than or equal to the PPE Cut-off specified in the table following paragraph 4(1), the basic fee as set out in the table following paragraph 5(2);

(b) in a trial where the number of pages of prosecution evidence is less than or equal to the PPE Cut-off specified in the table following paragraph 4(2), the basic fee specified in the table following paragraph 6(2) plus the length of trial proxy specified in the table following paragraph 6(3);

(c) in a cracked trial or guilty plea where the number of pages of prosecution evidence exceeds the PPE Cut-off specified in the table following paragraph 4(1), the final fee, as calculated in accordance with paragraph 7(2); and

(d) in a trial where the number of pages of prosecution evidence exceeds the PPE Cut-off specified in the table following paragraph 4(2), the final fee, as calculated in accordance with paragraph 8(2).

Retrials and Transfers			
Scenario	*Percentage of the total fee*	*Case type used to determine total fee*	*Claim period*
Cracked trial before retrial, where there is no change of litigator	25%	Cracked trial	—
Retrial, where there is no change of litigator	25%	Trial	—
Up to and including plea and case management hearing transfer (original litigator)	25%	Cracked trial	—
Up to and including plea and case management hearing transfer – guilty plea (new litigator)	100%	Guilty plea	—
Up to and including plea and case management hearing transfer – cracked trial (new litigator)	100%	Cracked trial	—
Up to and including plea and case management hearing transfer – trial (new litigator)	100%	Trial	—
Before trial transfer (original litigator)	75%	Cracked trial	—
Before trial transfer – cracked trial (new litigator)	100%	Cracked trial	—
Before trial transfer – trial (new litigator)	100%	Trial	—
During trial transfer (original litigator)	100%	Trial	Claim up to and including the day before the transfer
During trial transfer (new litigator)	50%	Trial	Claim for the full trial length
[Transfer after trial and before sentencing hearing (original litigator)	100%	Trial	Claim for the full trial length, excluding the length of the sentencing hearing
Transfer after trial and before sentencing hearing (new litigator)	10%	Trial	Claim for one day, or for the length of the sentencing hearing if longer than one day
Transfer before retrial (original litigator)	25%	Cracked trial	—
Transfer before cracked retrial (new litigator)	50%	Cracked trial	—
Transfer before retrial (new litigator)	50%	Trial	Claim for the full retrial length
Transfer during … retrial (original litigator)	25%	Trial	Claim up to and including the day before the transfer

Transfer during … retrial (new litigator)	50%	Trial	Claim for the full retrial length
Transfer after retrial and before sentencing hearing (original litigator)	25%	Trial	Claim for the full retrial length, excluding the length of the sentencing hearing
Transfer after retrial and before sentencing hearing (new litigator)	10%	Trial	Claim for one day, or for the length of the sentencing hearing if longer than one day

Fees for appeals and committals for sentence hearings

The fee payable to a litigator instructed in—

(a) an appeal against conviction from a magistrates' court;

(b) an appeal against sentence from a magistrates' court;

(c) a sentencing hearing following a committal for sentence to the Crown Court.

is that set out in the table below.

Fees for hearing subsequent to sentence

(1) The fee payable to a litigator instructed in relation to a hearing under an enactment listed in sub-paragraph (2) is that set out in the table below.

(2) The enactments are—

(a) section 1CA of the Crime and Disorder Act 1998 (variation and discharge of orders under section 1C);

(b) section 155 of the Powers of Criminal Courts (Sentencing) Act 2000 (alteration of Crown Court sentence);

(c) section 74 of the Serious Organised Crime and Police Act 2005 (assistance by defendant: review of sentence).]

Fees for committal proceedings

The fee payable to a litigator for work done in relation to committal proceedings, including any hearing in the magistrates' court, is that set out in the table below.

Fees for contempt proceedings

This paragraph applies to proceedings referred to in section 12(2)(f) of the Act in the Crown Court.

Where, in proceedings to which this paragraph applies, the contempt is alleged to have been committed by a person other than a defendant in a case to which this Schedule applies, remuneration for litigators must be at the rate set out in the table below.

Where, in proceedings to which this paragraph applies, the contempt is alleged to have been committed by the defendant in a case to which this Schedule applies, all work undertaken by the litigator is included within—

(a) the fee payable under Part 2, or

(b) in proceedings under paragraph 12 or 14, the fixed fee set out in the table below

Fees for alleged breaches of a Crown Court order

This paragraph applies to proceedings in the Crown Court against one assisted person arising out of a single alleged breach of an order of the Crown Court.

The fee payable to the litigator in respect of the proceedings to which this paragraph applies is that set out in the table below.

Fixed Fees		
Type of proceedings	*Paragraph providing for fee*	*Fee payable (£ per proceedings)*
Appeal against sentence from a Magistrates' Court	12	170.21
Appeal against conviction from a Magistrates' Court	12	382.98
Committal for sentence	12	255.32
Hearing subsequent to sentence	12A	170.21
Committal proceedings	12B	318
Contempt proceedings (where contempt is alleged to have been committed by a person other than the defendant)	13(2)	127.66
Alleged breach of a Crown Court order	14(3)	85.11

Fixed Fees		
Type of proceedings	*Paragraph providing for fee*	*Fee payable (£ per proceedings)*
Appeal against sentence from a Magistrates' Court	12	127.66
Appeal against conviction from a Magistrates' Court	12	340.43
Committal for sentence	12	212.77
Contempt proceedings (where contempt is alleged to have been committed by a person other than the defendant)	13(2)	127.66
Alleged breach of a Crown Court order	14(3)	85.11

Fees for special preparation

(1) This paragraph applies in any case on indictment in the Crown Court—

(a) in respect of which a fee is payable under Part 2, where any or all of the prosecution evidence, as defined in paragraph 1(2), is served in electronic form only; or

(b) in respect of which a fee is payable under Part 2 (other than paragraph 6), where the number of pages of prosecution evidence, as so defined, exceeds 10,000, and the appropriate officer considers it reasonable to make a payment in excess of the fee payable under Part 2.

(2) Where this paragraph applies, a special preparation fee may be paid, in addition to the fee payable under Part 2.

(3) The amount of the special preparation fee must be calculated from the number of hours which the appropriate officer considers reasonable—

(a) where sub-paragraph (1)(a) applies, to view the prosecution evidence; and

(b) where sub-paragraph (1)(b) applies, to read the excess pages,

and in each case using the rates specified in the table below headed 2Prescribed fee rates"

(4) A litigator claiming a special preparation fee must supply such information and documents as may be required by the appropriate officer in support of the claim.

(5) In determining a claim under this paragraph, the appropriate officer must take into account all the relevant circumstances of the case.

Discontinuance or dismissal of sent or transferred proceedings

(1) This paragraph applies to proceedings which are—

(a) sent for trial to the Crown Court under section 51 of the Crime and Disorder Act 1998 (no committal proceedings for indictable-only offences); or

(b) transferred to the Crown Court under—

(i) section 4 of the Criminal Justice Act 1987 (transfer of serious fraud cases); or

(ii) section 53 of the Criminal Justice Act 1991 (transfer of certain cases involving children).

(2) Where proceedings to which this paragraph applies are discontinued by a notice served under section 23A of the Prosecution of Offences Act 1985 (discontinuance of proceedings after accused has been sent for trial) at any time before the prosecution serves its evidence in accordance with the Crime and Disorder Act 1998 (Service of Prosecution Evidence) Regulations 2005 the litigator must be paid 50 percent of the Basic fee for a guilty plea, as specified in the table above headed "Cracked trial or guilty plea where the number of pages of prosecution evidence is less than or equal to the PPE Cut-off", as appropriate to the offence for which the assisted person is charged.

(3) Where proceedings to which this paragraph applies are discontinued by a notice served under section 23A of the Prosecution of Offences Act 1985 (discontinuance of proceedings after accused has been sent for trial) at any time after the prosecution serves its evidence in accordance with the Crime and Disorder Act 1998 (Service of Prosecution Evidence) Regulations 2005, the litigator must be paid a fee calculated in accordance for representing an assisted person in a guilty plea.

(4) Where an application for dismissal is made under paragraph 2 of Schedule 3 to the Crime and Disorder Act 1988, section 6 of the Criminal Justice Act 1987 or paragraph 5 of Schedule 6 to the Criminal Justice Act 1991, and—

(a) the charge, or charges are dismissed and the assisted person is discharged; or

(b) the charge, or charges, of an offence triable only on indictment are dismissed and the case is remitted to the magistrates' court in accordance with paragraph 10(3)(a) of Schedule 3 to the Crime and Disorder Act 1998 (procedure where no indictable offence remains),

the litigator instructed in the proceedings must be paid a fee calculated in accordance with above headed "Cracked trial or guilty plea where the number of pages of prosecution evidence is less than or equal to the PPE Cut-off", as appropriate for representing an assisted person in a guilty plea.

(5) Sub-paragraph (6) applies to—

(a) a plea and case management hearing that takes place after the prosecution serves its evidence; and

(b) any other hearing that takes place before a plea and case management hearing has taken place, but after the prosecution has served its evidence.

(6) Where, at a hearing to which this paragraph applies—

(a) the prosecution offers no evidence and the assisted person is discharged; or

(b) the assisted person is charged on an indictment which includes no offence that is triable only on indictment, and the case is remitted to the magistrates' court in accordance with paragraph 10(3)(a) of Schedule 3 to the Crime and Disorder Act 1998,

the litigator must be paid a fee calculated in accordance with the table above headed "Cracked trial or guilty plea where the number of pages of prosecution evidence is less than or equal to the PPE Cut-off", as appropriate for representing an assisted person in a guilty plea.

Defendant uplifts

(1) Where a litigator represents more than one assisted person in proceedings referred to in paragraph 16(2), (3), (4) or (5), a defendant uplift will be payable.

(2) The defendant uplift will be calculated in accordance with the table following this paragraph.

(3) In the table following this paragraph, the total fee means—

(a) the fee specified in sub-paragraph (2) where that sub-paragraph applies; or

(b) the Basic fee (B) specified in the table, where paragraph 16(3), (4) or (5) applies, as appropriate for the circumstances set out in that sub-paragraph.

Defendant uplifts	
Total number of defendants represented by litigator	Percentage uplift to total fee
2–4	20%
5+	30%

Warrant for arrest

(1) This paragraph applies where—

(a) the assisted person fails to attend a hearing;

(b) at that hearing the court issues a warrant for the arrest of the assisted person, pursuant to section 7(1) of the Bail Act 1976 ("the warrant");

(c) the case does not proceed in the absence of the assisted person.

(2) Where in a case on indictment the warrant is not executed within three months of the date on which it was issued, the fee payable to the litigator is—

(a) where the warrant is issued at or before the plea and case management hearing, the fee payable for a guilty plea in accordance with the table above headed "Cracked trial or guilty plea where the number of pages of prosecution evidence is less than or equal to the PPE Cut-off",;

(b) where the warrant is issued after the plea and case management hearing but before the trial, the fee payable for a cracked trial in accordance with the table above headed "Cracked trial or guilty plea where the number of pages of prosecution evidence is less than or equal to the PPE Cut-off", as appropriate to the class of offence with which the assisted person is charged;

(c) where the warrant is issued during the trial, and the trial is aborted as a result, the fee payable for a trial as if the trial had ended on the day the warrant was issued.

(3) Where the warrant is issued during the course of proceedings referred to in paragraph 12 or 14 the fee payable to the litigator is the fee set out in the table below, as appropriate to the type of proceedings.

(4) Sub-paragraph (5) applies where—

(a) a fee has been paid, or is payable, to the litigator in accordance with sub-paragraph (2);

(b) the warrant is executed within 15 months of the date on which it was issued;

(c) the case proceeds after the warrant has been executed; and

(d) the litigator submits a claim for fees for the determination of his overall remuneration in the case, in accordance with article 6.

(5) Where this sub-paragraph applies—

(a) the appropriate officer must deduct the amount paid or payable in accordance with sub-paragraph (2) from the amount payable to the litigator on the final determination of fees in the case;

(b) if the fee paid or payable in accordance with sub-paragraph (2) is greater than the amount payable to the litigator on the final determination of fees in the case, the appropriate officer may recover the amount of the difference by way of repayment by the litigator.

Fees for abuse of process, disclosure, admissibility and withdrawal of plea hearings

(1) This paragraph applies to—

(a) the hearing of an application to stay the case on indictment or any count on the ground that the proceedings constitute an abuse of the process of the court;

(b) any hearing relating to the question of whether any material should be disclosed by the prosecution to the defence or the defence to the prosecution (whether or not any claim to public interest immunity is made);

(c) the hearing of an application under section 2(1) of the Criminal Procedure (Attendance of Witnesses) Act 1965 (issue of witness summons on application to Crown Court) for disclosure of material held by third parties;

(d) any hearing relating to the question of the admissibility as evidence of any material; and

(e) the hearing of an application to withdraw a plea of guilty where the application is—

(i) made by an advocate other than the advocate who appeared at the hearing at which the plea of guilty was entered; and

(ii) unsuccessful.

(2) Where a hearing to which this paragraph applies is held on any day of the main hearing of a case on indictment, no separate fee is payable in respect of attendance at the hearing, but the hearing is included in the length of the main hearing for the purpose of calculating the fees payable.

(3) Where a hearing to which this paragraph applies is held prior to the first or only day of the main hearing, it is not included in the length of the main hearing for the purpose of calculating the fees payable and the trial advocate or substitute advocate must be remunerated for attendance at such a hearing—

(a) in respect of any day where the hearing begins before and ends after the luncheon adjournment, at the daily rate set out in the Table headed Noting brief fees as appropriate to the category of trial advocate or substitute advocate; or

(b) in respect of any day where the hearing begins and ends before the luncheon adjournment, or begins after the luncheon adjournment, at the half-daily rate set out in the Table headed Noting brief fees as appropriate to the category of trial advocate or substitute advocate

For proceedings in the Crown Court the appropriate officer must allow fees for work done at the following prescribed rates—

Prescribed fee rates

Table 1			
Class of work	*Grade of fee earner*	*Rate*	*Variations*
Preparation	Senior solicitor	£53.00 per hour	£55.75 per hour for a fee earner whose office is situated within the London region of the Commission
	Solicitor, legal executive or fee earner of equivalent experience	£45.00 per hour	£47.25 per hour for a fee earner whose office is situated within the London region of the Commission
	Trainee or fee earner of equivalent experience	£29.75 per hour	£34.00 per hour for a fee earner whose office is situated within the London region of the Commission
Attendance at court where more than one representative instructed	Senior solicitor	£42.25 per hour	—
	Solicitor, legal executive or fee earner of equivalent experience	£34.00 per hour	—
	Trainee or fee earner of equivalent experience	£20.50 per hour	—
Travelling and waiting	Senior solicitor	£24.75 per hour	—
	Solicitor, legal executive or fee earner of equivalent experience	£24. 75 per hour	—
	Trainee or fee earner of equivalent experience	£12.50 per hour	—
Writing routine letters and dealing with routine telephone calls		£3.45 per item	£3.60 per item for a fee earner whose office is situated within the London region of the Commission

Very High Cost Cases

This paragraph applies where, in a Very High Cost Case (in relation to fees claimed by advocates), a litigator instructs an advocate who is not a member of a Very High Cost Case (Crime) Panel, in accordance with the Very High Cost Case contract.

The litigator may claim payment from the Commission in respect of work undertaken by the advocate and authorised in accordance with the Very High Cost Case contract.

Where such a claim is made, the Commission—

(a) must pay the litigator at rates no higher than the rates set out in the tables following this paragraph; and

(b) where it considers that there are exceptional circumstances, may pay the litigator such fees as it considers reasonable and has agreed in advance with the litigator in respect of—

(i) travelling (in excess of four hours in one day);

(ii) accommodation; and

(iii) subsistence, up to a maximum of £20 per day.

In the tables following this paragraph—

(a) a reference in the first table to a category is a reference to that category as defined in the Very High Cost Case contract;

(b) a reference in the first table to a level A or B solicitor-advocate is a reference to a level A or B solicitor-advocate as defined in the Very High Cost Case contract;

(c) a reference in the second table to a junior includes a solicitor-advocate.

Preparation (hourly rates)	*Category 1*	*Category 2*	*Category 3*	*Category 4*
	£	£	£	£
Counsel				
QC	152.50	119.00	95.50	95.50
Leading junior	133.00	104.50	83.50	83.50
Led junior	95.50	76.00	65.00	65.00
Junior alone	104.50	85.50	74.00	74.00
2nd led junior	67.00	53.00	46.00	46.00
Solicitor-advocate				
Leading level A	152.50	119.00	95.50	95.50
Led level A	133.00	104.50	83.50	83.50
Leading level B	133.00	104.50	83.50	83.50
Led level B	110.00	90.50	69.00	69.00
Level A alone	138.00	115.00	93.50	93.50
Level B alone	116.00	99.50	78.50	78.50
Second advocate	67.00	53.00	46.00	46.00

Advocacy	*Preliminary hearing*	*Half day*	*Full day*
	£	£	£
QC	119.00	250.00	500.00
Leading junior	90.50	205.25	410.25
Led junior	61.00	132.75	265.50
Junior alone	70.00	150.00	300.00
Second led junior	35.50	67.50	135.00
Noter	30.50	57.50	115.00

Travelling, waiting and mileage

£25 per hour for travelling (up to a maximum of four hours in one day) or waiting

£0.45 per mile for mileage

Litigators' Fees for Proceedings in the Court of Appeal

The appropriate officer may allow work done in the following classes by fee earners—

(a) preparation, including taking instructions, interviewing witnesses, ascertaining the prosecution case, advising on plea and mode of trial, preparing and perusing documents, dealing with letters and telephone calls which are not routine, preparing for advocacy, instructing an advocate and expert witnesses, conferences, consultations, views and work done in connection with advice on appeal;

(b) advocacy, including applications for bail and other applications to the court;

(c) attending at court where an advocate is assigned, including conferences with the advocate at court;

(d) travelling and waiting; and

(e) writing routine letters and dealing with routine telephone calls.

(2) The appropriate officer must consider the claim, any further information or documents submitted by the fee earner under paragraph 2 and any other relevant information and must allow—

(a) such work as appears to him to have been reasonably done under the representation order (including any representation or advice which is deemed to be work done under that order) by a fee earner, classifying such work according to the classes specified in sub-paragraph (1) as he considers appropriate; and

(b) such time in each class of work allowed by him (other than routine letters written and routine telephone calls) as he considers reasonable.

(3) The fees allowed in accordance with this Schedule are those appropriate to such of the following grades of litigator as the appropriate officer considers reasonable—

(a) senior solicitor;

(b) solicitor, legal executive or fee earner of equivalent experience; or

(c) trainee or fee earner of equivalent experience.

For proceedings in the Court of Appeal the appropriate officer must allow fees for work by litigators at the following prescribed rates—

Class of work	*Grade of fee earner*	*Rate*	*Variations*
Preparation	Senior solicitor	£53.00 per hour	£55.75 per hour for a litigator whose office is situated within the London region of the Commission
	Solicitor, legal executive or fee earner of equivalent experience	£45.00 per hour	£47.25 per hour for a litigator whose office is situated within the London region of the Commission
	Trainee or fee earner of equivalent experience	£29.75 per hour	£34.00 per hour for a litigator whose office is situated within the London region of the Commission
Advocacy	Senior solicitor	£64.00 per hour	
	Solicitor	£56.00 per hour	
Attendance at court where more than one representative assigned	Senior solicitor	£42.25 per hour	
	Solicitor, legal executive or fee earner of equivalent experience	£34.00 per hour	
	Trainee or fee earner of equivalent experience	£20.50 per hour	
Travelling and waiting	Senior solicitor	£24.75 per hour	
	Solicitor, legal executive or fee earner of equivalent experience	£24. 75 per hour	
	Trainee or fee earner of equivalent experience	£12.50 per hour	
Routine letters written and routine telephone calls		£3.45 per item	£3.60 per item for a fee earner whose office is situated within the London region of the Commission

In respect of any item of work, the appropriate officer may allow fees at less than the relevant prescribed rate specified in paragraph 7 where it appears to him reasonable to do so having regard to the competence and despatch with which the work was done.

Upon a determination of fees the appropriate officer may, subject to the provisions of this paragraph, allow fees at more than the relevant prescribed rate specified in paragraph 7 for preparation, advocacy, attendance at court where more than one representative is assigned, routine letters written and routine telephone calls, in respect of offences in Class A, B, C, D, G, I, J or K in the Table of Offences in Part 6 of Schedule 1.

The appropriate officer may allow fees at more than the prescribed rate where it appears to him, taking into account all the relevant circumstances of the case, that—

(a) the work was done with exceptional competence, skill or expertise;

(b) the work was done with exceptional despatch; or

(c) the case involved exceptional complexity or other exceptional circumstances.

Paragraph 3 of Schedule 1 applies to litigators in respect of proceedings in the Court of Appeal as it applies to advocates.

(4) Where the appropriate officer considers that any item or class of work should be allowed at more than the prescribed rate, he must apply to that item or class of work a percentage enhancement in accordance with the following provisions of this paragraph.

(5) In determining the percentage by which fees should be enhanced above the prescribed rate the appropriate officer may have regard to—

(a) the degree of responsibility accepted by the fee earner;

(b) the care, speed and economy with which the case was prepared; and

(c) the novelty, weight and complexity of the case.

(6) The percentage above the relevant prescribed rate by which fees for work may be enhanced must not exceed 100 per cent.

(7) The appropriate officer may have regard to the generality of proceedings to which this Order applies in determining what is exceptional within the meaning of this paragraph.

Advocates' fees for proceedings in the Court of Appeal

For proceedings in the Court of Appeal the appropriate officer must allow fees for work by advocates at the following prescribed rates However, after taking into account all the relevant circumstances of the case, if it appears that owing to the exceptional circumstances of the case the amount payable by way of fees in accordance with the Table would not provide reasonable remuneration for some or all of the work he has allowed, he may allow such amounts as appear to him to be reasonable remuneration for the relevant work.

Junior counsel					
Type of proceedings	*Basic fee*	*Full day refresher*	*Subsidiary fees*		
			Attendance at consultation, conferences and views	*Written work*	*Attendance at pre-trial reviews, applications and other appearances*
All appeals	Maximum amount: £545.00 per case	Maximum amount: £178.75 per day	£33.50 per hour, minimum amount: £16.75	Maximum amount: £58.25 per item	Maximum amount: £110 per appearance
QC					
Type of proceedings	*Basic fee*	*Full day refresher*	*Subsidiary fees*		
			Attendance at consultation, conferences and views	*Written work*	*Attendance at pre-trial reviews, applications and other appearances*
All appeals	Maximum amount: £5,400.00 per case	Maximum amount: £330.50 per day	£62.50 per hour, Minimum amount: £32.00	Maximum amount: £119.50 per item	Maximum amount: £257.50 per appearance

Where an hourly rate is specified in the Table following paragraph 10, the appropriate officer must determine any fee for such work in accordance with that hourly rate; provided that the fee determined must not be less than the minimum amount specified.

Where a refresher fee is claimed in respect of less than a full day, the appropriate officer must allow such fee as appears to him reasonable having regard to the fee which would be allowable for a full day.

Witness Allowances in Criminal Proceedings

Contents

The CPS is responsible for paying allowances and expenses to witnesses who are called to give evidence in prosecutions conducted by the Service.

The Regulations

Allowances and expenses payable to prosecution witnesses attending court are governed by Regulations made by the Attorney General (the Regulations) (The Crown Prosecution Service (Witnesses' etc. Allowances) Regulations 1988), as amended from time to time.

Classes of Witnesses

There are three classes of witnesses:

- ordinary;
- professional; and
- expert.

Ordinary Witnesses

Witnesses may receive compensation for:

- travelling expenses
- money spent on refreshments and meals
- financial loss (e.g. loss of earnings)
- other expense incurred (e.g. childcare)

Limits on the amounts payable:

- bus and train fares (standard fare) are normally repaid in full;
- travel by bicycle is paid at 20p per mile;
- travel by motor vehicle is paid at a rate per mile;
- a higher rate per mile may be paid if it is necessary, as opposed to just convenient, to use a private motor vehicle;
- taxi fares are allowed where this was the only form of transport available or if a witness is disabled or infirm.
- set limits apply to refreshments and meals;
- maximum daily amounts apply to loss of earnings and other financial losses.

Professional Witnesses

These (doctors, dentists, veterinary surgeons, lawyers, accountants) may receive, subject to an upper limit, either:

- a compensatory allowance; or
- a sum to reimburse the cost of employing a locum.

Subsistence allowance is not payable, except when an overnight stay is necessary but travelling expenses are payable.

Expert Witnesses

These will receive a fee. The fee should, wherever possible, be agreed in advance. The fee is discretionary but scales of guidance exist.

Subsistence allowance is not payable, except when an overnight stay is necessary. Travelling expenses are payable.

Interpreters

Interpreters will receive a fee based on a fixed hourly rate.

Subsistence allowance is not payable, except when an overnight stay is necessary. Travelling expenses are payable.

Other People attending Court

Other people, in certain circumstances, may receive allowances just like ordinary witnesses. Examples are:

- parents accompanying child witnesses;
- people accompanying elderly or infirm witnesses.
- witnesses and their companions attending court for the purposes of familiarisation visits.

Provision of Claim Forms: Magistrates' Courts

Witnesses attending magistrates' court hearings will normally have received a witness expense claim form together with their warning notice. The claim form should have been accompanied by a "Current Rates" leaflet, giving information on the maximum amounts claimable.

Some witnesses may have lost their form; others may have been called too late for a warning notice, and thus a claim form may not been served. A supply of claim forms should, therefore, be available in the operational unit and at the court building.

Before sending or handing a claim form to a witness, ensure that the appropriate List of Witnesses to Attend Court (LWAC) reference number is entered on it as well as the full name and address of the witness. This is important and should be checked for accuracy with the witness, as it will be used by the Service Centre to despatch payment. The address must be full and clear, including the postcode, or it may result in payment or postal delivery being delayed, and further queries raised. Ensure that the "Current Rates" leaflet accompanies the expense claim form provided to the witness.

Allowances and expenses governed by the Regulations are:

- those payable to ordinary and professional witnesses; and
- overnight allowances and travelling expenses payable to expert witnesses and interpreters.

Allowances, expenses and fees not governed by the Regulations are:

- fees for expert witnesses;
- fees and expenses for interpreters; and
- those payable to people reasonably attending court, but not as witnesses, for example, parents of child witnesses, persons assisting people with disabilities, members of victim's family.

People who cannot be paid

No allowances, expenses or fees can be paid to:

- police officers (from Forces in England and Wales) attending in their official capacity;
- prison officers attending in their official capacity, (but see Payment of Witnesses Expenses & Allowances, 'travelling expenses' section elsewhere in this guidance,) and Costs elsewhere in this guidance, and
- prisoner witnesses brought to court in custody (from within the jurisdiction) Costs elsewhere in this guidance.
- Witnesses that attend court but refuse to give evidence.

Payments by the CPS are limited to expenses, allowances and fees incurred by attendance at court or elsewhere in connection with giving evidence. This includes attendance not specifically to give evidence, such as a visit made for familiarisation purposes.

Giving Evidence

Witnesses who attend to give evidence will be paid whether or not they actually give evidence. There is only one exception. A witness who attends but refuses to give evidence is not entitled to be paid.

Estimating Expense Claims for Costs Applications

Crown prosecutors and caseworkers should not attempt to calculate or confirm expense claims with the witness. This function is performed by the NFBC.

They will, however, need to be able to estimate witness expenses, so that applications for costs against convicted defendants can be properly assessed. Therefore, you should ask witnesses for an indication of the expenses they will claim. The estimated claim figure should be included in the total estimate of costs incurred.

Provision of Claim Forms: Crown Courts

There is no approved system for advance distribution of witness expense claim forms to witnesses. Caseworkers attending at the Crown Court are responsible for supplying claim forms to witnesses. Claim forms are not given to expert witnesses. They should send an invoice for their fees and expenses to the CPS office that instructed them to claim their fees and expenses.

Return of Claim Forms

The claim form tells witnesses to complete it at the end of the case. It also tells them to send the completed form to the relevant NFBC, using the prepaid envelope provided.

Release Times

The time of release of every witness must be recorded on the file copy LWAC. Witnesses are usually released, if recall is not likely, at the end of their evidence. Normally you should record the actual time of release on the LWAC. It may affect the amount of expenses to which they are entitled.

There is discretion to enter a later time in appropriate circumstances, such as:

- a complainant who needs to stay to seek a compensation order;
- a witness required to remain to advise on defence evidence;
- a witness sharing transport with other witnesses whose evidence is not completed; or
- a witness giving appropriate support to another.

Advance Payments

CPS Area staff can request a cheque or payable order payment or issue a travel warrant to a witness who needs an advance to pay for their journey to or from court. The Cashier will need to be provided with confirmation of the witness's identify, the case name and LWAC number to process an advance payment.

If there will not be enough time to send such a payment or travel warrant, the witness can contact their nearest police station. The police may provide a cash advance or travel warrant. If time permits, the police may first want confirmation from the CPS that the witness is required to attend court. Be prepared to give confirmation in appropriate cases.

Similar arrangements apply to witnesses needing a warrant for their return home:

- if the NFBC is nearby, and the witness can cash a cheque at a bank, arrange for a cheque to be issued;
- where a cash advance is required, or no warrant available for the CPS, send the witness to the nearest police station for a cash advance or travel warrant.

Advance payments from police stations are for real emergencies only. Any cash advanced must be limited to the amount needed for the journey to, or home from, court. Under no circumstances should you attempt to calculate and pay the full allowances due to a witness, even where the witness requests this.

Discretion to Exceed Allowances

There is a discretion, under the Regulations, to pay more than the entitlement which should only be used in exceptional circumstances. Authority of the NFBC, Chief Crown Prosecutor (Sector Director London) or designated officer for this purpose, with the necessary delegated financial authority must be obtained before such a payment is made.

Current rates

Ordinary and Professional witnesses

Subsistence Allowances

Day subsistence (Ordinary Witnesses only)

Attendance not exceeding 5 hours	£2.25
Attendance exceeding 5 hours but not exceeding 10 hours	£4.50
Attendance exceeding 10 hours	£9.75

These are fixed allowances towards the cost of meals and refreshments and the appropriate amount will be paid automatically. The period of attendance includes time spent travelling to and from court as well as the time spent at court.

Attendance overnight in London, Birmingham, Manchester, Leeds, Liverpool and Newcastle upon Tyne	£95.00 (Ordinary Witness)
	£85.25 (Professional Witness)
Attendance overnight elsewhere	£65.00 (Ordinary Witness)
	£55.25 (Professional Witness)
PLUS (Ordinary Witnesses only)	
Night Subsistence Allowance	£21.00
Personal Incidental Allowance	£5.00

The CPS will normally arrange the hotel accommodation for ordinary witnesses and pay for it. Where an evening meal is also included the witness is entitled to the Personal Incidental Allowance only. Where no evening meal is included the witness will also be entitled to the Night Subsistence Allowance. These are fixed amount towards the cost of meals, refreshments, accommodation and other expenses where the witness had to stay away from home. The overnight allowance covers an absence of 24 hours and day subsistence is then only paid if the witness were away for more than 24 hours.

Ordinary witnesses who stay with family or friends will receive, in place of the above, a single payment:

Night Subsistence Allowance	£25.00

Travel expenses

Public transport: Rail, bus, coach and tube fares at standard (second class) rates will be reimbursed in full.

Motor car: If the witness uses his own motor car, he will be paid 25p for each mile. In addition, if another witness who is required to attend court or other person authorised to accompany you, is given a lift a further 2p per mile will be paid for the first passenger and 1p per mile for each additional passenger. Exceptionally, if it can be shown that the witness had to use his own car instead of public transport because there was no public transport, or there was a considerable saving of time and money, or because he is disabled or infirm), then a higher rate of 45p per mile may be paid. The witness will need to justify using his own motor car to be eligible for the higher rate.

Motorcycles: Similar rules apply if the witness uses his own motorcycle. The rate per mile that will be paid is 23.8p. Exceptionally the higher rate of 25.4p per mile may also be paid if the witness can show it was necessary to use his own vehicle instead of public transport.

Bicycle: If the witness travels by bicycle he will be paid 20p per mile.

Car parking: Car parking charges will normally only be paid.

Congestion Charge: Congestion Charges will normally be reimbursed in full.

Taxis: The cost of taxi fares or other hired vehicles (including any reasonable tips) will only be paid in cases of emergency, illness, infirmity, or where no other reasonable means of transport was available. The cost of waiting time will not be paid.

Other transport: If the witness intends to use some other form of transport (eg aeroplane or ship), the witness is advised to contact the CPS Finance Business Centre for advice as to whether the cost will be allowed. The cost of travel by air or sea will be reimbursed at economy class fare only.

Loss of earnings – employed persons (Ordinary Witnesses only)

The maximum amount of earnings lost that may be repaid is:

For an absence from work not exceeding 4 hours	£33.50
For an absence from work exceeding 4 hours	£67.00

These payments are not subject to income tax or other statutory deductions. To claim loss of earnings, you must get your employer to complete this section of your claim certifying the earnings you have lost. Do this after you have attended court.

Loss of earnings – self-employed persons (Ordinary Witnesses only)

The maximum amount of earnings lost that may be repaid is:

For an absence from work not exceeding 4 hours	£42.95
For an absence from work exceeding 4 hours	£85.90

Compensatory Allowance (Professional Witnesses only)

Absence from practice/residence for up to 2 hours	£83.50
Absence from practice/residence between 2 and 4 hours	£117.00
Absence from practice/residence between 4 and 6 hours	£174.00
Absence from practice/residence over 6 hours	£234.00

Employing someone to work in witnesses' absence, as a locum or childcare costs

The maximum amount that can be repaid if someone is employed to work in the witnesses' absence or as a childminder is £67.00 for each day of attendance.

If the witness is a professional witness who wishes to claim for employing a locum you should ask the locum to complete this section.

The maximum amounts payable are:

Absence from practice for up to 2 hours	£89.00
Absence from practice between 2 and 4 hours	£125.00
Absence from practice over 4 hours or where locum necessarily covers more than 4 hours	£250.00

Other Costs (Ordinary Witnesses only)

If the witness incurs any other costs not covered by other sections of the claim full details should be given and receipts provided.

The maximum payable is:	£67.00 for each day of attendance.

Prosecution interpreter

The current rates and upper limits of allowances payable by the Crown Prosecution Service to interpreters required to provide interpreter services for a prosecution witness are set out below.

Minimum booking – Payment where attendance time is three hours or less	£85.00
Additional payment for attendance and travelling time beyond three hours per 15 minutes or part thereof	£7.50
Cancellation fee when cancelling a booking after 10am on the day before it is due to begin (i.e. a sum equal to the minimum booking fee)	£85.00

Subsistence Allowances

Overnight allowance: Where it is necessary to stay overnight an allowance is paid towards the cost of meals and accommodation. The allowance is:

Attendance overnight in London, Birmingham, Manchester, Leeds, Liverpool and Newcastle upon Tyne	£85.25
Attendance overnight elsewhere	£55.25

Travel allowances

Travel allowances are the same as shown above.

Expert witnesses

The current rates and upper limits of allowances payable by the Crown Prosecution Service to an expert witness are set out below.

Subsistence Allowances

Overnight allowance: Where it is necessary to stay overnight an allowance is paid towards the cost of meals and accommodation. The allowance is:

Attendance overnight in London, Birmingham, Manchester, Leeds, Liverpool and Newcastle upon Tyne	£85.25
Attendance overnight elsewhere	£55.25

Travel allowances

Travel allowances are the same as shown above.

Part 76 of the Criminal Procedure Rules 2011

Contents of this Part

Section 1: General

When this Part applies

76.1.—(1) This Part applies where the court can make an order about costs under—

(a) Part II of the Prosecution of Offences Act 1985 and Part II, IIA or IIB of The Costs in Criminal Cases (General) Regulations 1986;

(b) section 109 of the Magistrates' Courts Act 1980;

(c) section 52 of the Senior Courts Act 1981and rule 76.6;

(d) section 8 of the Bankers Books Evidence Act 1879;

(e) section 2C(8) of the Criminal Procedure (Attendance of Witnesses) Act 1965;

(f) section 36(5) of the Criminal Justice Act 1972;

(g) section 159(5) and Schedule 3, paragraph 11, of the Criminal Justice Act 1988;

(h) section 14H(5) of the Football Spectators Act 1989;

(i) section 4(7) of the Dangerous Dogs Act 1991; or

(j) Part 3 of The Serious Crime Act 2007 (Appeals under Section 24) Order 2008;

(2) In this Part, 'costs' means—

(a) the fees payable to a legal representative;

(b) the disbursements paid by a legal representative; and

(c) any other expenses incurred in connection with the case.

[Note. A costs order can be made under—

(a) section 16 of the Prosecution of Offences Act 1985 (defence costs), for the payment out of central funds of a defendant's costs (see rule 76.4);

(b) section 17 of the Prosecution of Offences Act 1985 (prosecution costs), for the payment out of central funds of a private prosecutor's costs (see rule 76.4);

(c) section 18 of the Prosecution of Offences Act 1985 (award of costs against accused), for the payment by a defendant of another person's costs (see rules 76.5 and 76.6);

(d) section 19(1) of the Prosecution of Offences Act 1985 and regulation 3 of The Costs in Criminal Cases (General) Regulations 1986, for the payment by a party of another party's costs incurred as a result of an unnecessary or improper act or omission by or on behalf of the first party (see rule 76.8);

(e) section 19A of the Prosecution of Offences Act 1985 (costs against legal representatives, etc.)—

(i) for the payment by a legal representative of a party's costs incurred as a result of an improper, unreasonable or negligent act or omission by or on behalf of the representative, or

(ii) disallowing the payment to that representative of such costs (see rule 76.9);

(f) section 19B of the Prosecution of Offences Act 1985 (provision for award of costs against third parties) and regulation 3F of The Costs in Criminal Cases (General) Regulations 1986, for the payment by a person who is not a party of a party's costs where there has been serious misconduct by the non-party (see rule 76.10);

(g) section 109 of the Magistrates' Courts Act 1980, section 52 of the Senior Courts Act 1981 and rule 76.6, for the payment by an appellant of a respondent's costs on abandoning an appeal to the Crown Court (see rule 76.6);

(h) section 52 of the Senior Courts Act 1981 and rule 76.6, for the payment by a party of another party's costs on an appeal to the Crown Court in any case not covered by (c) or (g) (see rule 76.6);

(i) section 8 of the Bankers Books Evidence Act 1879, for the payment of costs by a party or by the bank against which an application for an order is made (see rule 76.7);

(j) section 2C(8) of the Criminal Procedure (Attendance of Witnesses) Act 1965, for the payment by the applicant for a witness summons of the costs of a party who applies successfully under rule 28.7 to have it withdrawn (see rule 76.7);

(k) section 36(5) of the Criminal Justice Act 1972 or Schedule 3, paragraph 11, of the Criminal Justice Act 1988, for the payment out of central funds of a defendant's costs on a reference by the Attorney General of—

(i) a point of law, or

(ii) an unduly lenient sentence (see rule 76.4);

(l) section 159(5) of the Criminal Justice Act 1988, for the payment by a person of another person's costs on an appeal about a reporting or public access restriction (see rule 76.6);

(m) section 14H(5) of the Football Spectators Act 1989, for the payment by a defendant of another person's costs on an application to terminate a football banning order (see rule 76.7);

(n) section 4(7) of the Dangerous Dogs Act 1991, for the payment by a defendant of another person's costs on an application to terminate a disqualification for having custody of a dog (see rule 76.7);

(o) article 14 of The Serious Crime Act 2007 (Appeals under Section 24) Order 2008), corresponding with section 16 of the Prosecution of Offences Act 1985 (see rule 76.4);

(p) article 15 of The Serious Crime Act 2007 (Appeals under Section 24) Order 2008, corresponding with section 18 of the Prosecution of Offences Act 1985 (see rule 76.6);

(q) article 16 of The Serious Crime Act 2007 (Appeals under Section 24) Order 2008, corresponding with an order under section 19(1) of the 1985 Act (see rule 76.8);

(r) article 17 of The Serious Crime Act 2007 (Appeals under Section 24) Order 2008, corresponding with an order under section 19A of the 1985 Act (see rule 76.9); or

(s) article 18 of The Serious Crime Act 2007 (Appeals under Section 24) Order 2008, corresponding with an order under section 19B of the 1985 Act (see rule 76.10).

See also the Criminal Costs Practice Direction.

Part 68 (Appeal to the Court of Appeal about conviction or sentence) contains rules about appeals against costs orders made in the Crown Court under the legislation listed in (c) above.

Part 63 (Appeal to the Crown Court) and Part 68 (Appeal to the Court of Appeal about conviction or sentence) contain rules about appeals against costs orders made under the legislation listed in (e) and (f) above.

As to costs in restraint or receivership proceedings under Part 2 of the Proceeds of Crime Act 2002, see rules 61.19 to 61.22.

A costs order can be enforced—

(a) against a defendant, under section 41(1) or (3) of the Administration of Justice Act 1970;

(b) against a prosecutor, under section 41(2) or (3) of the Administration of Justice Act 1970;

(c) against a representative, under regulation 3D of The Costs in Criminal Cases (General) Regulations 1986 or article 18 of The Serious Crime Act 2007 (Appeals under Section 24) Order 2008; or

(d) against a non-party, under regulation 3I of The Costs in Criminal Cases (General) Regulations 1986 or article 31 of the Serious Crime Act 2007 (Appeals under Section 24) Order 2008.

See also section 58, section 150(1) and Part III of the Magistrates' Courts Act 1980 and Schedule 5 to the Courts Act 2003.]

Costs orders: general rules

76.2.—(1) The court must not make an order about costs unless each party and any other person directly affected—

(a) is present; or

(b) has had an opportunity—

(i) to attend, or

(ii) to make representations.

(2) The court may make an order about costs—

(a) at a hearing in public or in private; or

(b) without a hearing.

(3) In deciding what order, if any, to make about costs, the court must have regard to all the circumstances, including—

(a) the conduct of all the parties; and

(b) any costs order already made.

(4) If the court makes an order about costs, it must—

(a) specify who must, or must not, pay what, to whom; and

(b) identify the legislation under which the order is made, where there is a choice of powers.

(5) The court must give reasons if it—

(a) refuses an application for a costs order; or

(b) rejects representations opposing a costs order.

(6) If the court makes an order for the payment of costs—

(a) the general rule is that it will be for an amount that is sufficient reasonably to compensate the recipient for costs—

(i) actually, reasonably and properly incurred, and

(ii) reasonable in amount; but

(b) the court may order the payment of—

(i) a proportion of that amount,

(ii) a stated amount less than that amount,

(iii) costs from or until a certain date only,

(iv) costs relating only to particular steps taken, or

(v) costs relating only to a distinct part of the case.

(7) On an assessment of the amount of costs, relevant factors include—

(a) the conduct of all the parties;

(b) the particular complexity of the matter or the difficulty or novelty of the questions raised;

(c) the skill, effort, specialised knowledge and responsibility involved;

(d) the time spent on the case;

(e) the place where and the circumstances in which work or any part of it was done; and

(f) any direction or observations by the court that made the costs order.

(8) If the court orders a party to pay costs to be assessed under rule 76.11, it may order that party to pay an amount on account.

(9) An order for the payment of costs takes effect when the amount is assessed, unless the court exercises any power it has to order otherwise.

[Note. Under the powers to which apply rule 76.8 (costs resulting from unnecessary or improper act, etc.) and rule 76.9 (costs against a legal representative), specified conduct must be established for such orders to be made.

The amount recoverable under a costs order may be affected by the legislation under which the order is made.

Under section 141 of the Powers of Criminal Courts (Sentencing) Act 2000 and section 75 of the Magistrates' Courts Act 1980; the Crown Court and magistrates' court respectively can allow time for payment, or payment by instalments.]

Court's power to vary requirements under Sections 2, 3 and 4

76.3.—(1) The court may—

(a) extend a time limit for serving an application or representations under section 2, 3 or 4 of this Part, even after it has expired; and

(b) consider an application or representations—

(i) made in a different form to one set out in the Practice Direction, or

(ii) made orally instead of in writing.

(2) A person who wants an extension of time must—

(a) apply when serving the application or representations for which it is needed; and

(b) explain the delay.

Section 2: Costs Out of Central Funds

Costs out of central funds

76.4.—(1) This rule applies where the court can order the payment of costs out of central funds.

(2) In this rule, costs—

(a) include—

(i) on an appeal, costs incurred in the court that made the decision under appeal, and

(ii) at a retrial, costs incurred at the initial trial and on any appeal; but

(b) do not include costs funded by the Legal Services Commission.

(3) The court may make an order—

(a) on application by the person who incurred the costs; or

(b) on its own initiative.

(4) Where a person wants the court to make an order that person must—

(a) apply as soon as practicable; and

(b) outline the type of costs and the amount claimed, if that person wants the court to direct an assessment; or

(c) specify the amount claimed, if that person wants the court to assess the amount itself.

(5) The general rule is that the court will make an order, but—

(a) the court may decline to make a defendant's costs order if, for example—

(i) the defendant is convicted of at least one offence, or

(ii) the defendant's conduct led the prosecutor reasonably to think the prosecution case stronger than it was; and

(b) the court may decline to make a prosecutor's costs order if, for example, the prosecution was started or continued unreasonably.

(6) If the court makes an order—

(a) it may direct an assessment under, as applicable—

(i) regulations 4 to 12 of The Costs in Criminal Cases (General) Regulations 1986, or

(ii) articles 21 to 28 of The Serious Crime Act 2007 (Appeals under Section 24) Order 2008;

(b) it may assess the amount itself, if the recipient agrees;

(c) it must assess the amount itself, in a case in which it decides not to allow an amount that is reasonably sufficient to compensate the recipient for expenses properly incurred in the proceedings.

[Note. See also rule 76.2.

An order for the payment of costs out of central funds can be made—

(a) for a defendant—

(i) on acquittal,

(ii) where a prosecution does not proceed,

(iii) where the Crown Court allows any part of a defendant's appeal from a magistrates' court,

(iv) where the Court of Appeal allows any part of a defendant's appeal from the Crown Court,

(v) where the Court of Appeal decides a prosecutor's appeal under Part 66 (appeal to the Court of Appeal against ruling at preparatory hearing) or Part 67 (appeal to the Court of Appeal against ruling adverse to prosecution),

(vi) where the Court of Appeal decides a reference by the Attorney General under Part 70 (reference to the Court of Appeal of point of law or unduly lenient sentence), or

(vii) where the Court of Appeal decides an appeal by someone other than the defendant about a serious crime prevention order;

(See section 16 of the Prosecution of Offences Act 1985 and regulation 14 of The Costs in Criminal Cases (General) Regulations 1986; section 36(5) of the Criminal Justice Act 1972 and paragraph 11 of Schedule 3 to the Criminal Justice Act 1988; and article 14 of The Serious Crime Act 2007 (Appeals under Section 24) Order 2008.)

(b) for a private prosecutor, in proceedings in respect of an offence that must or may be tried in the Crown Court;

(See section 17 of the Prosecution of Offences Act 1985 and regulation 14 of The Costs in Criminal Cases (General) Regulations 1986.)

(c) for a person adversely affected by a serious crime prevention order, where the Court of Appeal—

(i) allows an appeal by that person about that order, or

(ii) decides an appeal about that order by someone else.

(See article 14 of The Serious Crime Act 2007 (Appeals under Section 24) Order 2008.)]

Section 3: Payment of Costs by One Party to Another

Costs on conviction and sentence

76.5.—(1) This rule applies where the court can order a defendant to pay the prosecutor's costs if the defendant is—

(a) convicted or found guilty;

(b) dealt with in the Crown Court after committal for sentence there; or

(c) dealt with for breach of a sentence.

(2) The court may make an order—

(a) on application by the prosecutor; or

(b) on its own initiative.

(3) Where the prosecutor wants the court to make an order—

(a) the prosecutor must—

(i) apply as soon as practicable, and

(ii) specify the amount claimed; and

(b) the general rule is that the court will make an order if it is satisfied that the defendant can pay; but

(c) the court may decline to do so.

(4) A defendant who wants to oppose an order must make representations as soon as practicable.

(5) If the court makes an order, it must assess the amount itself.

[Note. See—

(a) rule 76.2; and

(b) section 18 of the Prosecution of Offences Act 1985 and regulation 14 of The Costs in Criminal Cases (General) Regulations 1986.

Under section 18(4) and (5) of the 1985 Act, if a magistrates' court—

(a) imposes a fine, a penalty, forfeiture or compensation that does not exceed £5—

(i) the general rule is that the court will not make a costs order against the defendant, but

(ii) the court may do so;

(b) fines a defendant under 18, no costs order against the defendant may be for more than the fine.

Part 68 (Appeal to the Court of Appeal about conviction or sentence) contains rules about appeal against a Crown Court costs order to which this rule applies.]

Costs on appeal

76.6.—(1) This rule—

(a) applies where a magistrates' court, the Crown Court or the Court of Appeal can order a party to pay another person's costs on an appeal, or an application for permission to appeal;

(b) authorises the Crown Court, in addition to its other powers, to order a party to pay another party's costs on an appeal to that court, except on an appeal under—

(i) section 108 of the Magistrates' Courts Act 1980, or

(ii) section 45 of the Mental Health Act 1983.

(2) In this rule, costs include—

(a) costs incurred in the court that made the decision under appeal; and

(b) costs funded by the Legal Services Commission.

(3) The court may make an order—

(a) on application by the person who incurred the costs; or

(b) on its own initiative.

(4) A person who wants the court to make an order must—

(a) apply as soon as practicable;

(b) notify each other party;

(c) specify—

(i) the amount claimed, and

(ii) against whom; and

(d) where an appellant abandons an appeal to the Crown Court by serving a notice of abandonment—

(i) apply in writing not more than 14 days later, and

(ii) serve the application on the appellant and on the Crown Court officer.

(5) A party who wants to oppose an order must—

(a) make representations as soon as practicable; and

(b) where the application was under paragraph (4)(d), serve written representations on the applicant, and on the Crown Court officer, not more than 7 days after it was served.

(6) Where the application was under paragraph (4)(d), the Crown Court officer may—

(a) submit it to the Crown Court; or

(b) serve it on the magistrates' court officer, for submission to the magistrates' court.

(7) If the court makes an order, it may direct an assessment under rule 76.11, or assess the amount itself where—

(a) the appellant abandons an appeal to the Crown Court;

(b) the Crown Court decides an appeal, except an appeal under—

(i) section 108 of the Magistrates' Courts Act 1980, or

(ii) section 45 of the Mental Health Act 1983; or

(c) the Court of Appeal decides an appeal to which Part 69 applies (appeal to the Court of Appeal regarding reporting or public access restriction).

(8) If the court makes an order in any other case, it must assess the amount itself.

[Note. See also rule 76.2.

A magistrates' court can order an appellant to pay a respondent's costs on abandoning an appeal to the Crown Court.

The Crown Court can order—

(a) the defendant to pay the prosecutor's costs on dismissing a defendant's appeal—

(i) against conviction or sentence, under section 108 of the Magistrates' Courts Act 1980, or

(ii) where the magistrates' court makes a hospital order or guardianship order without convicting the defendant, under section 45 of the Mental Health Act 1983; and

(b) one party to pay another party's costs on deciding any other appeal to which Part 63 applies.

The Court of Appeal can order—

(a) the defendant to pay another person's costs on dismissing a defendant's appeal or application to which Part 66 (appeal to the Court of Appeal against ruling at preparatory hearing), Part 68 (appeal to the Court of Appeal about conviction or sentence) or Part 74 (appeal or reference to the Supreme Court) applies;

(b) the defendant to pay another person's costs on allowing a prosecutor's appeal to which Part 67 (appeal to the Court of Appeal against ruling adverse to the prosecution) applies;

(c) the appellant to pay another person's costs on dismissing an appeal or application by a person affected by a serious crime prevention order;

(d) one party to pay another party's costs on deciding an appeal to which Part 69 (appeal to the Court of Appeal regarding reporting or public access restriction) applies.

See section 109 of the Magistrates' Courts Act 1980; section 52 of the Senior Courts Act 1981 which allows rules of court to authorise the Crown Court to order costs); section 18 of the Prosecution of Offences Act 1985; section 159(5) of the Criminal Justice Act 1988; and article 15 of The Serious Crime Act 2007 (Appeals under Section 24) Order 2008.]

Costs on an application

76.7.—(1) This rule applies where the court can order a party to pay another person's costs in a case in which—

(a) the court decides an application for the production in evidence of a copy of a bank record;

(b) a magistrates' court or the Crown Court decides an application to terminate—

(i) a football banning order, or

(ii) a disqualification for having custody of a dog; or

(c) the Crown Court allows an application to withdraw a witness summons.

(2) The court may make an order—

(a) on application by the person who incurred the costs; or

(b) on its own initiative.

(3) A person who wants the court to make an order must—

(a) apply as soon as practicable;

(b) notify each other party; and

(c) specify—

(i) the amount claimed, and

(ii) against whom.

(4) A party who wants to oppose an order must make representations as soon as practicable.

(5) If the court makes an order, it may direct an assessment under rule 76.11, or assess the amount itself.

[Note. See—

(a) rule 76.2;

(b) section 8 of the Bankers Books Evidence Act 1879;

(c) section 14H(5) of the Football Spectators Act 1989;

(d) section 2C(8) of the Criminal Procedure (Attendance of Witnesses) Act 1965; and

(e) section 4(7) of the Dangerous Dogs Act 1991.]

Costs resulting from unnecessary or improper act, etc.

76.8.—(1) This rule applies where the court can order a party to pay another party's costs incurred as a result of an unnecessary or improper act or omission by or on behalf of the first party.

(2) In this rule, costs include costs funded by the Legal Services Commission.

(3) The court may make an order—

(a) on application by the party who incurred such costs; or

(b) on its own initiative.

(4) A party who wants the court to make an order must—

(a) apply in writing as soon as practicable after becoming aware of the grounds for doing so;

(b) serve the application on—

(i) the court officer (or, in the Court of Appeal, the Registrar), and

(ii) each other party;

(c) in that application specify—

(i) the party by whom costs should be paid,

(ii) the relevant act or omission,

(iii) the reasons why that act or omission meets the criteria for making an order,

(iv) the amount claimed, and

(v) those on whom the application has been served.

(5) Where the court considers making an order on its own initiative, it must—

(a) identify the party against whom it proposes making the order; and

(b) specify—

(i) the relevant act or omission,

(ii) the reasons why that act or omission meets the criteria for making an order, and

(iii) with the assistance of the party who incurred the costs, the amount involved.

(6) A party who wants to oppose an order must—

(a) make representations as soon as practicable; and

(b) in reply to an application, serve written representations on the applicant and on the court officer (or Registrar) not more than 7 days after it was served.

(7) If the court makes an order, it must assess the amount itself.

[Note. See—

(a) rule 76.2;

(b) section 19(1) of the Prosecution of Offences Act 1985 and regulation 3 of The Costs in Criminal Cases (General) Regulations 1986; and

(c) article 16 of The Serious Crime Act 2007 (Appeals under Section 24) Order 2008.

Under regulation 3(5) of the 1986 Regulations, if a magistrates' court fines a defendant under 17, no costs order to which this rule applies may be for more than the fine.

The Criminal Costs Practice Direction sets out a form of application for use in connection with this rule.]

Section 4: Other Costs Orders

Costs against a legal representative

76.9.—(1) This rule applies where—

(a) a party has incurred costs—

(i) as a result of an improper, unreasonable or negligent act or omission by a legal or other representative or representative's employee, or

(ii) which it has become unreasonable for that party to have to pay because of such an act or omission occurring after those costs were incurred; and

(b) the court can—

(i) order the representative responsible to pay such costs, or

(ii) prohibit the payment of costs to that representative.

(2) In this rule, costs include costs funded by the Legal Services Commission.

(3) The court may make an order—

(a) on application by the party who incurred such costs; or

(b) on its own initiative.

(4) A party who wants the court to make an order must—

(a) apply in writing as soon as practicable after becoming aware of the grounds for doing so;

(b) serve the application on—

(i) the court officer (or, in the Court of Appeal, the Registrar),

(ii) the representative responsible,

(iii) each other party, and

(iv) any other person directly affected;

(c) in that application specify—

(i) the representative responsible,

(ii) the relevant act or omission,

(iii) the reasons why that act or omission meets the criteria for making an order,

(iv) the amount claimed, and

(v) those on whom the application has been served.

(5) Where the court considers making an order on its own initiative, it must—

(a) identify the representative against whom it proposes making that order; and

(b) specify—

(i) the relevant act or omission,

(ii) the reasons why that act or omission meets the criteria for making an order, and

(iii) with the assistance of the party who incurred the costs, the amount involved.

(6) A representative who wants to oppose an order must—

(a) make representations as soon as practicable; and

(b) in reply to an application, serve written representations on the applicant and on the court officer (or Registrar) not more than 7 days after it was served.

(7) If the court makes an order—

(a) the general rule is that it will do so without waiting until the end of the case, but it may postpone making the order; and

(b) it must assess the amount itself.

(8) Instead of making an order, the court may make adverse observations about the representative's conduct for use in an assessment where—

(a) a party's costs are—

(i) funded by the Legal Services Commission, or

(ii) to be paid out of central funds; or

(b) there is to be an assessment under rule 76.11.

[Note. See—

(a) rule 76.2;

(b) section 19A of the Prosecution of Offences Act 1985;

(c) article 17 of The Serious Crime Act 2007 (Appeals under Section 24) Order 2008; and

(d) article 27 of The Criminal Defence Service (Funding) Order 2007.

The Criminal Costs Practice Direction sets out a form of application for use in connection with this rule.

Part 63 (Appeal to the Crown Court) and Part 68 (Appeal to the Court of Appeal about conviction or sentence) contain rules about appeals against a costs order to which this rule applies.]

Costs against a third party

76.10.—(1) This rule applies where—

(a) there has been serious misconduct by a person who is not a party; and

(b) the court can order that person to pay a party's costs.

(2) In this rule, costs include costs funded by the Legal Services Commission.

(3) The court may make an order—

(a) on application by the party who incurred the costs; or

(b) on its own initiative.

(4) A party who wants the court to make an order must—

(a) apply in writing as soon as practicable after becoming aware of the grounds for doing so;

(b) serve the application on—

(i) the court officer (or, in the Court of Appeal, the Registrar),

(ii) the person responsible,

(iii) each other party, and

(iv) any other person directly affected;

(c) in that application specify—

(i) the person responsible,

(ii) the relevant misconduct,

(iii) the reasons why the criteria for making an order are met,

(iv) the amount claimed, and

(v) those on whom the application has been served.

(5) Where the court considers making an order on its own initiative, it must—

(a) identify the person against whom it proposes making that order; and

(b) specify—

(i) the relevant misconduct,

(ii) the reasons why the criteria for making an order are met, and

(iii) with the assistance of the party who incurred the costs, the amount involved.

(6) A person who wants to oppose an order must—

(a) make representations as soon as practicable; and

(b) in reply to an application, serve written representations on the applicant and on the court officer (or Registrar) not more than 7 days after it was served.

(7) If the court makes an order—

(a) the general rule is that it will do so at the end of the case, but it may do so earlier; and

(b) it must assess the amount itself.

[Note. See—

(a) rule 76.2;

(b) section 19B of the Prosecution of Offences Act 1985 and regulation 3F of The Costs in Criminal Cases (General) Regulations 1986; and

(c) article 18 of The Serious Crime Act 2007 (Appeals under Section 24) Order 2008.

The Criminal Costs Practice Direction sets out a form of application for use in connection with this rule.

Part 63 (Appeal to the Crown Court) and Part 68 (Appeal to the Court of Appeal about conviction or sentence) contain rules about appeals against a costs order to which this rule applies.]

Section 5: Assessment of Costs

Assessment and re-assessment

76.11.—(1) This rule applies where the court directs an assessment under—

(a) rule 61.20 (Proceeds of Crime Act 2002 – rules applicable to restraint and receivership proceedings, assessment of costs);

(b) rule 76.6 (costs on appeal); or

(c) rule 76.7 (costs on an application).

(2) The assessment must be carried out by the relevant assessing authority, namely—

(a) the court officer, where the direction was given by a magistrates' court or by the Crown Court; or

(b) the Registrar of Criminal Appeals, where the direction was given by the Court of Appeal.

(3) The party in whose favour the court made the costs order ('the applicant') must—

(a) apply for an assessment—

(i) in writing, in any form required by the assessing authority, and

(ii) not more than 3 months after the costs order; and

(b) serve the application on—

(i) the assessing authority, and

(ii) the party against whom the court made the costs order ('the respondent').

(4) The applicant must—

(a) summarise the work done;

(b) specify—

(i) each item of work done, giving the date, time taken and amount claimed,

(ii) any disbursements or expenses, including the fees of any advocate, and

(iii) any circumstances of which the applicant wants the assessing authority to take particular account; and

(c) supply—

(i) receipts or other evidence of the amount claimed, and

(ii) any other information or document for which the assessing authority asks, within such period as that authority may require.

(5) A respondent who wants to make representations about the amount claimed must—

(a) do so in writing; and

(b) serve the representations on the assessing authority, and on the applicant, not more than 21 days after service of the application.

(6) The assessing authority must—

(a) if it seems likely to help with the assessment, obtain any other information or document;

(b) resolve in favour of the respondent any doubt about what should be allowed; and

(c) serve the assessment on the parties.

(7) Where either party wants the amount allowed re-assessed—

(a) that party must—

(i) apply to the assessing authority, in writing and in any form required by that authority,

(ii) serve the application on the assessing authority, and on the other party, not more than 21 days after service of the assessment,

(iii) explain the objections to the assessment,

(iv) supply any additional supporting information or document, and

(v) ask for a hearing, if that party wants one; and

(b) a party who wants to make representations about an application for re-assessment must—

(i) do so in writing,

(ii) serve the representations on the assessing authority, and on the other party, not more than 21 days after service of the application, and

(iii) ask for a hearing, if that party wants one;

(c) the assessing authority—

(i) must arrange a hearing, in public or in private, if either party asks for one,

(ii) subject to that, may re-assess the amount allowed with or without a hearing,

(iii) must re-assess the amount allowed on the initial assessment, taking into account the reasons for disagreement with that amount and any other representations,

(iv) may maintain, increase or decrease the amount allowed on the assessment,

(v) must serve the re-assessment on the parties, and

(vi) must serve written reasons on the parties, if not more than 21 days later either party asks for such reasons.

(8) A time limit under this rule may be extended even after it has expired—

(a) by the assessing authority, or

(b) by the Senior Costs Judge, if the assessing authority declines to do so.

Appeal to a costs judge

76.12.—(1) This rule applies where—

(a) the assessing authority has re-assessed the amount allowed under rule 76.11; and

(b) either party wants to appeal against that amount.

(2) That party must—

(a) serve an appeal notice on—

(i) the Senior Costs Judge,

(ii) the other party, and

(iii) the assessing authority

not more than 21 days after service of the written reasons for the re-assessment;

(b) explain the objections to the re-assessment;

(c) serve on the Senior Costs Judge with the appeal notice—

(i) the applications for assessment and re-assessment,

(ii) any other information or document considered by the assessing authority,

(iii) the assessing authority's written reasons for the re-assessment, and

(iv) any other information or document for which a costs judge asks, within such period as the judge may require; and

(d) ask for a hearing, if that party wants one.

(3) A party who wants to make representations about an appeal must—

(a) serve representations in writing on—

(i) the Senior Costs Judge, and

(ii) the applicant

not more than 21 days after service of the appeal notice; and

(b) ask for a hearing, if that party wants one.

(4) Unless a costs judge otherwise directs, the parties may rely only on—

(a) the objections to the amount allowed on the initial assessment; and

(b) any other representations and material considered by the assessing authority.

(5) A costs judge—

(a) must arrange a hearing, in public or in private, if either party asks for one;

(b) subject to that, may determine an appeal with or without a hearing;

(c) may—

(i) consult the assessing authority,

(ii) consult the court which made the costs order, and

(iii) obtain any other information or document;

(d) must reconsider the amount allowed by the assessing authority, taking into account the objections to the re-assessment and any other representations;

(e) may maintain, increase or decrease the amount allowed on the re-assessment;

(f) may provide for the costs incurred by either party to the appeal; and

(g) must serve reasons for the decision on—

(i) the parties, and

(ii) the assessing authority.

(6) A costs judge may extend a time limit under this rule, even after it has expired.

[Note. The Criminal Costs Practice Direction sets out a form for use in connection with this rule.]

Appeal to a High Court judge

76.13.—(1) This rule applies where—

(a) a costs judge has determined an appeal under rule 76.12; and

(b) either party wants to appeal against the amount allowed.

(2) A party who wants to appeal—

(a) may do so only if a costs judge certifies that a point of principle of general importance was involved in the decision on the review; and

(b) must apply in writing for such a certificate and serve the application on—

(i) the costs judge,

(ii) the other party

not more than 21 days after service of the decision on the review.

(3) That party must—

(a) appeal to a judge of the High Court attached to the Queen's Bench Division as if it were an appeal from the decision of a master under Part 52 of the Civil Procedure Rules 1998; and

(b) serve the appeal not more than 21 days after service of the costs judge's certificate under paragraph (2).

(4) A High Court judge—

(a) may extend a time limit under this rule even after it has expired;

(b) has the same powers and duties as a costs judge under rule 76.12; and

(c) may hear the appeal with one or more assessors.

[Note. See also section 70 of the Senior Courts Act 1981.]

Application for an extension of time under Section 5

76.14. A party who wants an extension of time under rule 76.11, 76.12 or 76.13 must—

(a) apply in writing;

(b) explain the delay; and

(c) attach the application, representations or appeal for which the extension of time is needed.

PART 3 MISCELLANEOUS RATES AND FEES

1. Motor Mileage

Motor Mileage Rates

From the 17th January 1986	31.8p per mile
From the 26th November 1990	35.7p per mile
From the 24th April 1995	36p per mile
From the 2nd April 2001	45p per mile

Motor Mileage Tax Allowances

Approved mileage rates

With effect from the 6th April 2011, the increase in the tax approved mileage rate for employees using their own cars on business is increased from 40p per mile (for the first 10,000 miles) to 45p per mile. The rate beyond 10,000 miles remains at 25p. The rate for passengers (now extended to volunteers) remains at 5p

The effective rates are therefore:

2011–2012	**First 10,000 business miles in the tax year**	**Each business mile over 10,000 in the tax year**
Cars and vans	45p	25p
Motor cycles	24p	24p
Bicycles	20p	20p

2. Value Added Tax Rates

From the 18th June 1979	15%
From the 1st April 1991	17.5%
From the 1st December 2008	15%
From the 1st January 2010	17.5%
From the 4th January 2011	20%

See also for guidance the Law Society's Practice Notes at:- http://www.lawsociety.org.uk

VAT on disbursements practice note – 10th March 2011

VAT on legal aid – 15th December 2009

3. Insurance Premium Tax Rates

From the 1st October 1994 to 31st March 1997 – a single rate of 2.5%.

From the 1st April 1997, two rates charged.

Standard rate:

From the 1st April 1997 to 30th June 1999	4%;
From the 1st July 1999 to 4th January 2011	5%
From the 4th January 2011	6%

Higher rate:

From the 1st April 1997 to date	17.5% (on certain types of insurance arranged through certain suppliers of other goods and services)
From 1st August 1998	17.5% on all taxable travel insurance, regardless of the type of supplier.
From 4th January 2011	20%.

4. Oath Fees

	Oath	Exhibit
From the 11th February 1980	£2.00	£0.50
From the 1st May 1984	£3.00	£0.75
From the 23rd May 1988	£3.50	£1.00
From the 18th October 1993	£5.00	£2.00
From the 1st October 2007	£10.00	£2.00

For the fees currently payable when oaths/ affidavits are sworn by officers of the courts see Part 6

PART 4 IMPORTANT CASES/DECISIONS

Kitchen v Burwell Reed & Kinghorn Ltd ... [2006] 1 Costs LR 82
Jones v Caradon Catnic Ltd ... [2006] 3 Costs LR 427
Various Claimants v Gower Chemicals Ltd and Others ... [2007] 4 Costs LR 647
Crane v Canons Leisure Centre ... [2008] 1 Costs LR 132

Conditional Fee Agreements

Hodgson and Others v Imperial Tobacco Ltd & Gallaher ... [1998] 1 Costs LR 14
Thai Trading Co (a Firm) v Taylor ... [1998] 1 Costs LR 122
Bevan Ashford (a Firm) v Geoff Yeandle (Contractors) Ltd (in Liquidation) ... [1998] 2 Costs LR 15
Hodgson and Others v Imperial Tobacco Ltd and Others (No. 2) ... [1998] 2 Costs LR 27
Geraghty & Co v Awwad and Another ... [2000] 1 Costs LR 105
Leeds City Council v Carr and Coles & Wells v Barnsley Metropolitan Borough Council ... [2000] 1 Costs LR 144
Callery v Gray (No. 1) ... [2001] 2 Costs LR 163
Callery v Gray (No. 2) ... [2001] 2 Costs LR 205
Halloran v Delaney ... [2002] 3 Costs LR 503
Burstein v Times Newspapers Ltd ... [2003] 1 Costs LR 111
Designers Guild Ltd v Russell Williams (Textiles) Ltd (t/a Washington DC) ... [2003] 1 Costs LR 128
Designers Guild Ltd v Russell Williams (Textiles) Ltd ... [2003] 2 Costs LR 204
Grupo Torras SA v Al-Sabah ... [2003] 2 Costs LR 294
Hollins v Russell and Related Appeals ... [2003] 3 Costs LR 423
Myler and Mirror Group Newspapers v Williams ... [2003] 4 Costs LR 566
Thornley v Lang ... [2004] 1 Costs LR 91
Nedlloyd Lines UK Ltd and Another v CEL Group Ltd ... [2004] 2 Costs LR 286
C v Merseyside Regional Ambulance Service NHS Trust ... [2004] 3 Costs LR 363
Spencer v Wood and Wood t/a Gordons Tyres (a Firm) ... [2004] 3 Costs LR 372
Smiths Dock Ltd v Edwards and Others ... [2004] 3 Costs LR 440
King v Telegraph Group Ltd ... [2004] 3 Costs LR 449
Atack v Lee and Grechan; Ellerton v Harris ... [2005] 2 Costs LR 308
Begum v Klarit ... [2005] 3 Costs LR 452
Kellar and Carib West Ltd v Williams ... [2005] 4 Costs LR 559
Arkin v Borchard Lines Ltd and Others ... [2005] 4 Costs LR 643
Kitchen v Burwell Reed & Kinghorn Ltd ... [2006] 1 Costs LR 82
Jones v Caradon Catnic Ltd ... [2006] 3 Costs LR 427
Sharratt and Others and Rowe Cohen (a Firm) v London Central Bus Company Ltd and Others ... [2006] 4 Costs LR 584
Cox and Carter v MGN Ltd and Others ... [2006] 5 Costs LR 764
Garrett v Halton Borough Council; Myatt and Others v National Coal Board ... [2006] 5 Costs LR 798
Knight v Beyond Properties Pty Ltd and Others ... [2007] 1 Costs LR 5
Gaynor v Central West London Buses Ltd ... [2007] 1 Costs LR 33
Al-Koronky and Another v Time-Life Entertainment Group Ltd and Another ... [2007] 1 Costs LR 57
Rogers v Merthyr Tydfil County Borough Council ... [2007] 1 Costs LR 77
Russell Young & Co v Brown and Others ... [2007] 4 Costs LR 552
Myatt and Others v National Coal Board ... [2007] 4 Costs LR 564
Various Claimants v Gower Chemicals Ltd and Others ... [2007] 4 Costs LR 647
Birmingham City Council v Crook and Others ... [2007] 5 Costs LR 732
Crane v Canons Leisure Centre ... [2008] 1 Costs LR 132
Jones v Wrexham Borough Council ... [2008] 1 Costs LR 147
Fenton v Holmes ... [2008] 2 Costs LR 238
Gloucestershire County Council v Evans and Others ... [2008] 2 Costs LR 308
Fosberry v Her Majesty's Revenue & Customs ... [2008] 3 Costs LR 380
Utting v McBain ... [2008] 3 Costs LR 442
Supperstone v Hurst and Hurst ... [2008] 4 Costs LR 572
Kilby v Gawith ... [2008] 6 Costs LR 959
Strachey v Ramage ... [2009] 1 Costs LR 9
Birmingham City Council v Forde ... [2009] 2 Costs LR 206
Oliver v Whipps Cross University Hospital NHS Trust and Waltham Forest Primary Care Trust ... [2009] 3 Costs LR 474
Kris Motor Spares Ltd v Fox Williams LLP ... [2009] 6 Costs LR 931
McCarthy v Essex Rivers Healthcare NHS Trust ... [2010] 1 Costs LR 59
Barr and Others v Biffa Waste Services Ltd and Another (Westmill Landfill Group Litigation) ... [2010] 3 Costs LR 291
Barr and Others v Biffa Waste Services Ltd (No. 2) (Westmill Landfill Group Litigation) ... [2010] 3 Costs LR 317
Silvera v Bray Walker Solicitors and Another ... [2010] 4 Costs LR 584

Kris Motor Spares Ltd v Fox Williams LLP ....[2010] 4 Costs LR 620

Costs Capping

A B and Others v Leeds Teaching Hospitals NHS Trust (In the Matter of the Nationwide Organ Group Litigation) ....[2003] 3 Costs LR 405
Ledward Claimants v Kent & Medway Health Authority and East Kent Hospitals NHS Trust; Cost Capping Application....................[2004] 1 Costs LR 101
Various Ledward Claimants v Kent & Medway Health Authority and East Kent Hospitals NHS Trust; Cost Capping Application....................[2004] 1 Costs LR 101
Smart v East Cheshire NHS Trust ....[2004] 1 Costs LR 124
Lynch v Paul Davidson Taylor (a Firm) ....[2004] 2 Costs LR 321
King v Telegraph Group Ltd ....[2004] 3 Costs LR 449
R (Corner House Research) v The Secretary of State for Trade and Industry ....[2005] 3 Costs LR 455
Sheppard v Essex Strategic Health Authority....................[2006] 1 Costs LR 8
Henry v British Broadcasting Corporation....................[2006] 3 Costs LR 412
Tierney v News Group Newspapers Ltd ....[2006] 4 Costs LR 606
Knight v Beyond Properties Pty Ltd and Others....................[2007] 1 Costs LR 5
Peacock v MGN Ltd ....[2009] 4 Costs LR 584
Eweida v British Airways plc ....[2010] 1 Costs LR 43
Barr and Others v Biffa Waste Services Ltd (No. 2) (Westmill Landfill Group Litigation) ....[2010] 3 Costs LR 317
HR Trustees Ltd v German and Another (In the Matter of the IMG Pension Plan)....................[2010] 3 Costs LR 443
R (Garner) v Elmbridge Borough Council and Others ....[2011] 1 Costs LR 48
Coedbach Action Team Ltd v Secretary of State for Energy and Climate Change and Others ....[2011] 1 Costs LR 70

Cracked Trials

R v Bellas and five other appeals ....(1986) Costs LR (Core) 479
R v Dawson ....[1999] 1 Costs LR 4
Lord Chancellor v Taylor....................[2000] 1 Costs LR 1
R v Fairhurst ....[2000] 1 Costs LR 34
R v Faulkner ....[2003] 1 Costs LR 148
R v Edwards....................[2004] 4 Costs LR 679
R v Frampton....................[2005] 3 Costs LR 527
R v Finn ....[2006] 3 Costs LR 525
R v Johnson ....[2006] 5 Costs LR 852
R v Johnson (Craig) ....[2007] 2 Costs LR 316
R v Alays and Others....................[2007] 2 Costs LR 321
Lord Chancellor v Frieze ....[2007] 5 Costs LR 684
R v Leigh (John)....................[2008] 1 Costs LR 191
R v Wallace ....[2008] 3 Costs LR 494
R v Sanghera and Others ....[2008] 5 Costs LR 823
R v Carty ....[2009] 3 Costs LR 500
R v Harris ....[2009] 3 Costs LR 507
R v Chowdhury ....[2009] 3 Costs LR 514
R v Hann ....[2009] 5 Costs LR 833
R v Phillips....................[2009] 6 Costs LR 993
Lord Chancellor v Purnell and McCarthy ....[2010] 1 Costs LR 81
R v Gkampos ....[2011] 1 Costs LR 142

Defendant's Costs Orders

R v Preston Crown Court ex parte Lancashire County Council....................[1999] 1 Costs LR 58
R v Smith (Philip)....................[2008] 4 Costs LR 656
R v Theobald ....[2008] 4 Costs LR 662

Detailed Assessment

Anthony v Ellis & Fairbairn (a Firm)....................[2000] 2 Costs LR 277
South Coast Shipping Company Ltd v Havant Borough Council....................[2002] 1 Costs LR 98
Pine v The Law Society ....[2002] 3 Costs LR 347
Nugent and Killick v Michael Goss Aviation and Others....................[2002] 3 Costs LR 359
Bufton v Hill ....[2002] 3 Costs LR 381
Ortwein v Rugby Mansions Ltd....................[2004] 1 Costs LR 26
Smart v East Cheshire NHS Trust ....[2004] 1 Costs LR 124

Disclosure

Discontinuance

R (Allbutt) v The Ministry of Defence and Others ....[2011] 1 Costs LR 1
Hoist UK Ltd v Reid Lifting Ltd ....[2011] 1 Costs LR 36

Discretion

R v Osagie ....(1984) Costs LR (Core) 433
London Borough of Southwark v Nejad and Others ....[1999] 1 Costs LR 62
Joseph v Boyd & Hutchinson..........[1999] 1 Costs LR 74
Griffiths and Others v Solutia (UK) Ltd ....[2001] 1 Costs LR 99
Amber v Stacey ....[2001] 2 Costs LR 325
Hall v Rover Financial Services Ltd (GB) t/a Land Rover Financial Services ....[2003] 1 Costs LR 70
Powell v Herefordshire Health Authority..........[2003] 2 Costs LR 185
CIBC Mellon Trust Company Ltd and Another v Mora Hotel Corporation NY and Others..........[2003] 3 Costs LR 334
Jackson v The Lord Chancellor ....[2003] 3 Costs LR 395
McIlwraith v McIlwraith ....[2004] 4 Costs LR 533
R (Davies) (No. 2) v HM Deputy Coroner for Birmingham ....[2004] 4 Costs LR 545
Fleming v Chief Constable of the Sussex Police Force ....[2005] 1 Costs LR 1
Gil v Baygreen Properties Ltd (in Liquidation) and Others ....[2005] 1 Costs LR 75
Arrowfield Services Ltd v BP Collins (a Firm) ....[2005] 2 Costs LR 171
Kundrath v Harry Kwatia & Gooding..........[2005] 2 Costs LR 279
Painting v University of Oxford ....[2005] 3 Costs LR 394
R v Smith (Thomas) ....[2006] 1 Costs LR 167
Haji-Ioannou v Frangos and Others..........[2007] 2 Costs LR 253
R v Bowles ....[2007] 3 Costs LR 514
Aspin v Metric Group Ltd ....[2008] 2 Costs LR 259
R v Griffin ....[2008] 3 Costs LR 483
Angel Airlines SA v Dean & Dean (QBD) ....[2009] 2 Costs LR 159
Angel Airlines SA v Dean & Dean (CA) ....[2009] 2 Costs LR 182
Morgan v UPS ....[2009] 3 Costs LR 384
Morgan and Baker v Hinton Organics (Wessex) Ltd and CAJE..........[2010] 1 Costs LR 1
Onay v Brown ....[2010] 1 Costs LR 29
Kunaka v Barclays Bank plc..........[2011] 2 Costs LR 179
Mortgage Express v Sawali ....[2011] 2 Costs LR 288

enforcement

Wallace and Wallace v Brian Gale & Associates (a Firm)..........[1998] 2 Costs LR 53
Mohammed v Alaga & Co..........[1999] 2 Costs LR 169
Chohan v Times Newspaper Ltd ....[2001] 1 Costs LR 127
Chohan v Times Newspapers Ltd..........[2002] 1 Costs LR 1
Myler and Mirror Group Newspapers v Williams ....[2003] 4 Costs LR 566
Spencer v Wood and Wood t/a Gordons Tyres (a Firm) ....[2004] 3 Costs LR 372
Kellar and Carib West Ltd v Williams ....[2005] 4 Costs LR 559
Holmes v Alfred McAlpine Homes (Yorkshire) Ltd ....[2006] 3 Costs LR 466
Garrett v Halton Borough Council; Myatt and Others v National Coal Board ....[2006] 5 Costs LR 798
Gaynor v Central West London Buses Ltd ....[2007] 1 Costs LR 33
Birmingham City Council v Crook and Others ....[2007] 5 Costs LR 732
Wilson v The Specter Partnership and Others ....[2007] 6 Costs LR 802
Utting v McBain..........[2008] 3 Costs LR 442
Amber Construction Services Ltd v London Interspace HG Ltd ....[2008] 5 Costs LR 715
Truex v Toll ....[2009] 5 Costs LR 758
Silvera v Bray Walker Solicitors and Another..........[2010] 4 Costs LR 584
Westlaw Services Ltd and Another v Boddy and Another ....[2010] 6 Costs LR 934

Enhancement

R v Backhouse ....(1986) Costs LR (Core) 445
R v Rycott ....(1992) Costs LR (Core) 449
Miller Gardner v The Lord Chancellor ....[1997] 2 Costs LR 29
R v Cevik ....[1998] 2 Costs LR 1
R v Walpole ....[2002] 1 Costs LR 199
Ali and Others v Lord Chancellor's Department ....[2002] 2 Costs LR 258
R v Oldcorn ....[2003] 2 Costs LR 310

Ex Post Facto Assessment

Exaggerated Claims

Expert Witnesses

Family Proceedings

A Local Authority v A Mother and Child ....[2001] 1 Costs LR 136
D v D ....[2002] 2 Costs LR 312
Norris v Norris; Haskins v Haskins ....[2003] 4 Costs LR 591
E C-L v DM ....[2005] 4 Costs LR 576
B (Children) ....[2005] 4 Costs LR 675
Currey v Currey ....[2007] 2 Costs LR 227
Baker v Rowe ....[2010] 2 Costs LR 175
Oxfordshire County Council v X and Others ....[2010] 5 Costs LR 751

Graduated Fee Scheme

R v Sturdy ....[1999] 1 Costs LR 1
R v Carlyle ....[2002] 1 Costs LR 192
R v Ayres ....[2002] 2 Costs LR 330
R v Chubb ....[2002] 2 Costs LR 333
Lord Chancellor v Singh ....[2003] 1 Costs LR 62
R v Faulkner ....[2003] 1 Costs LR 148
R v Knight ....[2003] 3 Costs LR 496
R v Dalziell ....[2003] 4 Costs LR 651
R v Brook ....[2004] 1 Costs LR 178
R v Smith ....[2004] 2 Costs LR 348
R v Foot ....[2004] 3 Costs LR 525
R v Edwards ....[2004] 4 Costs LR 679
R v Prenga ....[2004] 4 Costs LR 699
R v Briers (Michael) ....[2005] 1 Costs LR 146
R v Khan (Zulfi Al) ....[2005] 1 Costs LR 157
R v Shaw (Mark Anthony) ....[2005] 2 Costs LR 326
R v Staniland (Craig) ....[2005] 2 Costs LR 337
R v Frampton ....[2005] 3 Costs LR 527
R v Bond (Michael) ....[2005] 3 Costs LR 532
R v McGunigle (Thomas) ....[2005] 3 Costs LR 537
R v Hadley ....[2005] 3 Costs LR 548
R v Taylor ....[2005] 4 Costs LR 712
R v McClean ....[2005] 4 Costs LR 740
R v Despres ....[2005] 4 Costs LR 750
Meeke and Taylor v Secretary of State for Constitutional Affairs ....[2006] 1 Costs LR 1
Secretary of State for Constitutional Affairs v Stork ....[2006] 1 Costs LR 69
R v Marandola ....[2006] 1 Costs LR 184
R v Henshaw ....[2006] 1 Costs LR 191
R v Warren ....[2006] 2 Costs LR 336
R v Brinkworth ....[2006] 3 Costs LR 512
R v Rigelsford ....[2006] 3 Costs LR 518
R v Finn ....[2006] 3 Costs LR 525
R v Ismail ....[2006] 3 Costs LR 530
R v Ranjit ....[2006] 3 Costs LR 541
R v Maguire ....[2006] 4 Costs LR 678
R v Gill (Steven) ....[2006] 5 Costs LR 837
R v Johnson ....[2006] 5 Costs LR 852
R v Davies (Benjamin) ....[2007] 1 Costs LR 116
R v Chapple ....[2007] 2 Costs LR 310
R v Johnson (Craig) ....[2007] 2 Costs LR 316
R v Alays and Others ....[2007] 2 Costs LR 321
R v Matthews (Rosalind) and Others ....[2007] 2 Costs LR 328
Goodman and Farr v The Secretary of State for Constitutional Affairs ....[2007] 3 Costs LR 366
Lord Chancellor v Frieze ....[2007] 5 Costs LR 684
Lord Chancellor v Haggan and Others ....[2007] 5 Costs LR 722
R v Larsh ....[2007] 5 Costs LR 783
R v Hill and Dalton ....[2007] 5 Costs LR 788
R v Harper ....[2007] 6 Costs LR 862
R v Ainsworth ....[2007] 6 Costs LR 865
R v Solomka ....[2007] 6 Costs LR 868

Guilty Pleas

Hourly Rates

Impecunious Claimants

Indemnity Costs

Indemnity Principle

Interest

Judicial Review

Jurisdiction

Stubblefield and Others v Kemp and Others	[2001] 1 Costs LR 30
Sinclair v British Telecommunications plc	[2001] 1 Costs LR 40
Rosling King v Rothschild Trust	[2005] 2 Costs LR 165
Gray v Going Places Leisure Travel Ltd	[2005] 3 Costs LR 405
HM Revenue & Customs v Viewtopia Ltd	[2006] 2 Costs LR 344
Nicholas Drukker & Co v Pridie Brewster & Co	[2006] 3 Costs LR 439
Westland Helicopters Ltd v Sheikh Salah Al-Hejailan	[2006] 4 Costs LR 549
Goodwood Recoveries Ltd v Breen; Breen v Slater	[2007] 2 Costs LR 147
Currey v Currey	[2007] 2 Costs LR 227
Angel Airlines SA v Dean & Dean Solicitors	[2007] 3 Costs LR 355
Lahey v Pirelli Tyres Ltd	[2007] 3 Costs LR 462
Richardson Roofing Company Ltd v The Colman Partnership Ltd	[2009] 4 Costs LR 521
Dadourian Group International Inc and Others v Simms and Others	[2010] 1 Costs LR 89
Baker v Rowe	[2010] 2 Costs LR 175
Hoist UK Ltd v Reid Lifting Ltd	[2011] 1 Costs LR 36
R (Edwards and Another) v Environment Agency and Others	[2011] 2 Costs LR 151
Conservative and Unionist Party v The Election Commissioner and Others	[2011] 2 Costs LR 298

Legal Services Commission

R v Secretary of State for the Home Department ex parte Gunn	[2001] 2 Costs LR 263
Snowden v Ministry of Defence	[2002] 2 Costs LR 249
Howarth v Green	[2003] 2 Costs LR 160
Cavaliere v Legal Services Commission	[2003] 3 Costs LR 350
Hinde v Harbourne and Others	[2004] 2 Costs LR 289
R v Syed	[2004] 4 Costs LR 686
R v McGunigle (Thomas)	[2005] 3 Costs LR 537
R v Hadley	[2005] 3 Costs LR 548
R v McClean	[2005] 4 Costs LR 740
R v Henshaw	[2006] 1 Costs LR 191
W (a Child), Re; D and DW v Portsmouth Hospital NHS Trust	[2006] 5 Costs LR 742
Aehmed and Others v The Legal Services Commission	[2009] 3 Costs LR 425
Liverpool Freeport Electronics Ltd and Others v Habib Bank Ltd and The Legal Services Commission	[2009] 3 Costs LR 434
R (E) v Governing Body of JFS and Others	[2009] 4 Costs LR 695
R v O'Cuneff	[2010] 3 Costs LR 476
R v Burbidge	[2010] 4 Costs LR 639
Floyd v S and Legal Services Commission	[2010] 5 Costs LR 739
R v Rayan	[2010] 6 Costs LR 969
R v Charlery; R v Small	[2011] 2 Costs LR 331

Litigants in Person

Hart v Aga Khan Foundation (UK)	(1984) Costs LR (Core) 87
Law Society v Persaud	(1990) Costs LR (Core) 114
Mainwaring and Lisle and Goldtech Investments Ltd; Goldtech Investments Ltd and Mainwaring and Lisle	[1997] 1 Costs LR 143
Official Receiver (The) v Brunt and Others	[1998] 2 Costs LR 38
Official Receiver (The) v Brunt and Others	[1999] 2 Costs LR 97
Mealing-McLeod v The Common Professional Examination Board	[2000] 2 Costs LR 223
R v Mold Crown Court ex parte Khan	[2001] 2 Costs LR 336
Morris v Wiltshire and Woodspring District Council and the Supreme Court Costs Office	[2002] 1 Costs LR 167
R (Wulfsohn) v Legal Services Commission	[2002] 3 Costs LR 341
Khan v Lord Chancellor	[2003] 2 Costs LR 228
Sutton v Horsham District Council	[2005] 2 Costs LR 344
Szekeres v Alan Smeath & Co	[2005] 4 Costs LR 707
Agassi v Robinson (HM Inspector of Taxes) (Bar Council and Law Society Intervening)	[2006] 2 Costs LR 283
Paturel v Marble Arch Services Ltd	[2006] 4 Costs LR 556
Horsford v Bird and Others	[2007] 2 Costs LR 245
Kunaka v Barclays Bank plc	[2011] 2 Costs LR 179

London Solicitors

Wraith and Sheffield Forgemasters Ltd ....[1997] 1 Costs LR 23
Truscott v Truscott; Wraith v Sheffield Forgemasters Ltd ....[1997] 2 Costs LR 74
Sullivan v The Co-Operative Insurance Society Ltd ....[1999] 2 Costs LR 158
Griffiths and Others v Solutia (UK) Ltd ....[2001] 1 Costs LR 99
Solutia UK Ltd v Griffiths and 165 Others ....[2001] 2 Costs LR 247
Gazley v Wade and News Group Newspapers Ltd ....[2005] 1 Costs LR 129
A v The Chief Constable of South Yorkshire Police ....[2008] 6 Costs LR 935
Earles v Barclays Bank plc ....[2009] 6 Costs LR 906
Higgins v Ministry of Defence ....[2010] 6 Costs LR 867

Misconduct

Joseph v Boyd & Hutchinson ....[1999] 1 Costs LR 74
Mars UK Ltd v Teknowledge Ltd ....[1999] 2 Costs LR 44
Sony Music Entertainment Inc and Sony Music Entertainment (UK) Ltd v Prestige Records Ltd and Dancebuy Ltd (t/a Slam Music) ....[2000] 2 Costs LR 186
Reid Minty (a Firm) v Taylor ....[2002] 1 Costs LR 180
Hall v Rover Financial Services Ltd (GB) t/a Land Rover Financial Services ....[2003] 1 Costs LR 70
Adrian Alan Ltd v Fuglers (a Firm) ....[2003] 4 Costs LR 518
Burton Marsden Douglas (a Firm), In the Matter of; Marsden and Douglas v Guide Dogs for the Blind Association and Others ....[2004] 3 Costs LR 378
Aaron v Shelton ....[2004] 3 Costs LR 488
Fleming v Chief Constable of the Sussex Police Force ....[2005] 1 Costs LR 1
Painting v University of Oxford ....[2005] 3 Costs LR 394
Nicholas Drukker & Co v Pridie Brewster & Co ....[2006] 3 Costs LR 439
Northstar Systems Ltd and Others v Fielding and Others ....[2007] 2 Costs LR 264
Lahey v Pirelli Tyres Ltd ....[2007] 3 Costs LR 462
Baxendale-Walker v The Law Society ....[2007] 3 Costs LR 475
R v Newport ....[2009] 6 Costs LR 983
Fitzpatrick Contractors Ltd v Tyco Fire and Integrated Solutions (UK) Ltd (No. 3) ....[2010] 2 Costs LR 115
Governing Body of St Albans Girls' School and Hertfordshire County Council v Neary ....[2010] 2 Costs LR 191
Shah v Ul-Haq and Others ....[2010] 3 Costs LR 336
Widlake v BAA Ltd ....[2010] 3 Costs LR 353
Sulaman v Axa Insurance plc and Another ....[2010] 3 Costs LR 391
Owens v Noble ....[2010] 4 Costs LR 540
Bank of Tokyo-Mitsubishi UFJ Ltd and Another v Baskan Gida Sanayi Ve Pazarlama AS and Others ....[2010] 5 Costs LR 657

Non-Party Costs Orders

Metalloy Supplies Ltd v MA (UK) Ltd ....[1998] 1 Costs LR 85
Murphy and Another v Young & Co's Brewery and Another ....[1998] 1 Costs LR 94
Locabail (UK) Ltd v Bayfield Properties and Others and Emmanuel v Locabail (UK) Ltd and Another ....[2000] 2 Costs LR 169
Dymocks Franchise Systems (NSW) Pty Ltd v Todd and Others (No. 2) ....[2005] 1 Costs LR 52
Barndeal Ltd and Another v London Borough of Richmond-Upon-Thames ....[2006] 1 Costs LR 47
PR Records Ltd v Vinyl 2000 Ltd and Owlett (Susan) and Owlett (Adrian) ....[2008] 1 Costs LR 19
Adris and Others v The Royal Bank of Scotland plc and Others ....[2010] 4 Costs LR 598

Pages of Prosecution Evidence

R v Dhaliwal ....[2004] 4 Costs LR 689
R v Warren ....[2006] 2 Costs LR 336
R v Rigelsford ....[2006] 3 Costs LR 518
R v Austin ....[2006] 5 Costs LR 857
Goodman and Farr v The Secretary of State for Constitutional Affairs ....[2007] 3 Costs LR 366
R v Ainsworth ....[2007] 6 Costs LR 865
R v Coutts (Graham) ....[2007] 6 Costs LR 878
R v Tucker ....[2009] 5 Costs LR 850
R v Cadogan ....[2009] 5 Costs LR 853
R v Neil ....[2010] 2 Costs LR 283
R v O'Cuneff ....[2010] 3 Costs LR 476
R v Burbidge ....[2010] 4 Costs LR 639

Part 36 Offers

Permission to Appeal

Privilege

Proportionality

Representation Orders

Retainers

Special Preparation

Success Fees

Summary Assessment

Very High Costs Cases

Wasted Costs Orders

PART 5 ESSENTIAL SUPPORT INFORMATION

Civil Proceedings Fees Order 2008

SI 2008 No 1053

The following sets out the Fees payable under the Order (as amended) in force with effect from the 4th April 2011.

Citation and commencement

1

(1) This Order may be cited as the Civil Proceedings Fees Order 2008 and shall come into force on 1st May 2008.

(2) In this Order—

(a) "CCBC" means County Court Bulk Centre;

(b) "the CPR" means the Civil Procedure Rules 1998;

(c) "LSC" means the Legal Services Commission established under section 1 of the Access to Justice Act 1999;

(d) expressions also used in the CPR have the same meaning as in those Rules.

Fees payable

2 The fees set out in column 2 of Schedule 1 are payable in the Supreme Court and in county courts in respect of the items described in column 1 in accordance with and subject to the directions specified in that column.

3 No fee is payable in respect of—

(a) non-contentious probate business;

(b) the enrolment of documents;

(c) criminal proceedings (except proceedings on the Crown side of the Queen's Bench Division to which the fees in Schedule 1 are applicable);

(d) proceedings by sheriffs, under-sheriffs, deputy-sheriffs or other officers of the sheriff; or

(e) family proceedings in the High Court or in a county court.

4 Where by any convention entered into by Her Majesty with any foreign power it is provided that no fee is required to be paid in respect of any proceedings, the fees specified in this Order are not payable in respect of those proceedings.

Remissions and part remissions

5 Schedule 2 applies for the purpose of ascertaining whether a party is entitled to a remission or part remission of a fee prescribed by this Order.

Revocations

6 The instruments listed in column 1 of the table in Schedule 3 (which have the references listed in column 2) are revoked.

SCHEDULE 1: FEES TO BE TAKEN

Column 1	*Column 2*
Number and description of fee	*Amount of fee*
1 Starting proceedings (High Court and county court)	
1.1 On starting proceedings (including proceedings issued after permission to issue is granted but excluding Claim Production Centre cases brought by Centre users or cases brought by Money Claim On Line users) to recover a sum of money where the sum claimed:	
(a) does not exceed £300;	£35
(b) exceeds £300 but does not exceed £500;	£50
(c) exceeds £500 but does not exceed £1,000;	£70
(d) exceeds £1,000 but does not exceed £1,500;	£80
(e) exceeds £1,500 but does not exceed £3,000;	£95
(f) exceeds £3,000 but does not exceed £5,000;	£120
(g) exceeds £5,000 but does not exceed £15,000;	£245
(h) exceeds £15,000 but does not exceed £50,000;	£395
(i) exceeds £50,000 but does not exceed £100,000;	£685
(j) exceeds £100,000 but does not exceed £150,000;	£885
(k) exceeds £150,000 but does not exceed £200,000;	£1,080
(l) exceeds £200,000 but does not exceed £250,000;	£1,275
(m) exceeds £250,000 but does not exceed £300,000;	£1,475
(n) exceeds £300,000 or is not limited.	£1,670
1.2 On starting proceedings to recover a sum of money in Claim Production Centre cases brought by Centre users, where the sum claimed:	
(a) does not exceed £300;	£15
(b) exceeds £300 but does not exceed £500;	£30
(c) exceeds £500 but does not exceed £1,000;	£55
(d) exceeds £1,000 but does not exceed £1,500;	£65
(e) exceeds £1,500 but does not exceed £3,000;	£75
(f) exceeds £3,000 but does not exceed £5,000;	£85
(g) exceeds £5,000 but does not exceed £15,000;	£190
(h) exceeds £15,000 but does not exceed £50,000;	£310
(i) exceeds £50,000 but does not exceed £100,000.	£550
1.3 On starting proceedings to recover a sum of money brought by Money Claim On Line users where the sum claimed:	
(a) does not exceed £300;	£25
(b) exceeds £300 but does not exceed £500;	£35
(c) exceeds £500 but does not exceed £1,000;	£60
(d) exceeds £1,000 but does not exceed £1,500;	£70
(e) exceeds £1,500 but does not exceed £3,000;	£80
(f) exceeds £3,000 but does not exceed £5,000;	£100
(g) exceeds £5,000 but does not exceed £15,000;	£210

Column 1	*Column 2*
Number and description of fee	*Amount of fee*
(h) exceeds £15,000 but does not exceed £50,000;	£340
(i) exceeds £50,000 but does not exceed £100,000.	£595
Fees 1.1, 1.2 and 1.3.	
Where the claimant is making a claim for interest on a specified sum of money, the amount on which the fee is calculated is the total amount of the claim and the interest.	
1.4 On starting proceedings for the recovery of land:	
(a) in the High Court;	£465
(b) in the county court, other than where fee 1.4(c) applies;	£175
(c) using the Possession Claims Online website.	£100
1.5 On starting proceedings for any other remedy (including proceedings issued after permission to issue is granted):	
in the High Court;	£465
in the county court.	£175
Fees 1.1, 1.4 and 1.5. Recovery of land or goods.	
Where a claim for money is additional or alternative to a claim for recovery of land or goods, only fee 1.4 or 1.5 is payable.	
Fees 1.1and 1.5. Claims other than recovery of land or goods.	
Where a claim for money is additional to a non money claim (other than a claim for recovery of land or goods), then fee 1.1 is payable in addition to fee 1.5.	
Where a claim for money is alternative to a non money claim (other than a claim for recovery of land or goods), only fee 1.1 is payable in the High Court, and, in the county court, whichever is greater of fee 1.1 or fee 1.5 is payable.	
Fees 1.1 and 1.5.	
Where more than one non money claim is made in the same proceedings, fee 1.5 is payable once only, in addition to any fee which may be payable under fee 1.1.	
Fees 1.1 and 1.5 are not payable where fee 1.8(b), fee 1.9(a), fee 3 or fee 10.1 applies.	
Fees 1.1 and fee 1.5. Amendment of claim or counterclaim.	
Where the claim or counterclaim is amended, and the fee paid before amendment is less than that which would have been payable if the document, as amended, had been so drawn in the first instance, the party amending the document must pay the difference.	
1.6 On the filing of proceedings against a party or parties not named in the proceedings.	£45
Fee 1.6 is payable by a defendant who adds or substitutes a party or parties to the proceedings or by a claimant who adds or substitutes a defendant or defendants.	
1.7 On the filing of a counterclaim.	The same fee as if the remedy sought were the subject of separate proceedings

Column 1	*Column 2*
Number and description of fee	*Amount of fee*
No fee is payable on a counterclaim which a defendant is required to make under rule 57.8 of the CPR (requirement to serve a counterclaim if a defendant makes a claim or seeks a remedy in relation to a grant of probate of a will, or letters of administration of an estate, of a deceased person).	
1.8(a) On an application for permission to issue proceedings.	£45
(b) On an application for an order under Part 3 of the Solicitors Act 1974 for the assessment of costs payable to a solicitor by a client or on starting costs-only proceedings.	£45
1.9(a) For permission to apply for judicial review.	£60
Where the court has made an order giving permission to proceed with a claim for judicial review, there is payable by the claimant within 7 days of service on the claimant of that order:	
1.9(b) if the judicial review procedure has been started.	£215
1.9(c) if the claim for judicial review was started otherwise than by using the judicial review procedure.	£60
2 General Fees (High Court and county courts)	
2.1 On the claimant filing an allocation questionnaire; or	
where the court dispenses with the need for an allocation questionnaire, within 14 days of the date of despatch of the notice of allocation to track; or	
where the CPR or a Practice Direction provide for automatic allocation or provide that the rules on allocation do not apply, within 28 days of the filing of the defence (or the filing of the last defence if there is more than one defendant), or within 28 days of the expiry of the time permitted for filing all defences if sooner:	
(a) if the case is on the small claims track and the claim exceeds £1,500;	£40
(b) if the case is on the fast track or multi-track.	£220
Fee 2.1 is payable by the claimant except where the action is proceeding on the counterclaim alone, when it is payable by the defendant:	
on the defendant filing an allocation questionnaire; or	
where the court dispenses with the need for an allocation questionnaire, within 14 days of the date of despatch of the notice of allocation to track; or	
where the CPR or a Practice Direction provide for automatic allocation or provide that the rules on allocation do not apply, within 28 days of the filing of the defence to the counterclaim (or the filing of the last defence to the counterclaim if there is more than one party entitled to file a defence to the counterclaim), or within 28 days of the expiry of the time permitted for filing all defences to the counterclaim if sooner.	
Where fee 2.1 is payable on the filing of an allocation questionnaire, by the claimant or the defendant as the case may be, the fee payable is based on the track for the case specified in the allocation questionnaire. If the case is subsequently allocated to a track which attracts a higher fee then the difference in fee is payable, by the party liable to pay the fee, within 14 days of the date of despatch of notice of allocation to track. If the case is allocated to a track which attracts a lower fee the difference in fee will be refunded.	
2.2 On the claimant filing a pre-trial check list (listing questionnaire); or where the court fixes the trial date or trial week without the need for a pre-trial check list, within 14 days of the date of despatch of the notice (or the date when oral notice is given if no written notice is given) of the trial week or the trial date if no trial week is fixed.	£110
Fee 2.2 is payable by the claimant except where the action is proceeding on the counterclaim alone, when it is payable by the defendant:	
on the defendant filing a pre-trial check list; or	

Column 1	*Column 2*
Number and description of fee	*Amount of fee*
where the court fixes the trial date or trial week without the need for a pre-trial check list, within 14 days of the date of despatch of the notice (or the date when oral notice is given if no written notice is given) of the trial week or the trial date if no trial week is fixed.	
Fees 2.1 and 2.2 in the High Court and the county court.	
Fees 2.1 and 2.2 are payable as appropriate where the court allocates a case to track for a trial of the assessment of damages.	
Fees 2.1 and 2.2 are not payable in relation to claims managed under a Group Litigation Order after that Order is made.	
Fees 2.1 and 2.2 are payable once only in the same proceedings.	
Fee 2.1 is not payable where the procedure in Part 8 of the CPR is used.	
Fee 2.2 is not payable where the court fixed the hearing date on the issue of the claim.	
Fees 2.1 and 2.2 in the county court	
Fee 2.1 is not payable in proceedings where the only claim is a claim to recover a sum of money and the sum claimed does not exceed £1,500.	
Fee 2.2 is not payable in respect of a case on the small claims track.	
2.3 On the occasion of fee 2.2 becoming payable; or where the claim is on the small claims track, within 14 days of the date of despatch of the notice (or the date when oral notice is given if no written notice is given) of the trial week or the trial date if no trial week is fixed a fee payable for the hearing of:	
(a) a case on the multi-track;	£1,090
(b) a case on the fast track;	£545
(c) a case on the small claims track where the sum claimed:	
(i) does not exceed £300;	£25
(ii) exceeds £300 but does not exceed £500;	£55
(iii) exceeds £500 but does not exceed £1,000;	£80
(iv) exceeds £1,000 but does not exceed £1,500;	£110
(v) exceeds £1,500 but does not exceed £3,000;	£165
(vi) exceeds £3,000.	£325
Fee 2.3 is payable by the claimant except where the action is proceeding on the counterclaim alone, when it is payable by the defendant:	
on the defendant filing a pre-trial check list; or	
where the claim is on the small claims track or the court fixes the trial date or trial week without the need for a pre-trial check list, within 14 days of the date of despatch of the notice (or the date when oral notice is given if no written notice is given) of the trial week or the trial date if no trial week is fixed.	
Where a case is on the multi-track or fast track and, after a hearing date has been fixed, the court receives notice in writing from the party who paid the hearing fee that the case has been settled or discontinued then the following percentages of the hearing fee will be refunded:	
(i) 100% if the court is notified more than 28 days before the hearing;	
(ii) 75% if the court is notified between 15 and 28 days before the hearing;	
(iii) 50% if the court is notified between 7 and 14 days before the hearing.	
Where a case is on the small claims track and, after a hearing date has been fixed, the court receives notice in writing from the party who paid the hearing fee, at least 7 days before the date set for the hearing, that the case has been settled or discontinued the hearing fee will be refunded in full.	

Column 1	*Column 2*
Number and description of fee	*Amount of fee*
Fee 2.3 is not payable in respect of a case where the court fixed the hearing date on the issue of the claim.	
2.4 In the High Court on filing:	£235
an appellant's notice: or	
a respondent's notice where the respondent is appealing or wishes to ask the appeal court to uphold the order of the lower court for reasons different from or additional to those given by the lower court.	
2.5 In the county court on filing:	
an appellant's notice, or	
a respondent's notice where the respondent is appealing or wishes to ask the appeal court to uphold the order of the lower court for reasons different from or additional to those given by the lower court:	
(a) in a claim allocated to the small claims track;	£115
(b) in all other claims.	£135
Fees 2.4 and 2.5 do not apply on appeals against a decision made in detailed assessment proceedings.	
2.6 On an application on notice where no other fee is specified.	£80
2.7 On an application by consent or without notice where no other fee is specified.	£45
For the purpose of fee 2.7 a request for a judgment or order on admission or in default does not constitute an application and no fee is payable.	
Fee 2.7 is not payable in relation to an application by consent for an adjournment of a hearing where the application is received by the court at least 14 days before the date set for that hearing.	
Fees 2.6 and 2.7 are not payable when an application is made in an appeal notice or is filed at the same time as an appeal notice.	
2.8 On an application for a summons or order for a witness to attend court to be examined on oath or an order for evidence to be taken by deposition, other than an application for which fee 7.2 or 8.3 is payable.	£40
2.9 On an application to vary a judgment or suspend enforcement, including an application to suspend a warrant of possession.	£40
Where more than one remedy is sought in the same application only one fee is payable.	
2.10 Register of judgments, orders and fines kept under section 98 of the Courts Act 2003:	
On a request for the issue of a certificate of satisfaction.	£15
3 Companies Act 1985, Companies Act 2006 and Insolvency Act 1986 (High Court and county court)	
3.1 On entering a bankruptcy petition:	
(a) if presented by a debtor or the personal representative of a deceased debtor;	£175
(b) if presented by a creditor or other person.	£220
3.2 On entering a petition for an administration order.	£175
3.3 On entering any other petition.	£220
One fee only is payable where more than one petition is presented in relation to a partnership.	
3.4(a) On a request for a certificate of discharge from bankruptcy;	£70
(b) after the first certificate, for each copy.	£5
3.5 On an application under the Companies Act 1985, the Companies Act 2006 or the Insolvency Act 1986 other than one brought by petition and where no other fee is specified.	£155
Fee 3.5 is not payable where the application is made in existing proceedings.	

Column 1	*Column 2*
Number and description of fee	*Amount of fee*
3.6 On an application for the conversion of a voluntary arrangement into a winding up or bankruptcy under Article 37 of Council Regulation (EC) No 1346/2000.	£155
3.7 On an application, for the purposes of Council Regulation (EC) No 1346/2000, for an order confirming creditors' voluntary winding up (where the company has passed a resolution for voluntary winding up, and no declaration under section 89 of the Insolvency Act 1986 has been made).	£35
3.8 On filing:	£35
a notice of intention to appoint an administrator under paragraph 14 of Schedule B1 to the Insolvency Act 1986 or in accordance with paragraph 27 of that Schedule; or	
a notice of appointment of an administrator in accordance with paragraphs 18 or 29 of that Schedule.	
Where a person pays fee 3.8 on filing a notice of intention to appoint an administrator, no fee is payable on that same person filing a notice of appointment of that administrator.	
3.9 On submitting a nominee's report under section 2(2) of the Insolvency Act 1986.	£35
3.10 On filing documents in accordance with paragraph 7(1) of Schedule A1 to the Insolvency Act 1986.	£35
3.11 On an application by consent or without notice within existing proceedings where no other fee is specified.	£35
3.12 On an application with notice within existing proceedings where no other fee is specified.	£70
3.13 On a search in person of the bankruptcy and companies records, in a county court.	£45
Requests and applications with no fee:	
No fee is payable on a request or on an application to the Court by the Official Receiver when applying only in the capacity of Official Receiver to the case (and not as trustee or liquidator), or on an application to set aside a statutory demand.	
4 Copy Documents (Court of Appeal, High Court and county court)	
4.1 On a request for a copy of a document (other than where fee 4.2 applies):	
(a) for ten pages or less;	£5
(b) for each subsequent page.	50p
Note: The fee payable under fee 4.1 includes:	
where the court allows a party to fax to the court for the use of that party a document that has not been requested by the court and is not intended to be placed on the court file;	
where a party requests that the court fax a copy of a document from the court file;	
the court provides a subsequent copy of a document which it has previously provided.	
4.2 On a request for a copy of a document on a computer disk or in other electronic form, for each such copy.	£5
5 Determination of costs (Senior Court and county court)	
Fee 5 does not apply to the determination in the Senior Courts of costs incurred in the Court of Protection.	
5.1 On the filing of a request for detailed assessment where the party filing the request is legally aided or is funded by the LSC and no other party is ordered to pay the costs of the proceedings.	£145
5.2 On the filing of a request for detailed assessment in any case where fee 5.1 does not apply; or on the filing of a request for a hearing date for the assessment of costs payable to a solicitor by a client pursuant to an order under Part 3 of the Solicitors Act 1974 where the amount of the costs claimed:	
(a) does not exceed £15,000;	£325
(b) exceeds £15,000 but does not exceed £50,000;	£655

Column 1	*Column 2*
Number and description of fee	*Amount of fee*
(c) exceeds £50,000 but does not exceed £100,000;	£980
(d) exceeds £100,000 but does not exceed £150,000;	£1,310
(e) exceeds £150,000 but does not exceed £200,000;	£1,635
(f) exceeds £200,000 but does not exceed £300,000;	£2,455
(g) exceeds £300,000 but does not exceed £500,000;	£4,090
(h) exceeds £500,000.	£5,455
Where there is a combined party and party and legal aid, or a combined party and party and LSC, or a combined party and party, legal aid and LSC determination of costs, fee 5.2 will be attributed proportionately to the party and party, legal aid, or LSC (as the case may be) portions of the bill on the basis of the amount allowed.	
5.3 On a request for the issue of a default costs certificate.	£60
5.4 On commencing an appeal against a decision made in detailed assessment proceedings.	£205
5.5 On applying for the court's approval of a certificate of costs payable from the Community Legal Service Fund.	£50
Fee 5.5 is payable at the time of applying for the court's approval and is recoverable only against the Community Legal Service Fund.	
5.6 On a request or application to set aside a default costs certificate.	£105
6 Determination in the Senior Court of costs incurred in the Court of Protection	
6.1 On the filing of a request for detailed assessment:	
(a) where the amount of the costs to be assessed (excluding VAT and disbursements) does not exceed £3,000;	£110
(b) in all other cases.	£220
6.2 On an appeal against a decision made in detailed assessment proceedings.	£65
6.3 On a request or application to set aside a default costs certificate.	£65
7 Enforcement in the High Court	
7.1 On sealing a writ of execution/possession/delivery.	£60
Where the recovery of a sum of money is sought in addition to a writ of possession and delivery, no further fee is payable.	
7.2 On an application for an order requiring a judgment debtor or other person to attend court to provide information in connection with enforcement of a judgment or order.	£50
7.3(a) On an application for a third party debt order or the appointment of a receiver by way of equitable execution.	£100
(b) On an application for a charging order.	£100
Fee 7.3(a) is payable in respect of each third party against whom the order is sought.	
Fee 7.3(b) is payable in respect of each charging order applied for.	
7.4 On an application for a judgment summons.	£100
7.5 On a request or application to register a judgment or order, or for permission to enforce an arbitration award, or for a certificate or a certified copy of a judgment or order for use abroad.	£60
8 Enforcement in the county court	
8.1 On an application for or in relation to enforcement of a judgment or order of a county court or through a county court, by the issue of a warrant of execution against goods except a warrant to enforce payment of a fine:	

Column 1	*Column 2*
Number and description of fee	*Amount of fee*
(a) in cases other than CCBC cases;	£100
(b) in CCBC cases.	£70
8.2 On a request for a further attempt at execution of a warrant at a new address following a notice of the reason for non-execution (except a further attempt following suspension and CCBC cases brought by Centre users).	£30
8.3 On an application for an order requiring a judgment debtor or other person to attend court to provide information in connection with enforcement of a judgment or order.	£50
8.4(a) On an application for a third party debt order or the appointment of a receiver by way of equitable execution.	£100
(b) On an application for a charging order.	£100
Fee 8.4(a) is payable in respect of each third party against whom the order is sought.	
Fee 8.4(b) is payable in respect of each charging order applied for.	
8.5 On an application for a judgment summons.	£100
8.6 On the issue of a warrant of possession or a warrant of delivery.	£110
Where the recovery of a sum of money is sought in addition, no further fee is payable.	
8.7 On an application for an attachment of earnings order (other than a consolidated attachment of earnings order) to secure payment of a judgment debt.	£100
Fee 8.7 is payable for each defendant against whom an order is sought.	
Fee 8.7 is not payable where the attachment of earnings order is made on the hearing of a judgment summons.	
8.8 On a consolidated attachment of earnings order or on an administration order. For every £1 or part of a £1 of the money paid into court in respect of debts due to creditors –	10p
Fee 8.8 is calculated on any money paid into court under any order at the rate in force at the time when the order was made (or, where the order has been amended, at the time of the last amendment before the date of payment).	
8.9 On an application for the enforcement of an award for a sum of money or other decision made by any court, tribunal, body or person other than the High Court or a county court.	£40
8.10 On a request for an order to recover a sum that is:	
a specified debt within the meaning of the Enforcement of Road Traffic Debts Order 1993; or	£7
pursuant to an enactment, treated as a specified debt for the purposes of that Order.	
No fee is payable on:	
an application for an extension of time to serve a statutory declaration or a witness statement in connection with any such order; or	
a request to issue a warrant of execution to enforce any such order.	
8A Service in the county court	
8A.1 On a request for service by a bailiff of an order to attend court for questioning.	£100
9 Sale (county court only)	
9.1 For removing or taking steps to remove goods to a place of deposit.	The reasonable expenses incurred
Fee 9.1 is to include the reasonable expenses of feeding and caring for any animals.	

Column 1	*Column 2*
Number and description of fee	*Amount of fee*
9.2 For advertising a sale by public auction pursuant to section 97 of the County Courts Act 1984.	The reasonable expenses incurred
9.3 For the appraisement of goods.	5p in the £1 or part of a £1 of the appraised value
9.4 For the sale of goods (including advertisements, catalogues, sale and commission and delivery of goods).	15p in the £1 or part of a £1 on the amount realised by the sale or such other sum as the district judge may consider to be justified in the circumstances
9.5 Where no sale takes place by reason of an execution being withdrawn, satisfied or stopped.	(a) 10p in the £1 or part of a £1 on the value of the goods seized, the value to be the appraised value where the goods have been appraised or such other sum as the district judge may consider to be justified in the circumstances; and in addition (b) any sum payable under fee 9.1, 9.2 or 9.3
FEES PAYABLE IN HIGH COURT ONLY	
10 Miscellaneous proceedings or matters	
Bills of Sale	
10.1 On filing any document under the Bills of Sale Acts 1878 and the Bills of Sale Act (1878) Amendment Act 1882 or on an application under section 15 of the Bills of Sale Act 1878 for an order that a memorandum of satisfaction be written on a registered copy of the bill.	£25
Searches	
10.2 For an official certificate of the result of a search for each name, in any register or index held by the court; or in the Court Funds Office, for an official certificate of the result of a search of unclaimed balances for a specified period of up to 50 years.	£45
10.3 On a search in person of the bankruptcy and companies records, including inspection, for each 15 minutes or part of 15 minutes.	£7
Judge sitting as arbitrator	
10.4 On the appointment of:	
(a) a judge of the Commercial Court as an arbitrator or umpire under section 93 of the Arbitration Act 1996; or	£2,390
(b) a judge of the Technology and Construction Court as an arbitrator or umpire under section 93 of the Arbitration Act 1996.	£1,860
10.5 For every day or part of a day (after the first day) of the hearing before:	
(a) a judge of the Commercial Court; or	£2,390
(b) a judge of the Technology and Construction Court, so appointed as arbitrator or umpire.	£1,860

Column 1	*Column 2*
Number and description of fee	*Amount of fee*
Where fee 10.4 has been paid on the appointment of a judge of the Commercial Court or a judge of the Technology and Construction Court as an arbitrator or umpire but the arbitration does not proceed to a hearing or an award, the fee will be refunded.	
11 Fees payable in Admiralty matters	
In the Admiralty Registrar and Marshal's Office:	
11.1 On the issue of a warrant for the arrest of a ship or goods.	£220
11.2 On the sale of a ship or goods	
Subject to a minimum fee of £200:	
(a) for every £100 or fraction of £100 of the price up to £100,000;	£1
(b) for every £100 or fraction of £100 of the price exceeding £100,000.	50p
Where there is sufficient proceeds of sale in court, fee 11.2 will be payable by transfer from the proceeds of sale in court.	
11.3 On entering a reference for hearing by the Registrar.	£70
FEES PAYABLE IN HIGH COURT AND COURT OF APPEAL ONLY	
12 Affidavits	
12.1 On taking an affidavit or an affirmation or attestation upon honour in lieu of an affidavit or a declaration except for the purpose of receipt of dividends from the Accountant General and for a declaration by a shorthand writer appointed in insolvency proceedings:	
for each person making any of the above.	£11
12.2 For each exhibit referred to in an affidavit, affirmation, attestation or declaration for which fee 12.1 is payable.	£2
FEES PAYABLE IN COURT OF APPEAL ONLY	
13 Fees payable in appeals to the Court of Appeal	
13.1(a) Where in an appeal notice, permission to appeal or an extension of time for appealing is applied for (or both are applied for):	£235
on filing an appellant's notice; or	
where the respondent is appealing, on filing a respondent's notice.	
13.1(b) Where permission to appeal is not required or has been granted by the lower court:	£465
on filing an appellant's notice, or	
on filing a respondent's notice where the respondent is appealing.	
13.1(c) On the appellant filing an appeal questionnaire (unless the appellant has paid fee 13.1(b), or on the respondent filing an appeal questionnaire (unless the respondent has paid fee 13.1(b)).	£465
13.2 On filing a respondent's notice where the respondent wishes to ask the appeal court to uphold the order of the lower court for reasons different from or additional to those given by the lower court.	£235
13.3 On filing an application notice.	£235
Fee 13.3 is not payable for an application made in an appeal notice.]	

SCHEDULE 2: REMISSIONS AND PART REMISSIONS

Article 4

Interpretation

1

(1) In this Schedule—

"child" means a child or young person in respect of whom a party is entitled to receive child benefit in accordance with section 141, and regulations made under section 142, of the Social Security Contributions and Benefits Act 1992;

"child care costs" has the meaning given in the Criminal Defence Service (Financial Eligibility) Regulations 2006;

"couple" has the meaning given in section 3(5A) of the Tax Credits Act 2002;

"disposable monthly income" has the meaning given in paragraph 5;

"excluded benefits" means—

(a) any of the following benefits payable under the Social Security Contributions and Benefits Act 1992—

(i) attendance allowance paid under section 64;

(ii) severe disablement allowance;

(iii) carer's allowance;

(iv) disability living allowance;

(v) constant attendance allowance paid under section 104 or paragraph 4 or 7(2) of Schedule 8 as an increase to a disablement pension;

(vi) council tax benefit;

(vii) any payment made out of the social fund;

(viii) housing benefit;

(b) any direct payment made under the Community Care, Services for Carers and Children's Services (Direct Payments) (England) Regulations 2003 or the Community Care, Services for Carers and Children's Services (Direct Payments) (Wales) Regulations 2004;

(c) a back to work bonus payable under section [26] of the Jobseekers Act 1995;

(d) any exceptionally severe disablement allowance paid under the Personal Injuries (Civilians) Scheme 1983;

(e) any pension paid under the Naval, Military and Air Forces etc (Disablement and Death) Service Pension Order 2006;

(f) any payment made from the Independent Living Funds; and

(g) any financial support paid under an agreement for the care of a foster child;

"the Funding Code" means the code approved under section 9 of the Access to Justice Act 1999;

"gross annual income" means total annual income, for the 12 months preceding the application for remission or part remission, from all sources other than receipt of any of the excluded benefits;

"gross monthly income" means total monthly income, for the month in which the application for remission or part remission is made, from all sources other than receipt of any of the excluded benefits;

"the Independent Living Funds" has the meaning given in the Criminal Defence Service (Financial Eligibility) Regulations 2006;

"partner" means a person with whom the party lives as a couple and includes a person with whom the party is not currently living but from whom the party is not living separate and apart;

"party" means the individual who would, but for this Schedule, be liable to pay the fee required under this Order;

"restraint order" means—

(h) an order under section 42(1A) of the [Senior Courts Act 1981]; or

(i) a civil restraint order under rule 3.11 of the Civil Procedure Rules 1998 or a practice direction made under that rule.

(2) Paragraphs 2, 3 and 4—

(a) do not apply to a party who is in receipt of funding provided by the LSC for the purposes of the proceedings for which a certificate has been issued under the Funding Code; and

(b) are subject to the provisions of paragraphs 10 (vexatious litigants) and 11 (exception).

Full remission of fees—qualifying benefits

2

(1) No fee is payable under this Order if, at the time when a fee would otherwise be payable, the party is in receipt of a qualifying benefit.

(2) The following are qualifying benefits for the purposes of sub-paragraph (1)—

(a) income support under the Social Security Contributions and Benefits Act 1992;

(b) working tax credit, provided that no child tax credit is being paid to the party;

(c) income-based jobseeker's allowance under the Jobseekers Act 1995; and

(d) guarantee credit under the State Pension Credit Act 2002; and

(e) income-related employment and support allowance under the Welfare Reform Act 2007.

Full remission of fees—gross annual income

3

(1) No fee is payable under this Order if, at the time when the fee would otherwise be payable, the party has the number of children specified in column 1 of the following table and—

(a) if the party is single, the gross annual income of the party does not exceed the amount set out in the appropriate row of column 2; or

(b) if the party is one of a couple, the gross annual income of the couple does not exceed the amount set out in the appropriate row of column 3.

Column 1	*Column 2*	*Column 3*
Number of children of party paying fee	*Single*	*Couple*
no children	£13,000	£18,000
1 child	£15,930	£20,930
2 children	£18,860	£23,860
3 children	£21,790	£26,790
4 children	£24,720	£29,720

(2) If the party paying the fee has more than 4 children then the relevant amount of gross annual income is the amount specified in the table for 4 children plus the sum of £2,930 for each additional child.

Full and part remission of fees—disposable monthly income

4

(1) No fee is payable under this Order if, at the time when the fee would otherwise be payable, the disposable monthly income of the party is £50 or less.

(2) The maximum amount of fee payable is—

(a) if the disposable monthly income of the party is more than £50 but does not exceed £210, an amount equal to one-quarter of every £10 of the party's disposable monthly income up to a maximum of £50; and

(b) if the disposable monthly income is more than £210, an amount equal to £50 plus one-half of every £10 over £200 of the party's disposable monthly income.

(3) Where the fee that would otherwise be payable under this Order is greater than the maximum fee which a party is required to pay as calculated in sub-paragraph (2), the fee will be remitted to the amount payable under that sub-paragraph.

Disposable monthly income

5

(1) A party's disposable monthly income is the gross monthly income of the party for the month in which the fee becomes payable ("the period") less the deductions referred to in sub-paragraphs (2) and (3).

(2) There are to be deducted from the gross monthly income—

(a) income tax paid or payable in respect of the period;

(b) any contributions estimated to have been paid under Part 1 of the Social Security Contributions and Benefits Act 1992 in respect of the period;

(c) either—

(i) monthly rent or monthly payment in respect of a mortgage debt or hereditable security, payable in respect of the only or main dwelling of the party, less any housing benefit paid under the Social Security Contributions and Benefits Act 1992; or

(ii) the monthly cost of the living accommodation of the party;

(d) any child care costs paid or payable in respect of the period;

(e) if the party is making bona fide payments for the maintenance of a child who is not a member of the household of the party, the amount of such payments paid or payable in respect of the period; and

(f) any amount paid or payable by the party, in respect of the period, in pursuance of a court order.

(3) There will be deducted from the gross monthly income an amount representing the cost of living expenses in respect of the period being—

(a) £315; plus

(b) £244 for each child of the party; plus

(c) £159, if the party has a partner.

Resources of partners

6

(1) For the purpose of determining whether a party is entitled to the remission or part remission of a fee in accordance with this Schedule, the income of a partner, if any, is to be included as income of the party.

(2) The receipt by a partner of a qualifying benefit does not entitle a party to remission of a fee.

Application for remission or part remission of fees

7

(1) An application for remission or part remission of a fee must be made to the court officer at the time when the fee would otherwise be payable.

(2) Where a claim for full remission of fees is made, the party must provide documentary evidence of, as the case may be—

(a) entitlement to a qualifying benefit; or

(b) gross annual income and, if applicable, the children included for the purposes of paragraph 3.

(3) Where a claim for full or part remission of fees under paragraph 4 is made, the party must provide documentary evidence of—

(a) such of the party's gross monthly income as is derived from—

(i) employment;

(ii) rental or other income received from persons living with the party by reason of their residence in the party's home;

(iii) a pension; or

(iv) a state benefit, not being an excluded benefit; and

(b) any expenditure being deducted from the gross monthly income in accordance with paragraph 5(2).

Remission in exceptional circumstances

8 Where it appears to the Lord Chancellor that the payment of any fee prescribed by this Order would, owing to the exceptional circumstances of the particular case, involve undue financial hardship, the Lord Chancellor may reduce or remit the fee in that case.

Refunds

9

(1) Subject to sub-paragraph (3), where a party has not provided the documentary evidence required by paragraph 7 and a fee has been paid at a time when, under paragraphs 2, 3 or 4, it was not payable, the fee will be refunded if documentary evidence relating to the time when the fee became payable is provided at a later date.

(2) Subject to sub-paragraph (3), where a fee has been paid at a time where the Lord Chancellor, if all the circumstances had been known, would have reduced or remitted the fee under paragraph 8, the fee or the amount by which the fee would have been reduced, as the case may be, will be refunded.

(3) No refund will be made under this paragraph unless the party who paid the fee applies within 6 months of paying the fee.

(4) The Lord Chancellor may extend the period of 6 months mentioned in sub-paragraph (3) if the Lord Chancellor considers that there is a good reason for an application being made after the end of the period of 6 months.

Vexatious Litigants

10

(1) This paragraph applies where—

(a) a restraint order is in force against a party; and

(b) the party makes an application for permission to—

(i) issue proceedings or take a step in proceedings as required by the restraint order;

(ii) apply for amendment or discharge of the order; or

(iii) appeal the order.

(2) The fee prescribed for the application by Schedule 1 is payable in full.

(3) If the court grants the permission requested the applicant will be refunded the difference between—

(a) the fee paid; and

(b) the fee that would have been payable if this Schedule had been applied without reference to this paragraph.

Exception

11 This Schedule does not apply to fee 8.8 (fee payable on a consolidated attachment of earnings order or an administration order).

SCHEDULE 3: REVOCATIONS

(NOT HEREIN PRINTED)

Family Proceedings Fees Order 2008

SI 2008 No 1054

The following sets out the Fees payable under the Order (as amended) in force with effect from the 4th April 2011.

Citation and commencement

1

(1) This Order may be cited as the Family Proceedings Fees Order 2008 and shall come into force on 1st May 2008.

(2) In this Order—

(a) "LSC" means the Legal Services Commission established under section 1 of the Access to Justice Act 1999;

(b) "the FPR 2010"means the Family Proceedings Rules 2010;and

(c) expressions also used in the FPR 2010 have the same meaning as in those FPR 2010.

Fees payable

2 The fees set out in column 2 of Schedule 1 are payable in family proceedings in the High Court and in county courts in respect of the items described in column 1 in accordance with and subject to the directions specified in that column.

3 Where by any convention entered into by Her Majesty with any foreign power it is provided that no fee is required to be paid in respect of any proceedings, the fees specified in this Order are not payable in respect of those proceedings.

Remissions and part remissions

4 Schedule 2 applies for the purpose of ascertaining whether a party is entitled to a remission or part remission of a fee prescribed by this Order.

Revocations

5 The instruments listed in column 1 of the table in Schedule 3 (which have the references listed in column 2) are revoked.

Transitional provision

6 Fees 2.2(b) and (c) are not payable in respect of an issues resolution hearing, pre-hearing review or final hearing which has been listed on any day between 1st May 2008 and 14th May 2008 inclusive.

SCHEDULE 1: FEES TO BE TAKEN

Column 1: Number and description of fee	*Column 2: Amount of fee*
SECTION 1: FEES TO BE TAKEN IN THE HIGH COURT AND IN COUNTY COURTS	
1 Commencement of proceedings	
1.1 On filing an application to start proceedings where no other fee is specified.	£230
1.2 On presenting any application for-	
(a) a matrimonial or civil partnership order, other than an application to which rule7.7(1)(b) of the FPR 2010 applies;	
(b) a declaration to which Chapter 5 of Part 8 of the FPR2010 applies.	£340
1.3 On applying for a non-molestation order, an occupation order or a forced marriage protection order under Part 4 or Part 4A of the Family Law Act 1996 (or on applying for two or more of those orders).	£70
1.4 On amending an application for a matrimonial or civil partnership order, amending an application for a declaration to which Chapter 5of Part 8 of the FPR2010 applies, or making an application to which rule 7.7 (1)(b) of the FPR 2010 applies.	£90
1.5 On filing an answer to an application for a matrimonial or civil partnership order.	£230
1.6 On applying for an order under Part 3 of the Solicitors Act 1974 for the assessment of costs payable to a solicitor by a client; or on the commencement of costs-only proceedings.	£40

2 Proceedings under the Children Act 1989	
2.1 On an application for an order in form C1 or form C100 (free standing application), form C79 (application related to enforcement of a contact order), form C2 (application in existing proceedings) or a request for permission to apply for an order in form C2 under the following provisions of the Children Act 1989—	
(a) section 4(1)(c) or (3), 4A(1)(b) or (3) (parental responsibility);	£200
(b) section 4ZA (1)(c) or (6) (parental responsibility);	£200
(c) section 5(1) or 6(7) (guardians);	£200
(d) section 10(1) or (2) (section 8 orders);	£200
(e) section 11J(2) (enforcement orders);	£200
(f) section 11O(2) (compensation for financial loss);	£200
(g) section 13(1) (change of child's surname or removal from jurisdiction while residence order in force);	£200
(h) section 14A(3) or (6)(a), 14C(3) or 14D(1) (special guardianship orders);	£160

(i) section 25 (secure accommodation order);	£170
(j) section 33(7) (change of child's surname or removal from jurisdiction while care order in force);	£170
(k) section 34(2), (3), (4) or (9) (contact with child in care);	£170
(l) section 36(1) (education supervision order);	£170
(m) section 39 (variation or discharge etc of care and supervision orders);	£170
(n) section 43(1) (child assessment order);	£170
(o) sections 44, 45 and 46 (emergency protection orders);	£170
(p) section 48 (warrant to assist person exercising powers under emergency protection order);	£170
(q) section 50 (recovery order);	£170
(r) section 102 (warrant to assist person exercising powers to search for children or inspect premises);	£170
(s) paragraph 4(2), 6(2), 7(2) or 9(2) of Schedule A1[(i)] (applications in respect of enforcement orders);	£90
(t) paragraph 5(2) of Schedule A1 (amendment of enforcement order by reason of change of address);	£45
(u) paragraph 1(1) or (4), 2(1) or (5), 5(6), 6(5), (7) or (8), 8(2), 10(2), 11 or 14(1) of Schedule 1 (financial provision for children);	£200
(v) paragraph 19(1) of Schedule 2 (approval of court for child in care of local authority to live abroad);	£170
(w) paragraph 6 of Schedule 3 (extension of supervision order);	£170
(x) paragraph 15(2) or 17(1) of Schedule 3 (extension or discharge of education supervision order).	£170

2.2 In relation to proceedings under section 31 of the Children Act 1989 (care and supervision orders)—	
(a) on an application;	£2,225
(b) where an issues resolution hearing or pre-hearing review has been listed;	£700
(c) where a final hearing has been listed.	£1,900
Notes to fees 2.1 and 2.2	
Where an application requires the permission of the court, the relevant fee is payable when permission is sought but no further fee will be charged if permission is granted and the application is made.	
Where an application is made, permission is sought or an appeal is commenced under or relating to provisions of the Children Act 1989 which are listed in two or more different numbered fees, or require two or more different numbered forms, only one fee is payable, and if those fees are different, only the highest fee is payable.	
Where an application is made, permission is sought or an appeal is commenced under or relating to two or more provisions of the Children Act 1989 which are listed in the same numbered fee, that fee is payable only once.	
Where the same application is made, permission is sought or an appeal is commenced in respect of two or more children, who are siblings or children of the family, at the same time, only one fee is payable in respect of each numbered fee.	
Notes to fee 2.2 only	
Where a final order is made at a case management conference, £500 of the amount paid under fee 2.2(a) will be refunded.	
Where the court lists more than one issues resolution hearing or pre-hearing review, fee is payable only once.	
Where proceedings are consolidated with other proceedings, any fee which falls to be paid after the date on which the proceedings are consolidated is payable only once.	
Where a fee is paid under fee 2.2(b) or (c) in relation to a hearing that is cancelled, for example, because a final order is made at earlier hearing, the application is withdrawn, or the hearing is no longer needed, the fee will be refunded. A refund will not be given if the hearing is adjourned to a later date or to a date to be fixed.	
The fee in 2.2(b) and (c) is payable 14 days before the hearing or review.	

2.3 On commencing an appeal under section 94 of the Children Act 1989 relating to proceedings to which the following fees apply—	
(a) 2.1 (a) to (g) and (u);	£200
(b) 2.1 (h);	£160
(c) 2.1 (i) to (r), (v) to (x) and 2.2.	£170
2.4 On commencing an appeal under paragraph 23(11) of Schedule 2 to the Children Act 1989 (appeal against contribution order).	£170

3 Adoption and wardship applications	
3.1 On applying or requesting permission to apply under any provision in Part 1 of the Adoption and Children Act 2002, other than an application under section 22 of that Act.	£160
3.2 On applying under section 22 of the Adoption and Children Act 2002 (placement order).	£400
3.3 On applying for the exercise by the High Court of its inherent jurisdiction with respect to children.	£160
When an application requires the permission of the court, the relevant fee is payable when permission is sought but no further fee will be charged if permission is granted and the application is made.	
Where an application is made or permission is sought under or relating to two or more provisions of the Adoption and Children Act 2002 only one fee is payable.	
Where the same application is made or permission is sought in respect of two or more children, who are siblings or children of the same family, at the same time, only one fee is payable.	

4 Applications in proceedings	
4.1 On an application without notice or by consent (including an application to make a decree nisi absolute or a conditional order final) except where separately listed in this Schedule. Note: Fee 4.1 is not payable in relation to an application by consent for an adjournment of a hearing where the application is received by the court at least 14 days before the date set for that hearing.	£45
4.2 On an application under rule 7.19 of the FPR 2010 for the court to consider the making of a decree nisi, a conditional order, a decree of judicial separation or a separation order (other than in an undefended case where no fee is payable).	£45
4.3 On an application on notice except where separately listed in the schedule.	£90
4.4 On the filing of- (a) a notice of intention to proceed with an application for a financial order to which rule 9.4(a) of the FPR 2010 applies; or (b) an application for a financial order to which rule 9.4(b) of the FPR 2010 applies, other than an application for a consent order.	£240

5 Appeal from a district judge	
5.1 On filing an appeal notice from a district judge to a judge.	£115

6 Searches	
6.1 On making a search in the central index of decrees absolute or of final orders kept at the Principal Registry of the Family Division for any specified period of ten calendar years or, if no such period is specified, for the ten most recent years, and, if appropriate, providing a certificate of decree absolute or of final order, as the case may be.	£60
6.2 On making a search in the central index of parental responsibility agreements kept at the Principal Registry of the Family Division in accordance with regulations made under section 4(2) of the Children Act 1989 and, if appropriate, providing a copy of the agreement.	£40
6.3 On making a search in the index of decrees absolute or of final orders kept at any designated county court or district registry for any specified period of ten calendar years or, if no period is specified, for the ten most recent years, and if appropriate, providing a certificate of decree absolute or of final order, as the case may be.	£40

7 Copy documents	
7.1 On a request for a copy document (other than where fee 7.2 applies)—	
(a) for ten pages or less; and	£5
(b) for each subsequent page.	50p
Note: The fee payable under fee 7.1 includes—	
—where the court allows a party to fax to the court for the use of that party a document that has not been requested by the court and is not intended to be placed on the court file.	
—where a party requests that the court fax a copy of a document from the court file.	
—where the court provides a subsequent copy of a document which it has previously provided.	
7.2 On a request for a copy of a document on a computer disk or in other electronic form, for each such copy.	£5

8 Determination of costs	
8.1 On filing a request for detailed assessment where the party filing the request is legally aided or is funded by the LSC and no other party is ordered to pay the costs of the proceedings.	£145
8.2 On filing a request for detailed assessment in any case where fee 8.1 does not apply; or on filing a request for a hearing date for the assessment of costs payable to a solicitor by a client pursuant to an order under Part 3 of the Solicitors Act 1974 where the amount of the costs claimed—	
(a) does not exceed £15,000;	£325
(b) exceeds £15,000 but does not exceed £50,000;	£655
(c) exceeds £50,000 but does not exceed £100,000;	£980
(d) exceeds £100,000 but does not exceed £150,000;	£1,310
(e) exceeds £150,000 but does not exceed £200,000;	£1,635
(f) exceeds £200,000 but does not exceed £300,000;	£2,455
(g) exceeds £300,000 but does not exceed £500,000;	£4,090
(h) exceeds £500,000.	£5,455
Where there is a combined standard basis and legal aid, or a combined standard basis and LSC, or a combined standard basis, legal aid and LSC determination of costs, fee 8.2 will be attributed proportionately to the standard basis, legal aid or LSC (as the case may be) portions of the bill on the basis of the amount allowed.	
8.3 On a request for the issue of a default costs certificate.	£60
8.4 On commencing an appeal against a decision made in detailed assessment proceedings.	£205
8.5 On applying for the court's approval of a certificate of costs payable from the Community Legal Service Fund.	
Fee 8.5 is payable at the time of applying for approval and is recoverable only against the Community Legal Service Fund.	£50
8.6 On an application to set aside a default costs certificate.	£105

9 Registration of maintenance orders	
9.1 On an application for a maintenance order to be registered under the Maintenance Orders Act 1950 or the Maintenance Orders Act 1958.	£40
9.2 On an application for a Maintenance order to be sent abroad for enforcement under the Maintenance Orders (Reciprocal Enforcement) Act 1972.	£40

10 Enforcement	
10.1 On an application to question a judgment debtor or other person on oath in connection with enforcement of a judgment, or on an application to which rule 33.3 (2)(b) of the FPR2010 applies.	£50
10.2 On an application for a third party debt order or the appointment of a receiver by way of equitable execution.	
Note: Fee 10.2 is payable in respect of each third party against whom the order is sought.	£100
10.3 On an application for a charging order.	
Note: Fee 10.3 is payable in respect of each charging order applied for.	£100
10.4 On an application for a judgment summons.	£100

SECTION 2. FEES TO BE TAKEN IN A COUNTY COURT ONLY	
11 Service	
11.1 On a request for service by bailiff of any document except—	£105
(a) an order for a debtor to attend the adjourned hearing of a judgment summons;	
(b) an interpleader summons under an execution;	
(c) an order made under section 23 of the Attachment of Earnings Act 1971 (enforcement provisions); or	
(d) an order for a debtor to attend an adjourned oral examination of means.	

12 Enforcement in the County Courts	
12.1 On an application for or in relation to enforcement of a judgment or order of a county court or through a county court, by the issue of a warrant of execution against goods except a warrant to enforce payment of a fine.	£100
12.2 On a request for further attempt at execution of a warrant at a new address where the warrant has been returned to the court not executed (except where the warrant has been returned after it has been suspended by the court).	£30
12.3 On the issue of a warrant of possession or a warrant of delivery.	
Where the recovery of a sum of money is sought in addition, no further fee is payable.	£110
12.4 On an application for an attachment of earnings order to secure money due under an order made in family proceedings.	
Fee 12.4 is payable in respect of each defendant against whom an order is sought.	
Fee 12.4 is not payable where the attachment of earnings order is made on the hearing of a judgment summons.	£100

13 Sale	
13.1 For removing or taking steps to remove goods to a place of deposit.	
Fee 13.1 is to include the reasonable expenses of feeding and caring for animals.	The reasonable expenses incurred.
13.2 For advertising a sale by public auction pursuant to section 97 of the County Courts Act 1984.	The reasonable expenses incurred.
13.3 For the appraisement of goods.	5p in the £1 or part of a £1 of the appraised value.

13.4 For the sale of goods (including advertisements, catalogues, sale and commission and delivery of goods).	15p in the £1 or part of a £1 on the amount realised by the sale or such other sum as the district judge may consider to be justified in the circumstances.
13.5 Where no sale takes place by reason of an execution being withdrawn, satisfied or stopped.	(a) 10p in the £1 or part of a £1 on the value of the goods seized, the value to be the appraised value where the goods have been appraised or such other sum as the district judge may consider to be justified in the circumstances; and in addition (b) any sum payable under fee 13.1, 13.2 or 13.3.

SECTION 3: FEES TO BE TAKEN IN THE HIGH COURT ONLY	
14 Enforcement in the High Court	
14.1 On sealing a writ of execution/possession/delivery. Where the recovery of a sum of money is sought in addition to a writ of possession and delivery, no further fee is payable.	£60
14.2 On a request or application to register a judgment or order; or for permission to enforce an arbitration award; or for a certified copy of a judgment or order for use abroad.	£60

15 Affidavits	
15.1 On taking an affidavit or an affirmation or attestation upon honour in lieu of an affidavit or a declaration.	£10
15.2 For each exhibit referred to and required to be marked.	£2

SCHEDULE 2: REMISSIONS AND PART REMISSIONS

Interpretation

1

(1) In this Schedule—

"child" means a child or young person in respect of whom a party is entitled to receive child benefit in accordance with section 141, and regulations made under section 142, of the Social Security Contributions and Benefits Act 1992;

"child care costs" has the meaning given in the Criminal Defence Service (Financial Eligibility) Regulations 2006;

"couple" has the meaning given in section 3(5A) of the Tax Credits Act 2002;

"disposable monthly income" has the meaning given in paragraph 5;

"excluded benefits" means—

(a) any of the following benefits payable under the Social Security Contributions and Benefits Act 1992—

(i) attendance allowance paid under section 64;

(ii) severe disablement allowance;

(iii) carer's allowance;

(iv) disability living allowance;

(v) constant attendance allowance paid under section 104 or paragraph 4 or 7(2) of Schedule 8 as an increase to a disablement pension;

(vi) council tax benefit;

(vii) any payment made out of the social fund;

(viii) housing benefit;

(b) any direct payment made under the Community Care, Services for Carers and Children's Services (Direct Payments)

(England) Regulations 2003 or the Community Care, Services for Carers and Children's Services (Direct Payments) (Wales) Regulations 2004;

(c) a back to work bonus payable under section 26 of the Jobseekers Act 1995;

(d) any exceptionally severe disablement allowance paid under the Personal Injuries (Civilians) Scheme 1983;

(e) any pension paid under the Naval, Military and Air Forces etc (Disablement and Death) Service Pension Order 2006;

(f) any payment made from the Independent Living Funds; and

(g) any financial support paid under an agreement for the care of a foster child;

"the Funding Code" means the code approved under section 9 of the Access to Justice Act 1999;

"gross annual income" means total annual income, for the 12 months preceding the application for remission or part remission, from all sources other than receipt of any of the excluded benefits;

"gross monthly income" means total monthly income, for the month in which the application for remission or part remission is made, from all sources other than receipt of any of the excluded benefits;

"the Independent Living Funds" has the meaning given in the Criminal Defence Service (Financial Eligibility) Regulations 2006;

"partner" means a person with whom the party lives as a couple and includes a person with whom the party is not currently living but from whom the party is not living separate and apart;

"party" means the individual who would, but for this Schedule, be liable to pay the fee required under this Order;

"restraint order" means—

(a) an order under section 42(1A) of the Senior Courts Act 1981;

(b) a civil restraint order under rule 3.11 of the Civil Procedure Rules 1998 or a practice direction made under that rule; or

(c) a civil restraint order under rule 4.8 of the FPR 2010 or the practice direction referred to in that rule.

(2) Paragraphs 2, 3 and 4—

(a) do not apply to a party who is in receipt of funding provided by the LSC for the purposes of the proceedings for which a certificate has been issued under the Funding Code; and

(b) are subject to the provisions of paragraph 10 (vexatious litigants).

Full remission of fees—qualifying benefits

2

(1) No fee is payable under this Order if, at the time when a fee would otherwise be payable, the party—

(a) is in receipt of a qualifying benefit; or

(b) is not a beneficiary of a trust fund in court of a value of more than £50,000 and is—

(i) under the age of eighteen; or

(ii) a person for whose financial relief an order under paragraph 2 of Schedule 1 to the Children Act 1989 is in force or being applied for.

(2) The following are qualifying benefits for the purposes of sub-paragraph (1)(a)—

(a) income support under the Social Security Contributions and Benefits Act 1992;

(b) working tax credit, provided that no child tax credit is being paid to the party;

(c) income-based jobseeker's allowance under the Jobseekers Act 1995; and

(d) guarantee credit under the State Pension Credit Act 2002; and

(e) income-related employment and support allowance under the Welfare Reform Act 2007.

Full remission of fees—gross annual income

3

(1) No fee is payable under this Order if, at the time when the fee would otherwise be payable, the party has the number of children specified in column 1 of the following table and—

(a) if the party is single, the gross annual income of the party does not exceed the amount set out in the appropriate row of column 2; or

(b) if the party is one of a couple, the gross annual income of the couple does not exceed the amount set out in the appropriate row of column 3.

Column 1	*Column 2*	*Column 3*
Number of children of party paying fee	*Single*	*Couple*
no children	£13,000	£18,000
1 child	£15,930	£20,930
2 children	£18,860	£23,860
3 children	£21,790	£26,790
4 children	£24,720	£29,720

(2) If the party paying the fee has more than 4 children then the relevant amount of gross annual income is the amount specified in the table for 4 children plus the sum of £2,930 for each additional child.

Full and part remission of fees—disposable monthly income

4

(1) No fee is payable under this Order if, at the time when the fee would otherwise be payable, the disposable monthly income of the party is £50 or less.

(2) The maximum amount of fee payable is—

(a) if the disposable monthly income of the party is more than £50 but does not exceed £210, an amount equal to one-quarter of every £10 of the party's disposable monthly income up to a maximum of £50; and

(b) if the disposable monthly income is more than £210, an amount equal to £50 plus one-half of every £10 over £200 of the party's disposable monthly income.

(3) Where the fee that would otherwise be payable under this Order is greater than the maximum fee which a party is required to pay as calculated in sub-paragraph (2), the fee will be remitted to the amount payable under that sub-paragraph.

Disposable monthly income

5

(1) A party's disposable monthly income is the gross monthly income of the party for the month in which the fee becomes payable ("the period") less the deductions referred to in sub-paragraphs (2) and (3).

(2) There are to be deducted from the gross monthly income—

(a) income tax paid or payable in respect of the period;

(b) any contributions estimated to have been paid under Part 1 of the Social Security Contributions and Benefits Act 1992 in respect of the period;

(c) either—

(i) monthly rent or monthly payment in respect of a mortgage debt or hereditable security, payable in respect of the only or main dwelling of the party, less any housing benefit paid under the Social Security Contributions and Benefits Act 1992; or

(ii) the monthly cost of the living accommodation of the party;

(d) any child care costs paid or payable in respect of the period;

(e) if the party is making bona fide payments for the maintenance of a child who is not a member of the household of the party, the amount of such payments paid or payable in respect of the period; and

(f) any amount paid or payable by the party, in respect of the period, in pursuance of a court order.

(3) There will be deducted from the gross monthly income an amount representing the cost of living expenses in respect of the period being—

(a) £315; plus

(b) £244 for each child of the party; plus

(c) £159, if the party has a partner.

Resources of partners

6

(1) For the purpose of determining whether a party is entitled to the remission or part remission of a fee in accordance with this Schedule, the income of a partner, if any, is to be included as income of the party.

(2) The receipt by a partner of a qualifying benefit does not entitle a party to remission of a fee.

Application for remission or part remission of fees

7

(1) An application for remission or part remission of a fee must be made to the court officer at the time when the fee would otherwise be payable.

(2) Where a claim for full remission of fees is made, the party must provide documentary evidence of, as the case may be—

(a) entitlement to a qualifying benefit; or

(b) gross annual income and, if applicable, the children included for the purposes of paragraph 3.

(3) Where a claim for full or part remission of fees under paragraph 4 is made, the party must provide documentary evidence of—

(a) such of the party's gross monthly income as is derived from—

(i) employment;

(ii) rental or other income received from persons living with the party by reason of their residence in the party's home;

(iii) a pension; or

(iv) a state benefit, not being an excluded benefit; and

(b) any expenditure being deducted from the gross monthly income in accordance with paragraph 5(2).

Remission in exceptional circumstances

8

Where it appears to the Lord Chancellor that the payment of any fee prescribed by this Order would, owing to the exceptional circumstances of the particular case, involve undue financial hardship, the Lord Chancellor may reduce or remit the fee in that case.

Refunds

9

(1) Subject to sub-paragraph (3), where a party has not provided the documentary evidence required by paragraph 7 and a fee has been paid at a time when, under paragraphs 2, 3 or 4, it was not payable, the fee will be refunded if documentary evidence relating to the time when the fee became payable is provided at a later date.

(2) Subject to sub-paragraph (3), where a fee has been paid at a time where the Lord Chancellor, if all the circumstances had been known, would have reduced or remitted the fee under paragraph 8, the fee or the amount by which the fee would have been reduced, as the case may be, will be refunded.

(3) No refund will be made under this paragraph unless the party who paid the fee applies within 6 months of paying the fee.

(4) The Lord Chancellor may extend the period of 6 months mentioned in sub-paragraph (3) if the Lord Chancellor considers that there is a good reason for an application being made after the end of the period of 6 months.

Vexatious Litigants

10

(1) This paragraph applies where—

(a) a restraint order is in force against a party; and

(b) the party makes an application for permission to—

(i) issue proceedings or take a step in proceedings as required by the restraint order;

(ii) apply for amendment or discharge of the order; or

(iii) appeal the order.

(2) The fee prescribed for the application by Schedule 1 is payable in full.

(3) If the court grants the permission requested the applicant will be refunded the difference between—

(a) the fee paid; and

(b) the fee that would have been payable if this Schedule had been applied without reference to this paragraph.

SCHEDULE 3: REVOCATIONS

(NOT HEREIN PRINTED)

Magistrates' Courts Fees Order 2008

SI 2008 No 1052

The following sets out the Fees payable under the Order (as amended) in force with effect from the 1st September 2010.

Citation and commencement

1 This Order may be cited as the Magistrates' Courts Fees Order 2008 and shall come into force on 1st May 2008.

Fees payable

2 The fees set out in column 2 of Schedule 1 are payable in magistrates' courts in respect of the items described in column 1 in accordance with and subject to the directions specified in that column.

(1) No fee is payable in respect of—

(a) criminal proceedings (except for documents that were used in, or result from, criminal proceedings that are subsequently required for civil or family proceedings);

(b) any summons, warrant, notice or order issued, given or made under sections 83(1) or (2), 88, 89 or 136 of the Magistrates' Courts Act 1980, or under any rule made for the purpose of those provisions; or

(c) binding over proceedings.

(2) In this article, "binding over proceedings" means any proceedings instituted (whether by way of complaint under section 115 of the Magistrates' Courts Act 1980 or otherwise) with a view to obtaining from a magistrates' court an order requiring a person to enter into a recognizance to keep the peace or to be of good behaviour.

4 Where by any convention entered into by Her Majesty with any foreign power it is provided that no fee is required to be paid in respect of any proceedings, the fees specified in this Order are not payable in respect of those proceedings.

Remissions and part remissions

5 Schedule 2 applies for the purpose of ascertaining whether a party is entitled to a remission or part remission of a fee prescribed by this Order.

Revocations

6 The instruments listed in column 1 of the table in Schedule 3 (which have the references listed in column 2) are revoked.

Transitional provision

7 Fees 10.2(b) and (c) are not payable in respect of an issues resolution hearing, pre-hearing review or final hearing which has been listed on any day between 1st May 2008 and 14th May 2008 inclusive

SCHEDULE 1: FEES TO BE TAKEN

Fee No	*Item*	£
1. Attendance		
1.1	On an application which requires a justice of the peace to perform a function away from the court premises.	£50
	Note: Fee 1.1 is payable in addition to other payable fees.	
2. Appeals		
2.1	On an application to state a case for the opinion of the High Court under section 111(1) of the Magistrates' Courts Act 1980.	£500
	Note: Where fee 2.1 is payable, no further fee is payable in respect of the preparation of a draft case by the justices' clerk, providing copies, taking recognisance as required by s.114 of that Act and enlargement and renewal of such recognisance	
2.2	Proceedings under the Child Support Act 1991—	
	(a) On commencing an appeal under section 20.	£150
	(b) On commencing an appeal against a deduction from earnings order	£90
2.3	Proceedings under Schedule 5 to the Licensing Act 2003—	
	on commencing an appeal under paragraph 1, 2(2), 3(2)(a), 4(2), 7(2), 8(2)(b), 8A(2)(b), 10, 11(2), 12(2), 13(2)(b), 14, 16(2), 17(1), and (4) or 18(2)(a) of Schedule 5 to the Licensing Act 2003.	£400
2.4	On commencing an appeal where no other fee is specified.	£200
3. Certificates and Certified Documents		
3.1	On a request for a certificate of refusal to state a case.	£100
3.2	Register of judgments, orders and fines kept under section 98 of the Courts Act 2003—	
	on a request for a certificate of satisfaction.	£15
3.3	On a request for a certified copy of a memorandum of conviction.	£60
3.4	On a request for a certificate or certified document where no other fee is specified.	£60
	Note: Fee 3.4 includes any copy of a document certified by the court as a genuine copy of the original document.	
4. Liability Orders		
4.1	Proceedings under the Council Tax (Administration and Enforcement) Regulations 1992 or the Non-Domestic Rating(Collection and Enforcement)(Local Lists) Regulations 1989—	£3
	on an application for a liability order	
	Note: Fee 4.1 is payable in respect of each defendant against whom the liability order is sought.	
4.2	Proceedings under the Child Support Act 1991—	
	on an application for a liability order.	£40
	Note: Fee 4.2 is payable in respect of each liability order applied for.	
5. Copy Documents		
5.1	On a request for a copy of a document (other than where fee 5.2 applies)—	
	(a) of ten pages or less;	£5 and
	(b) for each subsequent page	50p
	Note: The fee payable under fee 5.1 includes where:	

Fee No	Item	£
	the court allows a party to fax to the court for the use of that party a document that has not been requested by the court and is not intended to be place on the court file;	
	a party requests that the court fax a copy of a document from the court file;	
	the court provides a subsequent copy of a document which it has previously provided.	
5.2	On a request for a copy of a document on a computer disk or in other electronic form, for each such copy.	£5
6. Financial Provision		
6.1	Proceedings under the Domestic Proceedings and Magistrates' Courts Act 1978 or Schedule 6 to the Civil Partnership Act 2004 —	
	On an application for an order for financial provision (other than an application to vary or revoke such an order, or an application for an order for financial provision made for the benefit of, or against, a person residing outside the United Kingdom).	£200
7. Proceedings under the Family Law Act 1986		
7.1	On an application for a declaration of parentage (each child).	£150
8. Proceedings under the Children Act 1989		
8.1	On an application for an order in form C1 or form C100 (freestanding application), form C79 (application related to enforcement of a contact order), form C2 (application in existing proceedings) or a request for permission to apply for an order in form C2 under the following provisions of the Children Act 1989—	
	(a) section 4(1)(c) or (3) or 4A(1)(b) or (3) (parental responsibility);	£200
	(b) section 4ZA(1)(c) or (6) (parental responsibility);	£200
	(c) section 5(1) or 6(7) (guardians);	£200
	(d) section 10(1) or (2) (section 8 orders);	£200
	(e) section 11J(2) (enforcement orders);	£200
	(f) section11O(2)(compensation for financial loss);	£200
	(g) section 13(1) (change of child's surname or removal from jurisdiction while residence order in force);	£200
	(h) section 14A(3) or (6)(a), 14C(3) or 14D(1) (special guardianship orders);	£160
	(i) section 25 (secure accommodation order);	£170
	(j) section 33(7) (change of child's surname or removal from jurisdiction while care order in force);	£170
	(k) section 34(2), (3), (4) or (9) (contact with child in care);	£170
	(l) section 36(1) (education supervision order);	£170
	(m) section 39 (variation or discharge etc of care and supervision orders);	£170
	(n) section 43(1) (child assessment order);	£170
	(o) sections 44, 45 and 46 (emergency protection order);	£170
	(p) section 48 (warrant to assist person exercising powers under emergency protection order);	£170
	(q) section 50 (recovery order);	£170
	(r) section 79K (cancellation, variation or removal or imposition of condition of registration of child minder or day carer);	£170
	(s) paragraph 4(2), 6(2), 7(2) or 9(2) of Schedule A1 (applications in respect of enforcement orders);	£90
	(t) paragraph 5(2) of Schedule A1 (amendment of enforcement order by reason of change of	£45

Fee No	*Item*	£
	(u) section 102 (warrant to assist person exercising powers to search for children or inspect premises);	£170
	(v) paragraph 1(1) or (4), 2(1) or (5), 5(6), 6(5), (7) or (8), 8(2), 10(2), 11 or 14(1) of Schedule 1 (financial provision for children);	£200
	(w) paragraph 19(1) of Schedule 2 (approval of court for child in care of local authority to live abroad);	£170
	(x) paragraph 6 of Schedule 3 (extension of supervision order);.	£170
	(y) paragraph 15(2) or 17(1) of Schedule 3 (extension or discharge of education supervision order);	£170
	(z) paragraph 8(1) of Schedule 8 (appeals concerning foster parenting)	£170
8.2	In relation to proceedings under section 31 of the Children Act 1989 (care and supervision orders)—	
	(a) on an application;	£2,225
	(b) where an issues resolution hearing or a pre-hearing review has been listed;	£700
	(c) where a final hearing has been listed;	£1900
	Notes to fees 8.1 and 8.2:	
	Where an application requires the permission of the court, the relevant fee is payable when permission is sought but no further fee will be charged if permission is granted and the application is made. Where an application is made or permission is sought under or relating to provisions of the Children Act 1989 which are listed in two or more different numbered fees, or require two or more different numbered forms, only one fee is payable, and if those fees are different, only the highest fee is payable.	
9. Proceedings under the Human Fertilisation and Embryology Act 2008		
9.1	On an application under section 54 (parental order)	£200
10. Proceedings under the Adoption and Children Act 2002		
10.1	On an application or a request for permission to apply under any provision in Part 1 of the Adoption and Children Act 2002, other than an application under section 22 of that Act.	£160
10.2	On an application under section 22 of the Adoption and Children Act 2002 (placement order).	£400
	Notes: Where an application requires the permission of the court, the relevant fee is payable when permission is sought but no further fee will be charged if permission is granted and the application is made.	
	Where an application is made or permission is sought under or relating to two or more provisions of the Adoption and Children Act 2002 only one fee is payable.	
	Where the same application is made or permission is sought in respect of two or more children at the same time, and these children are siblings or children of the family, only one fee is payable.	
11. Proceedings under the Children and Adoption Act 2006		
11.1	On an application for a warning notice to be attached to a contact Order	£45
	Notes: Where an application is made or permission is sought under or relating to provisions of the Children Act 1989 and the Children and Adoption Act 2006 which are listed in two or more different numbered fees, only one fee is payable.	
	Where the same application is made or permission is sought in respect of two or more children at the same time, and those children are siblings or children of the family, only one fee is payable in respect of each numbered fee.	

Fee No	Item	£
12. Proceedings to vary, extend or revoke an order made in family proceedings		
12.1	On an application to vary, extend or revoke an order made in family proceedings where no other fee is specified.	£20
13. Licences		
13.1	On a request for a licence, consent or authority where no other fee is specified	£25
13.2	On an application for the renewal or variation of an existing Licence	£25
13.3	On an application for the revocation of a licence where no other fee is specified	£25
14. Oaths		
14.1	On taking the attestation of a constable or special constable under the Police Act 1996	£10
	Note: Fee 14.1 is payable for every attestation made by every constable or special constable at or away from court premises.	
14.2	For every oath, affirmation, solemn declaration or statutory declaration where no other fee is specified.	
	Note: No fee is payable for the swearing in of witnesses or in any case where an enactment directs that no fee will be taken.	
15. Other civil proceedings		
15.1	On commencing proceedings where no other fee is specified and where leave or permission is not required	£200
15.2	On commencing proceedings where leave or permission is required—	
	(a) on an application for leave or permission to commence proceedings where no other fee is specified.	£100
	(b) on commencing proceedings where leave or permission has been granted following payment of fee 15.2(a).	£100
	Note: Fees 15.1 and 15.2 do not apply to family proceedings.	
15.3	Contested hearing—	
	For a hearing at which the proceedings are contested	£500
	Note: Fee 15.3—	
	applies only to hearings in proceedings to which fee 15.1 or 15.2 apply.	
	is payable by the party who commenced the proceedings.	
	is payable on the day that the hearing commences.	
	is payable only once in the same proceedings.	
16. Warrants		
16.1	On an application for a warrant of entry	£18
16.2	On an application for any other warrant where no other fee is specified	£75
	Note: Fee 16.2 includes an application for a warrant made during a hearing. No fee is payable if the court issues a warrant of its own initiative.	
17. Commitment		
17.1	Proceedings under the Council Tax (Administration and Enforcement) Regulations 1992 or the Non-Domestic Rating(Collection and Enforcement)(Local Lists) Regulations 1989—	
	on an application for a warrant for commitment	£240

Fee No	Item	£
17.2	Proceedings under the Child Support Act 1991–on an application for a warrant for commitment	£240
	Note: Fees 17.1 and 17.2 do not include a warrant of arrest which is provided for under fee 16.2.	

SCHEDULE 2: REMISSIONS AND PART-REMISSIONS

Interpretation

1

(1) In this Schedule—

"child" means a child or young person in respect of whom a party is entitled to receive child benefit in accordance with section 141, and regulations made under section 142, of the Social Security Contributions and Benefits Act 1992;

"child care costs" has the meaning given in the Criminal Defence Service (Financial Eligibility) Regulations 2006;

"couple" has the meaning given in section 3(5A) of the Tax Credits Act 2002;

"disposable monthly income" has the meaning given in paragraph 5;

"excluded benefits" means—

(a) any of the following benefits payable under the Social Security Contributions and Benefits Act 1992—

(i) attendance allowance paid under section 64;

(ii) severe disablement allowance;

(iii) carer's allowance;

(iv) disability living allowance;

(v) constant attendance allowance paid under section 104 or paragraph 4 or 7(2) of Schedule 8 as an increase to a disablement pension;

(vi) council tax benefit;

(vii) any payment made out of the social fund;

(viii) housing benefit;

(b) any direct payment made under the Community Care, Services for Carers and Children's Services (Direct Payments) (England) Regulations 2003 or the Community Care, Services for Carers and Children's Services (Direct Payments) (Wales) Regulations 2004;

(c) a back to work bonus payable under section 26 of the Jobseekers Act 1995;

(d) any exceptionally severe disablement allowance paid under the Personal Injuries (Civilians) Scheme 1983;

(e) any pension paid under the Naval, Military and Air Forces etc (Disablement and Death) Service Pension Order 2006;

(f) any payment made from the Independent Living Funds; and

(g) any financial support paid under an agreement for the care of a foster child;

"the Funding Code" means the code approved under section 9 of the Access to Justice Act 1999;

"gross annual income" means total annual income, for the 12 months preceding the application for remission or part remission, from all sources other than receipt of any of the excluded benefits;

"gross monthly income" means total monthly income, for the month in which the application for remission or part remission is made, from all sources other than receipt of any of the excluded benefits;

"the Independent Living Funds" has the meaning given in the Criminal Defence Service (Financial Eligibility) Regulations 2006;

"LSC" means the Legal Services Commission established under section 1 of the Access to Justice Act 1999;

"partner" means a person with whom the party lives as a couple and includes a person with whom the party is not currently living but from whom the party is not living separate and apart;

"party" means the individual who would, but for this Schedule, be liable to pay the fee required under this Order;

"restraint order" means—

(a) an order under section 42(1A) of the Senior Courts Act 1981]; or

(b) a civil restraint order under rule 3.11 of the Civil Procedure Rules 1998 or a practice direction made under that rule.

(2) Paragraphs 2, 3 and 4—

(a) do not apply to a party who is in receipt of funding provided by the LSC for the purposes of the proceedings for which a certificate has been issued under the Funding Code; and

(b) are subject to the provisions of paragraph 10 (vexatious litigants).

Full remission of fees—qualifying benefits

2

(1) No fee is payable under this Order if, at the time when a fee would otherwise be payable, the party—

(a) is in receipt of a qualifying benefit; or

(b) is not a beneficiary of a trust fund in court of a value of more than £50,000 and is—

(i) under the age of eighteen; or

(ii) a person for whose financial relief an order under paragraph 2 of Schedule 1 to the Children Act 1989 is in force or being applied for.

(2) The following are qualifying benefits for the purposes of sub-paragraph (1)(a)—

(a) income support under the Social Security Contributions and Benefits Act 1992;

(b) working tax credit, provided that no child tax credit is being paid to the party;

(c) income-based jobseeker's allowance under the Jobseekers Act 1995; and

(d) guarantee credit under the State Pension Credit Act 2002[; and

(e) income-related employment and support allowance under the Welfare Reform Act 2007.

(3) Sub-paragraph (1)(b) applies to—

(a) an application to which fee 8, 9, 10, 11, 12, 13, 14 or 15 applies;

(b) an application or request to which fee 2, 3, 6 or 7 applies where the application or request is made in relation to proceedings to which fee 8, 9, 10, 11, 12, 13, 14 or 15 applies.

Full remission of fees—gross annual income

3

(1) No fee is payable under this Order if, at the time when the fee would otherwise be payable, the party has the number of children specified in column 1 of the following table and—

(a) if the party is single, the gross annual income of the party does not exceed the amount set out in the appropriate row of column 2; or

(b) if the party is one of a couple, the gross annual income of the couple does not exceed the amount set out in the appropriate row of column 3.

Column 1	*Column 2*	*Column 3*
Number of children of party paying fee	*Single*	*Couple*
no children	£13,000	£18,000
1 child	£15,930	£20,930
2 children	£18,860	£23,860
3 children	£21,790	£26,790
4 children	£24,720	£29,720

(2) If the party paying the fee has more than 4 children then the relevant amount of gross annual income is the amount specified in the table for 4 children plus the sum of £2,930 for each additional child.

Full and part remission of fees—disposable monthly income

4

(1) No fee is payable under this Order if, at the time when the fee would otherwise be payable, the disposable monthly income of the party is £50 or less.

(2) The maximum amount of fee payable is—

(a) if the disposable monthly income of the party is more than £50 but does not exceed £210, an amount equal to one-quarter of every £10 of the party's disposable monthly income up to a maximum of £50; and

(b) if the disposable monthly income is more than £210, an amount equal to £50 plus one-half of every £10 over £200 of the party's disposable monthly income.

(3) Where the fee that would otherwise be payable under this Order is greater than the maximum fee which a party is required to pay as calculated in sub-paragraph (2), the fee will be remitted to the amount payable under that sub-paragraph.

Disposable monthly income

5

(1) A party's disposable monthly income is the gross monthly income of the party for the month in which the fee becomes payable ("the period") less the deductions referred to in sub-paragraphs (2) and (3).

(2) There are to be deducted from the gross monthly income—

(a) income tax paid or payable in respect of the period;

(b) any contributions estimated to have been paid under Part 1 of the Social Security Contributions and Benefits Act 1992 in respect of the period;

(c) either—

(i) monthly rent or monthly payment in respect of a mortgage debt or hereditable security, payable in respect of the only or main dwelling of the party, less any housing benefit paid under the Social Security Contributions and Benefits Act 1992; or

(ii) the monthly cost of the living accommodation of the party;

(d) any child care costs paid or payable in respect of the period;

(e) if the party is making bona fide payments for the maintenance of a child who is not a member of the household of the party, the amount of such payments paid or payable in respect of the period; and

(f) any amount paid or payable by the party, in respect of the period, in pursuance of a court order.

(3) There will be deducted from the gross monthly income an amount representing the cost of living expenses in respect of the period being—

(a) £315; plus

(b) £244 for each child of the party; plus

(c) £159, if the party has a partner.

Resources of partners

6

(1) For the purpose of determining whether a party is entitled to the remission or part remission of a fee in accordance with this Schedule, the income of a partner, if any, is to be included as income of the party.

(2) The receipt by a partner of a qualifying benefit does not entitle a party to remission of a fee.

Application for remission or part remission of fees

7

(1) An application for remission or part remission of a fee must be made to the court officer at the time when the fee would otherwise be payable.

(2) Where a claim for full remission of fees is made, the party must provide documentary evidence of, as the case may be—

(a) entitlement to a qualifying benefit; or

(b) gross annual income and, if applicable, the children included for the purposes of paragraph 3.

(3) Where a claim for full or part remission of fees under paragraph 4 is made, the party must provide documentary evidence of—

(a) such of the party's gross monthly income as is derived from—

(i) employment;

(ii) rental or other income received from persons living with the party by reason of their residence in the party's home;

(iii) a pension; or

(iv) a state benefit, not being an excluded benefit; and

(b) any expenditure being deducted from the gross monthly income in accordance with paragraph 5(2).

Remission in exceptional circumstances

8 Where it appears to the Lord Chancellor that the payment of any fee prescribed by this Order would, owing to the exceptional circumstances of the particular case, involve undue financial hardship, the Lord Chancellor may reduce or remit the fee in that case.

Refunds

9

(1) Subject to sub-paragraph (3), where a party has not provided the documentary evidence required by paragraph 7 and a fee has been paid at a time when, under paragraphs 2, 3 or 4, it was not payable, the fee will be refunded if documentary evidence relating to the time when the fee became payable is provided at a later date.

(2) Subject to sub-paragraph (3), where a fee has been paid at a time where the Lord Chancellor, if all the circumstances had been known, would have reduced or remitted the fee under paragraph 8, the fee or the amount by which the fee would have been reduced, as the case may be, will be refunded.

(3) No refund will be made under this paragraph unless the party who paid the fee applies within 6 months of paying the fee.

(4) The Lord Chancellor may extend the period of 6 months mentioned in sub-paragraph (3) if the Lord Chancellor considers that there is a good reason for an application being made after the end of the period of 6 months.

Vexatious Litigants

10

(1) This paragraph applies where—

(a) a restraint order is in force against a party; and

(b) the party makes an application for permission to—

(i) issue proceedings or take a step in proceedings as required by the restraint order;

(ii) apply for amendment or discharge of the order; or

(iii) appeal the order.

(2) The fee prescribed for the application by Schedule 1 is payable in full.

(3) If the court grants the permission requested the applicant will be refunded the difference between—

(a) the fee paid; and

(b) the fee that would have been payable if this Schedule had been applied without reference to this paragraph.

Non-Contentious Probate Fees Order 2004

SI 2004 No 3120

The following sets out the Fees payable under the Order (as amended) in force with effect from the 4th April 2011.

Citation, commencement and interpretation

1

(1) This Order may be cited as the Non-Contentious Probate Fees Order 2004 and shall come into force on the 4th January 2005.

(2) In this Order—

(a) a fee referred to by number means the fee so numbered in Schedule 1 to this Order;

(b) "assessed value" means the value of the net real and personal estate (excluding settled land if any) passing under the grant as shown—

(i) in the Inland Revenue affidavit (for a death occurring before 13th March 1975), or

(ii) in the Inland Revenue account (for a death occurring on or after 13th March 1975), or

(iii) in the case in which, in accordance with arrangements made between the President of the Family Division and the Commissioners of the Inland Revenue, or regulations made under section 256(1)(a) of the Inheritance Tax Act 1984 and from time to time in force, no such affidavit or account is required to be delivered, in the oath which is sworn to lead to the grant,

and in the case of an application to reseal means the value, as shown, passing under the grant upon its being resealed;

(c) "authorised place of deposit" means any place in which, by virtue of a direction given under section 124 of the Senior Courts Act 1981 original wills and other documents under the control of the High Court (either in the principal registry or in any district registry) are deposited and preserved;

(d) "grant" means a grant of probate or letters of administration;

(e) "district registry" includes the probate registry of Wales, any district probate registry and any sub-registry attached to it;

(f) "the principal registry" means the Principal Registry of the Family Division and any sub-registry attached to it.

Fees to be taken

2 The fees set out in column 2 of Schedule 1 to this Order shall be taken in the principal registry and in each district registry in respect of the items described in column 1 in accordance with and subject to any directions specified in column 1.

Exclusion of certain death gratuities

3 In determining the value of any personal estate for the purposes of this Order there shall be excluded the value of a death gratuity payable under section 17(2) of the Judicial Pensions Act 1981 or section 4(3) of the Judicial Pensions and Retirement Act 1993, or payable to the personal representatives of a deceased civil servant by virtue of a scheme made under section 1 of the Superannuation Act 1972.

Remission of fees

4 Schedule 1A applies for the purpose of ascertaining whether a party is entitled to a remission or part remission of a fee prescribed by this Order.

5 The Lord Chancellor may, on the ground of financial hardship or for other reasonable cause, remit in whole or in part any fee prescribed by this Order.

6

(1) Where by any convention entered into by Her Majesty with any foreign power it is provided that no fee shall be required to be paid in respect of any proceedings, the fees specified in this Order shall not be taken in respect of those proceedings.

(2) Where any application for a grant is withdrawn before the issue of a grant, a registrar may reduce or remit a fee.

(3) Fee 7 shall not be taken where a search is made for research or similar purposes by permission of the President of the Family Division for a document over 100 years old filed in the principal registry or a district registry or another authorised place of deposit.

Special exemption—Armed Forces

7 Where a fee has been paid or fees have been paid for the application of a grant (other than fee 3.2) and at the time of payment of that fee or those fees—

(a) the application for the grant was in respect of an estate exempt from Inheritance Tax by virtue of section 154 of the Inheritance Tax Act 1984 (exemption for members of the armed forces etc); and

(b) was in respect of a death occurring before 20th March 2003;

the Lord Chancellor shall upon receiving a written application refund the difference between any fee or fees paid and fee 3.2.

Revocation

8 The Order specified in Schedule 2 in so far as it was made under section 128 of the Finance Act 1990 shall be revoked.

SCHEDULE 1: FEES TO BE TAKEN

Article 2

Column 1	*Column 2*
Number and description of fee	*Amount of fee*
1 Application for a grant On an application for a grant (or for resealing a grant) other than on an application to which fee 3 applies, where the assessed value of the estate exceeds £5,000	£45
2 Personal application fee Where the application under fee 1 is made by a personal applicant (not being an application to which fee 3 applies) fee 2 is payable in addition to fee 1 where the assessed value of the estate exceeds £5,000.	£60
3 Special applications 3.1 For a duplicate or second or subsequent grant (including one following a revoked grant) in respect of the same deceased person, other than a grant preceded only by a grant limited to settled land, to trust property, or to part of the estate.	£20
3.2 On an application for a grant relating to a death occurring on or after 20th March 2003 in respect of an estate exempt from inheritance tax by virtue of section 154 of the Inheritance Tax Act 1984 (exemption for members of the armed forces etc).	£10
4 Caveats For the entry or the extension of a caveat.	£20
5 Search On an application for a standing search to be carried out in an estate, for each period of six months including the issue of a copy grant and will, if any (irrespective of the number of pages).	£6
6 Deposit of wills On depositing a will for safe custody in the principal registry or a district registry.	£20
7 Inspection On inspection of any will or other document retained by the registry (in the presence of an officer of the registry).	£20
8 Copy documents On a request for a copy of any document whether or not provided as a certified copy:	
(a) for the first copy;	£6
(b) for every subsequent copy of the same document if supplied at the same time;	£1
(c) where copies of any document are made available on a computer disk or in other electronic form, for each such copy;	£4
(d) where a search of the index is required, in addition to fee 8(a), (b) or (c) as appropriate, for each period of 4 years searched after the first 4 years.	£4
9 Oaths Except on a personal application for a grant, for administering an oath:	
9.1 for each deponent to each affidavit;	£6
9.2 for marking each exhibit.	£2
10 Determination of costs For determining costs.	The same fees as are payable from time to time for determining costs under the Civil Proceedings Fees Order 2008, (the relevant fees are set out in fee 5 in Schedule 1 to that Order)
11 Settling documents For perusing and settling citations, advertisements, oaths, affidavits, or other documents, for each document settled.	£12

SCHEDULE 1A: REMISSIONS AND PART-REMISSIONS

Article 4

Interpretation

1

(1) In this Schedule—

"child" means a child or young person in respect of whom a party is entitled to receive child benefit in accordance with section 141, and regulations made under section 142, of the Social Security Contributions and Benefits Act 1992;

"child care costs" has the meaning given in the Criminal Defence Service (Financial Eligibility) Regulations 2006;

"couple" has the meaning given in section 3(5A) of the Tax Credits Act 2002;

"disposable monthly income" has the meaning given in paragraph 5;

"excluded benefits" means—

(a) any of the following benefits payable under the Social Security Contributions and Benefits Act 1992—

(i) attendance allowance paid under section 64;

(ii) severe disablement allowance;

(iii) carer's allowance;

(iv) disability living allowance;

(v) constant attendance allowance paid under section 104 or paragraph 4 or 7(2) of Schedule 8 as an increase to a disablement pension;

(vi) council tax benefit;

(vii) any payment made out of the social fund;

(viii) housing benefit;

(b) any direct payment made under the Community Care, Services for Carers and Children's Services (Direct Payments) (England) Regulations 2003 or the Community Care, Services for Carers and Children's Services (Direct Payments) (Wales) Regulations 2004;

(c) a back to work bonus payable under section 26 of the Jobseekers Act 1995;

(d) any exceptionally severe disablement allowance paid under the Personal Injuries (Civilians) Scheme 1983;

(e) any pension paid under the Naval, Military and Air Forces etc (Disablement and Death) Service Pensions Order 2006;

(f) any payment made from the Independent Living Funds; and

(g) any financial support paid under an agreement for the care of a foster child;

"the Funding Code" means the code approved under section 9 of the Access to Justice Act 1999;

"gross annual income" means total annual income, for the 12 months preceding the application for remission or part remission, from all sources other than receipt of any of the excluded benefits;

"gross monthly income" means total monthly income, for the month in which the application for remission or part remission is made, from all sources other than receipt of any of the excluded benefits;

"the Independent Living Funds" has the meaning given in the Criminal Defence Service (Financial Eligibility) Regulations 2006;

"LSC" means the Legal Services Commission established under section 1 of the Access to Justice Act 1999;

"partner" means a person with whom the party lives as a couple and includes a person with whom the party is not currently living but from whom the party is not living separate and apart;

"party" means the individual who would, but for this Schedule, be liable to pay the fee required under this Order;

(2) Paragraphs 2, 3 and 4 do not apply to a party who is in receipt of funding provided by the LSC for the purposes of the proceedings for which a certificate has been issued under the Funding Code.

Full remission of fees—qualifying benefits

2

(1) No fee is payable under this Order if, at the time when a fee would otherwise be payable, the party is in receipt of a qualifying benefit.

(2) The following are qualifying benefits for the purpose of sub-paragraph (1)—

(a) income support under the Social Security Contributions and Benefits Act 1992;

(b) working tax credit, provided that no child tax credit is being paid to the party;

(c) income-based jobseeker's allowance under the Jobseekers Act 1995;

(d) guarantee credit under the State Pension Credit Act 2002; and

(e) income-related employment and support allowance under the Welfare Reform Act 2007.

Full remission of fees—gross annual income

3

(1) No fee is payable under this Order if, at the time when the fee would otherwise be payable, the party has the number of children specified in column 1 of the following table and—

(a) if the party is single, the gross annual income of the party does not exceed the amount set out in the appropriate row of column 2; or

(b) if the party is one of a couple, the gross annual income of the couple does not exceed the amount set out in the appropriate row of column 3.

Column 1	*Column 2*	*Column 3*
Number of children of fee-paying party	*Single*	*Couple*
no children	£13,000	£18,000
1 child	£15,930	£20,930
2 children	£18,860	£23,860
3 children	£21,790	£26,790
4 children	£24,720	£29,720

(2) If the party paying the fee has more than 4 children then the relevant amount of gross annual income is the amount specified in the table for 4 children plus the sum of £2,930 for each additional child.

Full and part remission of fees—disposable monthly income

4

(1) No fee is payable under this Order if, at the time when the fee would otherwise be payable, the disposable monthly income of the party is £50 or less.

(2) The maximum amount of fee payable is—

(a) if the disposable monthly income of the party is more than £50 but does not exceed £210, an amount equal to one-quarter of every £10 of the party's disposable monthly income up to a maximum of £50; and

(b) if the disposable monthly income is more than £210, an amount equal to £50 plus one-half of every £10 over £200 of the party's disposable monthly income.

(3) Where the fee that would otherwise be payable under this Order is greater than the maximum fee which a party is required to pay as calculated in sub-paragraph (2), the fee will be remitted to the amount payable under that sub-paragraph.

Disposable monthly income

5

(1) A party's disposable monthly income is the gross monthly income of the party for the month in which the fee becomes payable ("the period") less the deductions referred to in sub-paragraphs (2) and (3).

(2) There is to be deducted from the gross monthly income—

(a) income tax paid or payable in respect of the period;

(b) any contributions estimated to have been paid under Part 1 of the Social Security Contributions and Benefits Act 1992 in respect of the period;

(c) either—

(i) monthly rent or monthly payment in respect of a mortgage debt or hereditable security, payable in respect of the only or main dwelling of the party, less any housing benefit paid under the Social Security Contributions and Benefits Act 1992; or

(ii) the monthly cost of the living accommodation of the party;

(d) any child care costs paid or payable in respect of the period;

(e) if the party is making bona fide payments for the maintenance of a child who is not a member of the household of the party, the amount of such payments paid or payable in respect of the period; and

(f) any amount paid or payable by the party, in respect of the period, in pursuance of a court order.

(3) There will be deducted from the gross monthly income an amount representing the cost of living expenses in respect of the period being—

(a) £315; plus

(b) £244 for each child of the party; plus

(c) £159, if the party has a partner.

Resources of partners

6

(1) For the purpose of determining whether a party is entitled to the remission or part remission of a fee in accordance with this Schedule, the income of a partner, if any, is to be included as income of the party.

(2) The receipt by a partner of a qualifying benefit does not entitle a party to remission of a fee.

Application for remission or part remission of fees

7

(1) An application for remission or part remission of a fee must be made to the court officer at the time when the fee would otherwise be payable.

(2) Where a claim for full remission of fees is made, the party must provide documentary evidence of, as the case may be—

(a) entitlement to a qualifying benefit; or

(b) gross annual income and, if applicable, the children included for the purposes of paragraph 3.

(3) Where a claim for full or part remission of fees under paragraph 4 is made, the party must provide documentary evidence of—

(a) such of the party's gross monthly income as is derived from—

(i) employment;

(ii) rental or other income received from persons living with the party by reason of their residence in the party's home;

(iii) a pension; or

(iv) a state benefit, not being an excluded benefit; and

(b) any expenditure being deducted from the gross monthly income in accordance with paragraph 5(2).

Remission in exceptional circumstances

8

Where it appears to the Lord Chancellor that the payment of any fee prescribed by this Order would, owing to the exceptional circumstances of the particular case, involve undue financial hardship, the Lord Chancellor may reduce or remit the fee in that case.

Refunds

9

(1) Subject to sub-paragraph (3), where a party has not provided the documentary evidence required by paragraph 7 and a fee has been paid at a time when, under paragraphs 2, 3 or 4, it was not payable, the fee will be refunded if documentary evidence relating to the time when the fee became payable is provided at a later date.

(2) Subject to sub-paragraph (3), when a fee has been paid at a time where the Lord Chancellor, if all the circumstances had been known, would have reduced or remitted the fee under paragraph 8, the fee or the amount by which the fee would have been reduced, as the case may be, will be refunded.

(3) No refund will be made under this paragraph unless the party who paid the fee applies within 6 months of paying the fee.

(4) The Lord Chancellor may extend the period of 6 months mentioned in sub-paragraph (3) if the Lord Chancellor considers that there is a good reason for an application being made after the end of the period of 6 months.

Public Guardian (Fees Etc) Regulations 2007

SI 2007 No 2051

The following sets out the Fees payable under the Regulations (as amended) in force with effect from the 1st April 2009.

1 Citation and commencement

These Regulations may be cited as the Public Guardian (Fees, etc) Regulations 2007 and shall come into force on 1 October 2007.

2 Interpretation

In these Regulations—

"the Act" means the Mental Capacity Act 2005;

"court" means the Court of Protection;

"office copy" means a true copy of the original marked by the Public Guardian as being an office copy;

"P" means the person in respect of whom a deputy has been appointed under section 16 of the Act; and

"Public Guardian" means the officer appointed in accordance with section 57 of the Act;

"the registers" means—

(a) the register of lasting powers of attorney,

(b) the register of enduring powers of attorney, and

(c) the register of court orders appointing deputies,

established and maintained by the Public Guardian under section 58(1)(a) and (b) of and paragraph 14 of Schedule 4 to the Act.

3 Schedule of fees

The fees set out in the Schedule to these Regulations shall apply in accordance with the following provisions of these Regulations.

4 Enduring power of attorney registration fee

(1) A fee for the registration of an enduring power of attorney shall be payable by the person seeking to register the enduring power of attorney under regulation 24 of the Lasting Powers of Attorney, Enduring Powers of Attorney and Public Guardian Regulations 2007 (application for registration).

(2) The fee prescribed by paragraph (1) shall be payable upon the application to register the enduring power of attorney.

4A Enduring power of attorney office copy fee

(1) A fee for an office copy of an enduring power of attorney registered under paragraph 13 in Part 4 of Schedule 4 to the Mental Capacity Act 2005 shall be payable by the person requesting the office copy.

(2) The fee prescribed by paragraph (1) shall be payable at the time the request for an office copy is made.

5 Lasting power of attorney registration fee

(1) A fee for the registration of a lasting power of attorney shall be payable by the person seeking to register the lasting power of attorney under regulation 11 of the Lasting Powers of Attorney, Enduring Powers of Attorney and Public Guardian Regulations 2007 (application for registration).

(2) The fee prescribed by paragraph (1) shall be payable upon the application to register the lasting power of attorney.

5A Lasting power of attorney office copy fee

(1) A fee for an office copy of a lasting power of attorney registered under Part 2 of Schedule 1 to the Mental Capacity Act 2005 shall be payable by the person requesting the office copy.

(2) The fee prescribed by paragraph (1) shall be payable at the time the request for an office copy is made.

6 Application to search the registers fee

(1) A fee for an application to search the registers made under regulation 31 of the Lasting Powers of Attorney, Enduring Powers of Attorney and Public Guardian Regulations 2007 (disclosure of information on a register: search by the Public Guardian) shall be payable by the person making the application.

(2) The fee prescribed by paragraph (1) shall be payable upon the application to search the registers.

(3) The fee prescribed by paragraph (1) shall not be payable where the person making the application is a:

(a) registered health care professional; or

(b) a representative of a public authority.

(4) In paragraph (3) "registered health care professional" means a person who is a member of a profession regulated by a body mentioned in section 25(3) of the National Health Service Reform and Health Care Professions Act 2002.

7 Appointment of deputy fee

(1) This regulation applies where—

(a) the court has appointed a deputy under section 16 of the Act (powers to make decisions and appoint deputies: general).

(b) omitted.

(2) Where paragraph (1) applies a fee shall be payable by P.

(3) The fee prescribed by paragraph (2) shall be payable by P within 30 days of the date of the invoice for the fee.

8 Appointment of deputy: supervision fees

(1) This regulation applies where—

(a) the court has appointed a deputy under section 16 of the Act (powers to make decisions and appoint deputies: general).

(b) omitted

(2) Where paragraph (1) applies the Public Guardian shall determine the level of supervision required under section 58(1)(c) of the Act.

(3) The levels of supervision are—

(a) type I (highest);

(aa) type IIA (intermediate);

(b) type II (lower); and

(c) type III (minimal).

(4) Where the level of supervision determined by the Public Guardian in accordance with paragraph (2) is type I (highest)[, type IIA (intermediate)] or type II (lower) an annual supervision fee shall be payable by P until the appointment of the deputy is terminated.

(5) Subject to paragraphs (6) and (7), the appropriate supervision fee prescribed by paragraph (2) shall be due on 31 March each year and shall be payable by P within 30 days of the date of the invoice for the fee.

(6) Where the period for which the fee prescribed by paragraph (4) is payable is less than one year, the amount of the fee payable shall be such proportion of the full fee as that period bears to one year.

(7) Where the deputy's appointment terminates, the appropriate fee prescribed by paragraph (4) shall be due on the date of termination and shall be payable within 30 days of the date of the invoice for the fee.

(8) In the event of termination of the appointment due to P's death, the appropriate fee prescribed by paragraph (2) shall be payable by P's estate.

9 Exemptions

(1) Subject to paragraph (2) no fee shall be payable under these regulations when, at the time when the fee would otherwise become payable, the relevant person is in receipt of any qualifying benefit.

(2) Paragraph (1) does not apply to a person who has an award of damages in excess of £16,000 which has been disregarded for the purposes of determining eligibility for that benefit.

(3) For the purposes of regulation 4 the relevant person is the donor of the enduring power of attorney.

(4) For the purposes of regulation 5 the relevant person is the donor of the lasting power of attorney.

(5) For the purposes of regulation 6 the relevant person is the person making the application.

(6) For the purposes of regulations 7 and 8 the relevant person is P.

(7) The following are qualifying benefits for the purposes of paragraph (1)—

(a) income support under the Social Security Contributions and Benefits Act 1992;

(b) working tax credit, provided that—

(i) child tax credit is being paid to the relevant person, or to a couple (as defined in section 3(5)(A) of the Tax Credits Act 2002) which includes the relevant person; or

(ii) there is a disability element or severe disability element (or both) to the tax credit received by the relevant person;

(c) income-based job-seeker's allowance under the Jobseekers Act 1995;

(d) guarantee credit under the State Pensions Credit Act 2002;

(e) council tax benefit under the Social Security Contributions and Benefits Act 1992;

(f) housing benefit under the Social Security Contributions and Benefits Act 1992; and

(g) income-related employment and support allowance under Part 1 of the Welfare Reform Act 2007.

10 Reductions and remissions in exceptional circumstances

(1) Where it appears to the Public Guardian that the payment of any fee prescribed by these Regulations would, owing to the exceptional circumstances of the particular case, involve undue hardship, he may reduce or remit the fee in that case.

(2) An application for the reduction or remission of any fee paid under regulation 8 (appointment of deputy: supervision fees) must be made to the Public Guardian within 6 months after the date of the invoice in respect of that fee.

11 Transitional provision

(1) In respect of the administration fee that would have been payable under rule 78 of the Court of Protection Rules 2001 on 31 March 2008, the appropriate proportion of that fee shall be due on 30 September 2007 and shall be payable within 30 days of the date of the invoice for the fee.

(2) Where the period for which the fee prescribed by paragraph (1) is payable is less than six months, the amount of the fee payable shall be such proportion of that fee as that period bears to six months.

12 Amendment to Schedule 7 of the Lasting Powers of Attorney, Enduring Powers of Attorney and Public Guardian Regulations 2007

(1) Schedule 7 of the Lasting Powers of Attorney, Enduring Powers of Attorney and Public Guardian Regulations 2007 is amended as follows.

(2) For paragraph 1 of Form EP1PG substitute "You have the right to object to the proposed registration on one or more of the grounds set out below. You must notify the Office of the Public Guardian of your objection within five weeks from the day this notice was given to you. You may make an application to the Court of Protection under rule 68 of the Court of Protection Rules 2007 for a decision on the matter. No fee is payable for such an application. If you do not make such an application, the Public Guardian will ask for the court's directions about registration."

SCHEDULE: FEES TO BE TAKEN

Regulation 3

Column 1	*Column 2*
Enduring power of attorney registration (regulation 4)	£120.00
[Enduring power of attorney office copy fee (regulation 4A)	£25
Lasting power of attorney registration (regulation 5)	£120
[Lasting power of attorney office copy fee (regulation 5A)	£25
Application to search the registers (regulation 6)	£25.00
Appointment of deputy (regulation 7)	£100
Type I (highest) supervision (regulation 8)	£800.00 per annum
Type IIA (intermediate) supervision (regulation 8)	£350 per annum
Type II (lower) supervision (regulation 8)	£175.00 per annum
Type III (minimal) supervision (regulation 8)	No fee

Court of Protection Fees Order 2007

SI 2007 No 1745

The following sets out the Fees payable under the Order (as amended) in force with effect from the 1st April 2009.

1 Citation and commencement

This Order may be cited as the Court of Protection Fees Order 2007 and comes into force on 1 October 2007.

2 Interpretation

In this Order—

"the Act" means the Mental Capacity Act 2005;'

"appellant" means the person who brings or seeks to bring an appeal;

"court" means the Court of Protection;

"P" means any person (other than a protected party) who lacks or, so far as consistent with the context, is alleged to lack capacity to make a decision or decisions in relation to any matter that is the subject of an application to the court and references to a person who lacks capacity are to be construed in accordance with the Act;

"protected party" means a party or an intended party (other than P or a child) who lacks capacity to conduct the proceedings;

"the Regulations" means the Lasting Powers of Attorney, Enduring Powers of Attorney and Public Guardian Regulations 2007; and

"the Rules" means the Court of Protection Rules 2007.

3 Schedule of fees

The fees set out in the Schedule to this Order shall apply in accordance with the following provisions of this Order.

4 Application fee

(1) An application fee shall be payable by the applicant on making an application under Part 9 of the Rules (how to start proceedings) in accordance with the following provisions of this article.

(2) Where permission to start proceedings is required under Part 8 of the Rules (permission), the fee prescribed by paragraph (1) shall be payable on making an application for permission.

(3) The fee prescribed by paragraph (1) shall not be payable where the application is made under—

(a) rule 67 of the Rules (applications relating to lasting powers of attorney) by—

(i) the donee of a lasting power of attorney, or

(ii) a person named in a statement made by the donor of a lasting power of attorney in accordance with paragraph 2(1)(c)(i) of Part 1 of Schedule 1 to the Act,

and is solely in respect of an objection to the registration of a lasting power of attorney; or

(b) rule 68 of the Rules (applications relating to enduring powers of attorney) by—

(i) a donor of an enduring power of attorney,

(ii) an attorney under an enduring power of attorney, or

(iii) a person listed in paragraph 6(1) of Part 3 of Schedule 4 to the Act,

and is solely in respect of an objection to the registration of an enduring power of attorney.

(4) The fee prescribed by paragraph (1) shall not be payable where the application is made by the Public Guardian.

(5) Where a fee has been paid under paragraph (1) it shall be refunded where P dies within five days of the application being filed.

5 Appeal fee

(1) An appeal fee shall be payable by the appellant on the filing of an appellant's notice under Part 20 of the Rules (appeals) in accordance with the following provisions of this article.

(2) The fee prescribed by paragraph (1) shall not be payable where the appeal is—

(a) brought by the Public Guardian; or

(b) an appeal against a decision of a nominated officer made under rule 197 of the Rules (appeal against a decision of a nominated officer).

(3) The fee prescribed by paragraph (1) shall be refunded where P dies within five days of the appellant's notice being filed.

6 Hearing fees

(1) A hearing fee shall be payable by the applicant where the court has—

(a) held a hearing in order to determine the case; and

(b) made a final order, declaration or decision.

(2) A hearing fee shall be payable by the appellant in relation to an appeal where the court has—

(a) held a hearing in order to determine the appeal; and

(b) made a final order, declaration or decision in relation to the appeal.

(3) The fees prescribed by paragraphs (1) and (2) shall not be payable where the hearing is in respect of an application or appeal brought by the Public Guardian.

(4) The fee prescribed by paragraph (2) shall not be payable where the hearing is in respect of an appeal against a decision of a nominated officer made under rule 197 of the Rules (appeal against a decision of a nominated officer).

(5) The fee prescribed by paragraph (1) shall not be payable where the applicant was not required to pay an application fee under Article 4(1) by virtue of Article 4(3).

(6) The fees prescribed by paragraphs (1) and (2) shall be payable by the applicant or appellant as the case may be within 30 days of the date of the invoice for the fee.

7 Fee for request for copy of court document

(1) A fee for a copy of a court document shall be payable by the person requesting the copy of the document.

(2) Omitted

(3) The fee prescribed by paragraph (1) shall be payable at the time the request for the copy is made to the court.

8 Exemptions

(1) Subject to paragraph (2) no fee shall be payable under this Order by a person who, at the time when a fee would otherwise become payable, is in receipt of any qualifying benefit.

(2) Paragraph (1) does not apply to a person who has an award of damages in excess of £16,000 which has been disregarded for the purposes of determining eligibility for that benefit.

(3) The following are qualifying benefits for the purposes of paragraph 1 above—

(a) income support under the Social Security Contributions and Benefits Act 1992;

(b) working tax credit, provided that—

(i) child tax credit is being paid to the person, or to a couple (as defined in section 3(5)(A) of the Tax Credits Act 2002) which includes the person; or

(ii) there is a disability element or severe disability element (or both) to the tax credit received by the person;

(c) income-based jobseeker's allowance under the Jobseekers Act 1995;

(d) guarantee credit under the State Pensions Credit Act 2002;

(e) council tax benefit under the Social Security Contributions and Benefits Act 1992;

(f) housing benefit under the Social Security Contributions and Benefits Act 1992; and

(g) income-related employment and support allowance under Part 1 of the Welfare Reform Act 2007.

9 Reductions and remissions in exceptional circumstances

Where it appears to the Lord Chancellor that the payment of any fee prescribed by this Order would, owing to the exceptional circumstances of the particular case, involve undue hardship, he may reduce or remit the fee in that case.

10 Transitional provision

(1) In this article "Court of Protection" means the office of the Supreme Court called the Court of Protection which ceases to exist under section 45(6) of the Act.

(2) Where a hearing that takes place on or after 1 October 2007 was listed by the Court of Protection before 1 October 2007, no hearing fee shall be payable under Article 6.

SCHEDULE: FEES TO BE TAKEN

Article 3

Column 1	*Column 2*
Application fee (Article 4)	£400.00
Appeal fee (Article 5)	£400.00
Hearing fees (Article 6)	£500.00
Copy of a document fee (Article 7(1))	£5.00

Insolvency Fees Order 2004

SI 2004 No 593

The following sets out the Fees payable under the Order (as amended) in force with effect from the 6th April 2010.

1 Citation and commencement

This Order may be cited as the Insolvency Proceedings (Fees) Order 2004 and shall come into force on 1st April 2004.

2 Interpretation

(1) In this Order—

"the Act" means the Insolvency Act 1986 (any reference to a numbered section being to the section so numbered in that Act);

"the commencement date" is the date referred to in Article 1;

"individual voluntary arrangement" means a voluntary arrangement pursuant to Part VIII of the Act; and "the Rules" means the Insolvency Rules 1986 (any reference to a numbered Rule being to the Rule so numbered in the Rules).

(2) A reference to a fee by a means of letters and a number is a reference to the fee so designated in the table in Schedule 2.

3 Revocations and Transitional Provisions

The instruments listed in the Schedule 1 to this Order are revoked to the extent set out in that Schedule.

4 Fees payable in connection with bankruptcies, debt relief orders, individual voluntary arrangements and winding up

(1) Subject to paragraphs (2) and (3) and article 8, the fees payable to the Secretary of State in respect of the costs of persons acting as approved intermediaries under Part 7A of the Act, proceedings under Parts I to XI of the Act and the performance by the official receiver or Secretary of State of functions under those Parts shall be determined in accordance with the provisions of Schedule 2 to this Order.

(2) Paragraph (1) and the provisions of Schedule 2 shall not apply to a bankruptcy where the bankruptcy order was made before the commencement date except insofar as is necessary to enable the charging of—

(a) fee INV1; or

(b) as regards an individual voluntary arrangement proposed by, or entered into by, the bankrupt, fees IVA1, IVA2 or IVA3.

(3) Paragraph (1) and the provisions of Schedule 2 shall not apply to a winding up by the court where the winding-up order was made before the commencement date except insofar as is necessary to enable the charging of fee INV1.

(4) Each request for the purchase of any government securities made by a trustee in bankruptcy under the Bankruptcy Act 1914 or a liquidator in a winding up under the provisions of the Companies Act 1985 shall be accompanied by the appropriate amount of fee INV1.

5 Fees payable to an insolvency practitioner appointed under section 273

Where a court appoints an insolvency practitioner under section 273(2) to prepare and submit a report under section 274 the court shall, on submission of the report, pay to the practitioner a fee of £450 (that sum being inclusive of Value Added Tax).

6 Deposits—winding up by the court and bankruptcy

(1) In this Article—

"appropriate deposit" means—

(a) in relation to a winding-up petition to be presented under the Act the sum of £1,165;

(b) in relation to a bankruptcy petition to be presented under section 264(1)(b) the sum of £525; or

(c) in relation to a bankruptcy petition to be presented under sections 264(1)(a), (ba), (bb), (c) or (d) the sum of £700;

"order" means a winding-up, or as the case may be, bankruptcy order;

"petition" means a winding-up, or as the case may be, bankruptcy petition;

"relevant assets" means the assets of the company or, as the case may be the assets comprised in the estate of the bankrupt; and

"relevant fees" means in relation to winding-up proceedings fee W1 and in relation to bankruptcy proceedings fee B1 together with any fees payable under section 273.

(2) Where a bankruptcy or winding-up petition is presented the appropriate deposit is payable by the petitioner and the deposit shall be security for the payment of the relevant fees and shall be used to discharge those fees to the extent that the relevant assets are insufficient for that purpose.

(3) Where a deposit is paid to the court, the court shall (except to the extent that a fee is payable by virtue of Article 5) transmit the deposit paid to the official receiver attached to the court.

(4) A deposit shall be repaid to the person who made it in a case where a petition is dismissed or withdrawn except in the case of a bankruptcy petition where it is required to pay any fees arising under Article 5.

(5) In any case where an order is made (including any case where the order is subsequently annulled, rescinded or recalled), any deposit made shall be returned to the person who made it save to the extent that the relevant assets are insufficient to discharge the fees for which the deposit is security.

7 Deposits—official receiver acting as nominee in individual voluntary arrangement

(1) Where a proposal for an individual voluntary arrangement with the official receiver acting as nominee is notified to the official receiver, the notification shall be accompanied by a deposit of £315 as security for fee IVA1 and fee IVA2.

(2) The deposit shall be used to discharge fee IVA1 and fee IVA2.

(3) Where the official receiver declines to act in relation to a proposal of the kind mentioned in paragraph (1) the deposit mentioned in that paragraph shall be refunded to the person entitled to it

(4) Where the official receiver agrees to act as nominee in relation to a proposal of the kind mentioned in paragraph (1) but the proposal is rejected by the bankrupt's creditors, any balance of the deposit after deducting fee IVA2 shall be returned to the person who is entitled to it.

8 Reduction and refund of fees—individual voluntary arrangement following bankruptcy

Where proposals made by a bankrupt for an individual voluntary arrangement with the official receiver acting as supervisor are approved by the bankrupt's creditors, fee B1 shall be reduced to £857.50 and any payments made in respect of fee B1 which exceed that amount shall be refunded to the credit of the estate of the bankrupt.

9 Value Added Tax

Where Valued Added Tax is chargeable in respect of the provision of a service for which a fee is prescribed by virtue of any provision of this Order (other than Article 5), there shall be payable in addition to that fee the amount of the Value Added Tax.

SCHEDULE 1: REVOCATIONS

(NOT HEREIN PRINTED)

SCHEDULE 2: FEES PAYABLE IN INSOLVENCY PROCEEDINGS

Article 4

1

(1) In this Schedule—

"the bankruptcy ceiling" means in relation to a bankruptcy, the sum which is arrived at by adding together—

(a) the bankruptcy debts required to be paid under the Rules

(b) any interest payable by virtue of sections 328(4) and 329(2)(b); and

(c) the expenses of the bankruptcy as set out in Rule 6.224 other than—

(i) any sums spent out of money received in carrying on the business of the bankrupt; and

(ii) fee B2 in the Table set out in paragraph 2;

"chargeable receipts" means those sums which are paid into the Insolvency Services Account after first deducting any amounts paid into the Insolvency Services Account which are subsequently paid out to secured creditors in respect of their securities or in carrying on the business of the company or the bankrupt; and

"the insolvency legislation" means the Insolvency Act 1986, the Insolvency Rules 1986 and the Insolvency Regulations 1994.

(2) In this Schedule, references to the performance of the "general duties" of the official receiver on the making of a winding-up or bankruptcy order—

(a) include the payment by the official receiver of any fees, costs or disbursements except for those associated with the realisation of assets or the distribution of funds to creditors; but

[(b)does not include anything done by the official receiver in connection with or for the purposes of—

(i) the appointment of agents for the purposes of, or in connection with, the realisation of assets;

(ii) the making of a distribution to creditors (including preferential or secured creditors or both such classes of creditor);

(iii)the realisation of assets on behalf of the holder of a fixed or floating charge or both types of those charges; or

(iv) the supervision of a special manager.

2

Fees payable to the Secretary of State in respect of proceedings under Parts I to XI of the Act and the performance by the official receiver and the Secretary of State of functions under those Parts shall be determined in accordance with the provisions of the Table of Fees set out below—

Fees payable in respect of individual voluntary arrangements only

Designation of Fee	*Description of fee and circumstances in which it is charged*	*Amount of fee or applicable %*
IVA1	**Individual voluntary arrangement registration fee**	
	On the registration of an individual voluntary arrangement by the Secretary of State there is payable a fee of—	£15
IVA2	**Individual voluntary arrangement—official receiver's nominee fee**	
	For the performance by the official receiver in relation to an individual voluntary arrangement of the functions of nominee there shall be payable on the agreement of the official receiver so to act a fee of—	£300
IVA3	**Individual voluntary arrangement—official receiver's supervisor fee**	
	For the performance by the official receiver in relation to an individual voluntary arrangement of the functions of supervisor, there shall be payable, a fee calculated as a percentage of any monies realised whilst he acts as supervisor at the rate of—	15%

Fees payable in bankruptcies only

Designation of Fee	*Description of fee and circumstances in which it is charged*	*Amount of fee or applicable %*
B1	**Bankruptcy—Official receiver's administration fee**	
	For the performance by the official receiver of his general duties as official receiver on the making of a bankruptcy order there shall be payable a fee of—	£1,715
B2	**Bankruptcy—Secretary of State's administration fee**	
	For the performance of the Secretary of State's general duties under the insolvency legislation in relation to the administration of the estate of each bankrupt, there shall be payable a fee calculated in accordance with the following scale as a percentage of chargeable receipts relating to the bankruptcy (but ignoring that part of the chargeable receipts which exceeds the bankruptcy ceiling at the rate of—	0% of the first £2,000, 100% of the next £1,700, 75% of the next £1,500, 15% of the next £396,000, 1% of the remainder, subject to a maximum of £80,000.

Fees payable in relation to debt relief orders

Designation of Fee	*Description of fee and circumstances in which it is charged*	*Amount of fee*
DRO1	**Application for a debt relief order – official receiver's administration fee and costs of persons acting as approved intermediaries**	
	For the performance by the official receiver of his functions, and for the payment of an amount not exceeding £10 in respect of the costs of persons acting as approved intermediaries, under Part 7A of the Act, there shall be payable in connection with an application for a debt relief order, a fee of—	£90

Fees payable in relation to winding up by the court only

Designation of Fee	*Description of fee and circumstances in which it is charged*	*Amount of fee or applicable %*
W1	**Winding up by the court—official receiver's administration fee**	
	For the performance by the official receiver of his general duties as official receiver on the making of a winding-up order there shall be payable a fee of—	£2,235
W2	**Winding up by the court—Secretary of State's administration fee**	
	For the performance of the Secretary of State's general duties under the insolvency legislation in relation to the administration of the affairs of each company which is being wound up by the court, there shall be payable a fee calculated in accordance with the following scale as a percentage of chargeable receipts relating to the company at the rate of —	0% of the first £2,500,100% of the next £1,700, 75% of the next £1,500, 15% of the next £396,000, 1% of the remainder, subject to a maximum of £80,000.

Fees payable in bankruptcies and both types of winding up

Designation of Fee	*Description of fee and circumstances in which it is charged*	*Amount of fee or applicable %*
INV1	**Investment fee—all cases**	£50
	Each request made by a trustee in bankruptcy or a liquidator in a compulsory or a voluntary winding up for the purchase of any government securities shall be accompanied by a fee of —	
	For each purchase or sale of any government securities made at the request of a trustee in bankruptcy or a liquidator in a compulsory or voluntary winding up—	
	(a) in respect of a purchase, where the cost of the securities (including accrued interest, if any)—	
	(i) does not exceed £5,000, a fee of—	£50
	(ii) exceeds £5,000, a fee of—	£50 plus 0.3% of the cost in excess of £5,000
	(b) in respect of a sale, where the proceeds of sale of the securities (including accrued interest, if any) exceed £5,000, a fee of—	£50 plus 0.3% of the proceeds in excess of £5,000